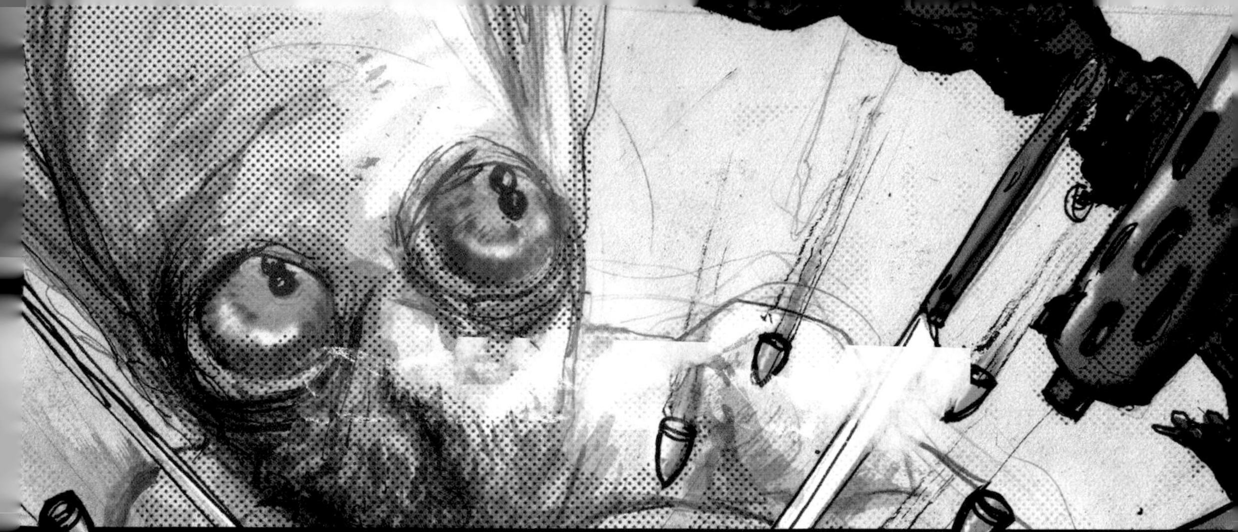

PROOF
THE COMPANY OF MEN

CREATED BY **ALEXANDER GRECIAN** & **RILEY ROSSMO**

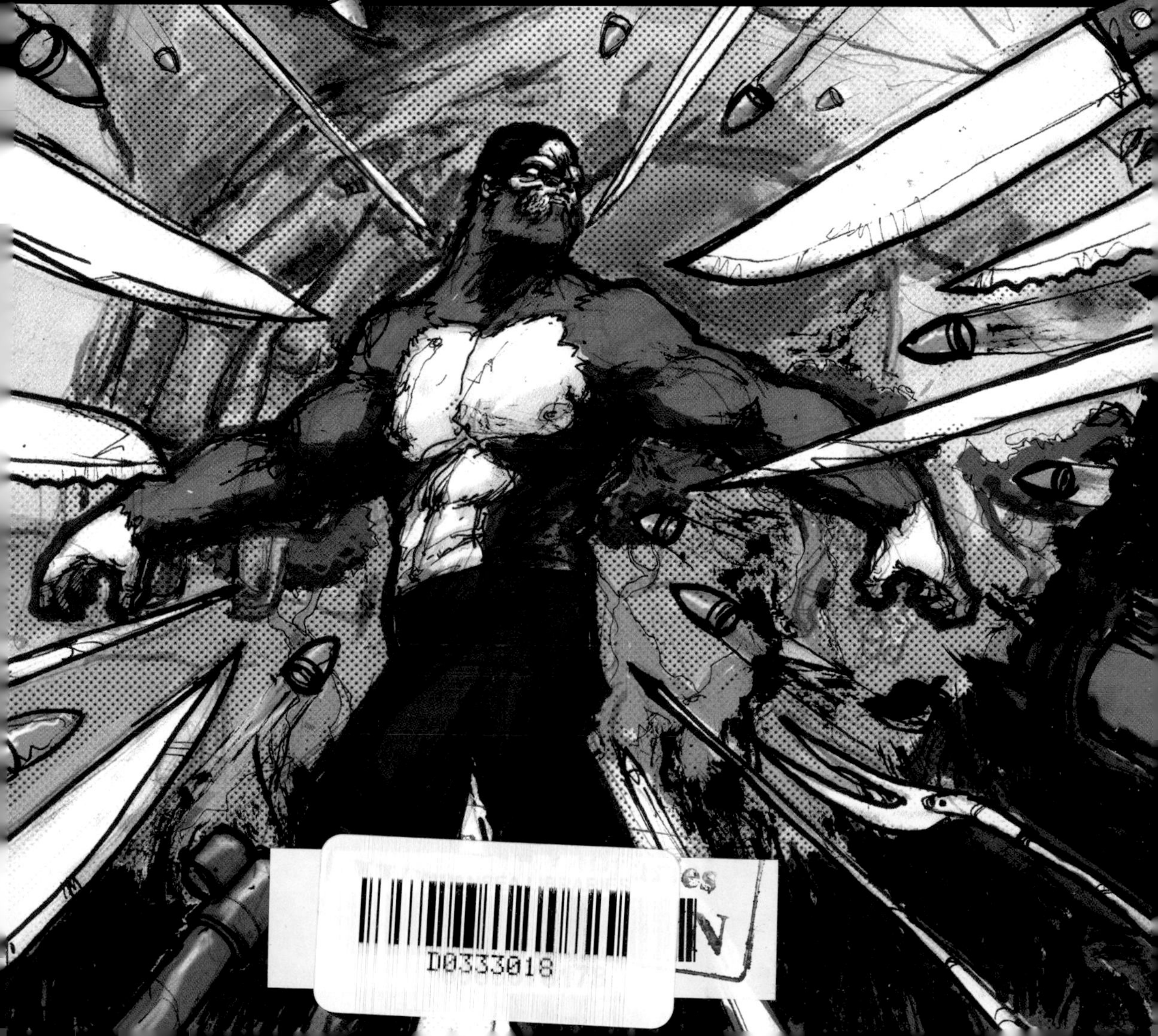

IMAGE COMICS, INC.

ROBERT KIRKMAN Chief Operating Officer **ERIK LARSEN** Chief Financial Officer **TODD McFARLANE** President
MARC SILVESTRI Chief Executive Officer **JIM VALENTINO** Vice-President

ericstephenson Publisher **JOE KEATINGE** PR & Marketing Coordinator **BRANWYN BIGGLESTONE** Accounts Manager
TYLER SHAINLINE Administrative Assistant **TRACI HUI** Traffic Manager **ALLEN HUI** Production Manager
DREW GILL Production Artist **JONATHAN CHAN** Production Artist **MONICA HOWARD** Production Artist

www.imagecomics.com

PROOF BOOK 2: THE COMPANY OF MEN
ISBN: 978-1-60706-017-8

ALEXANDER GRECIAN
script & letters

RILEY ROSSMO
art

with FIONA STAPLES & ADAM GUZOWSKI
colors

Special Thanks to
Frazer Irving, Kelly Tindall, Todd Dezago
and our Monster Pile-Up friends

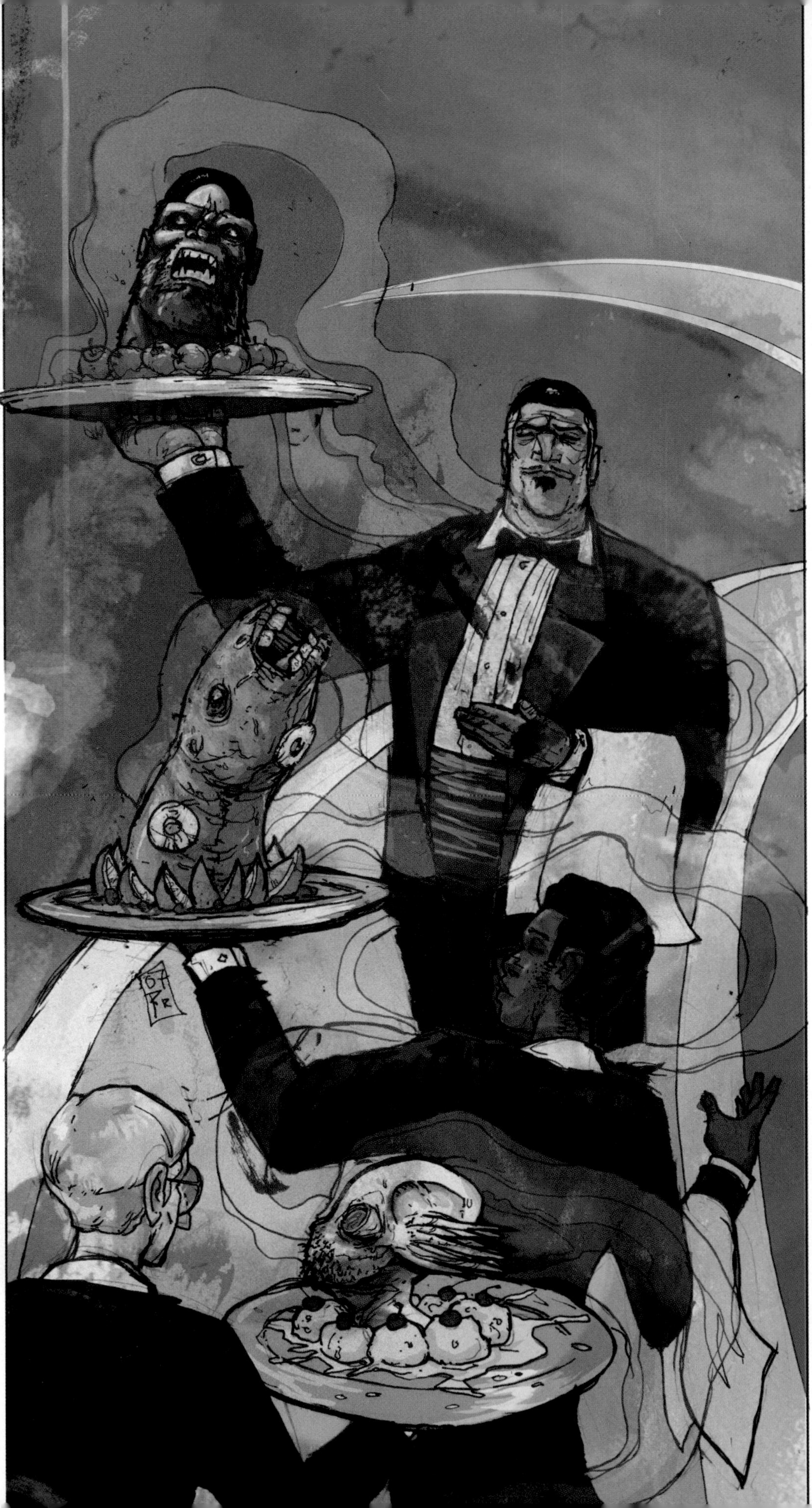

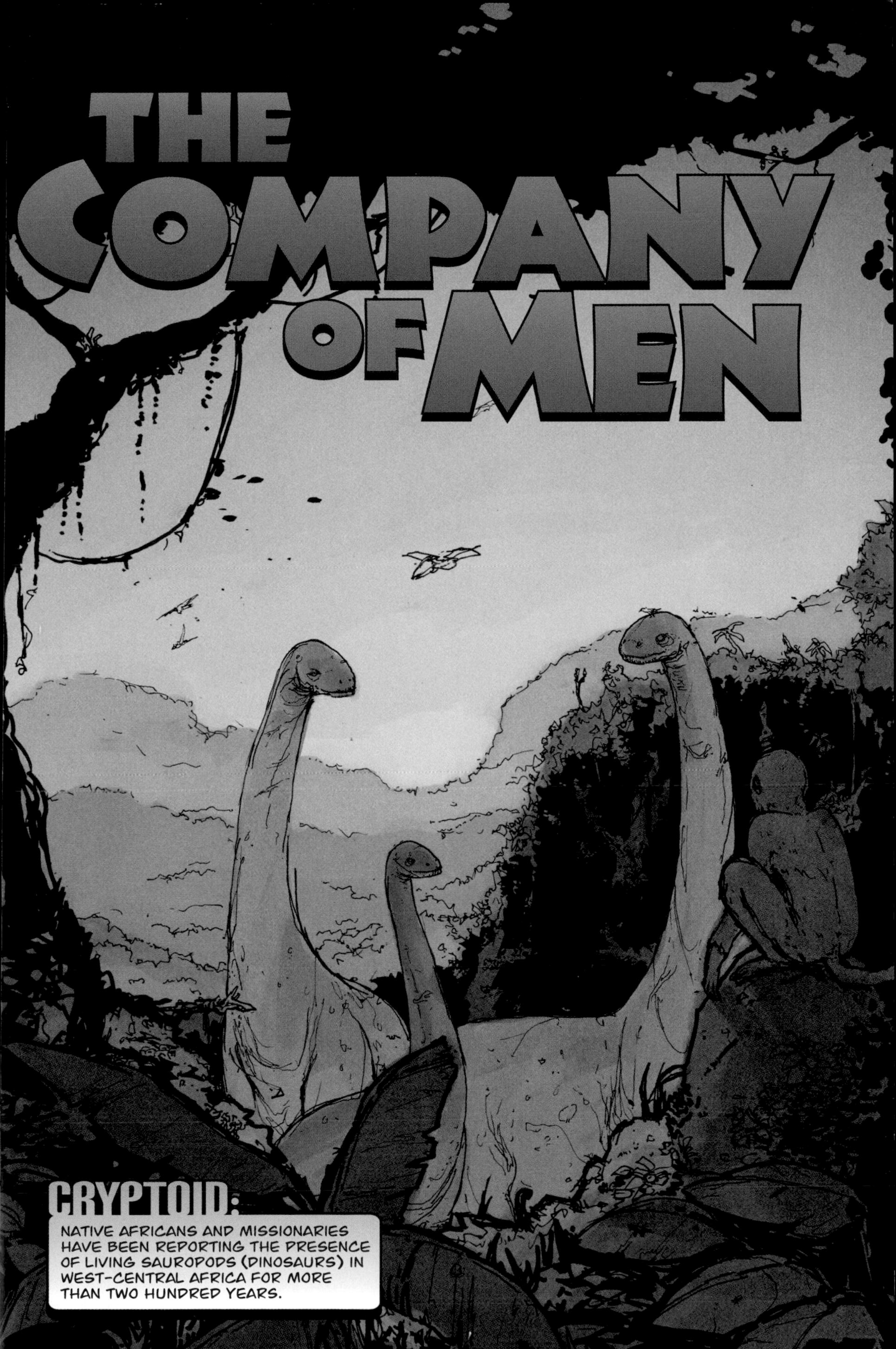
THE COMPANY OF MEN
CRYPTOID:
NATIVE AFRICANS AND MISSIONARIES HAVE BEEN REPORTING THE PRESENCE OF LIVING SAUROPODS (DINOSAURS) IN WEST-CENTRAL AFRICA FOR MORE THAN TWO HUNDRED YEARS.

MONDAY
THE DEMOCRATIC REPUBLIC OF THE CONGO

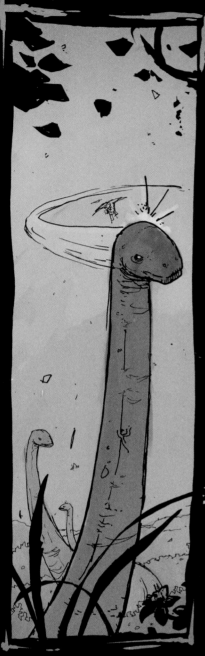

"...WHILE ANIMALS SURVIVE BY ADJUSTING THEMSELVES TO THEIR BACKGROUND, MAN SURVIVES BY ADJUSTING HIS BACKGROUND TO HIMSELF."
—AYN RAND

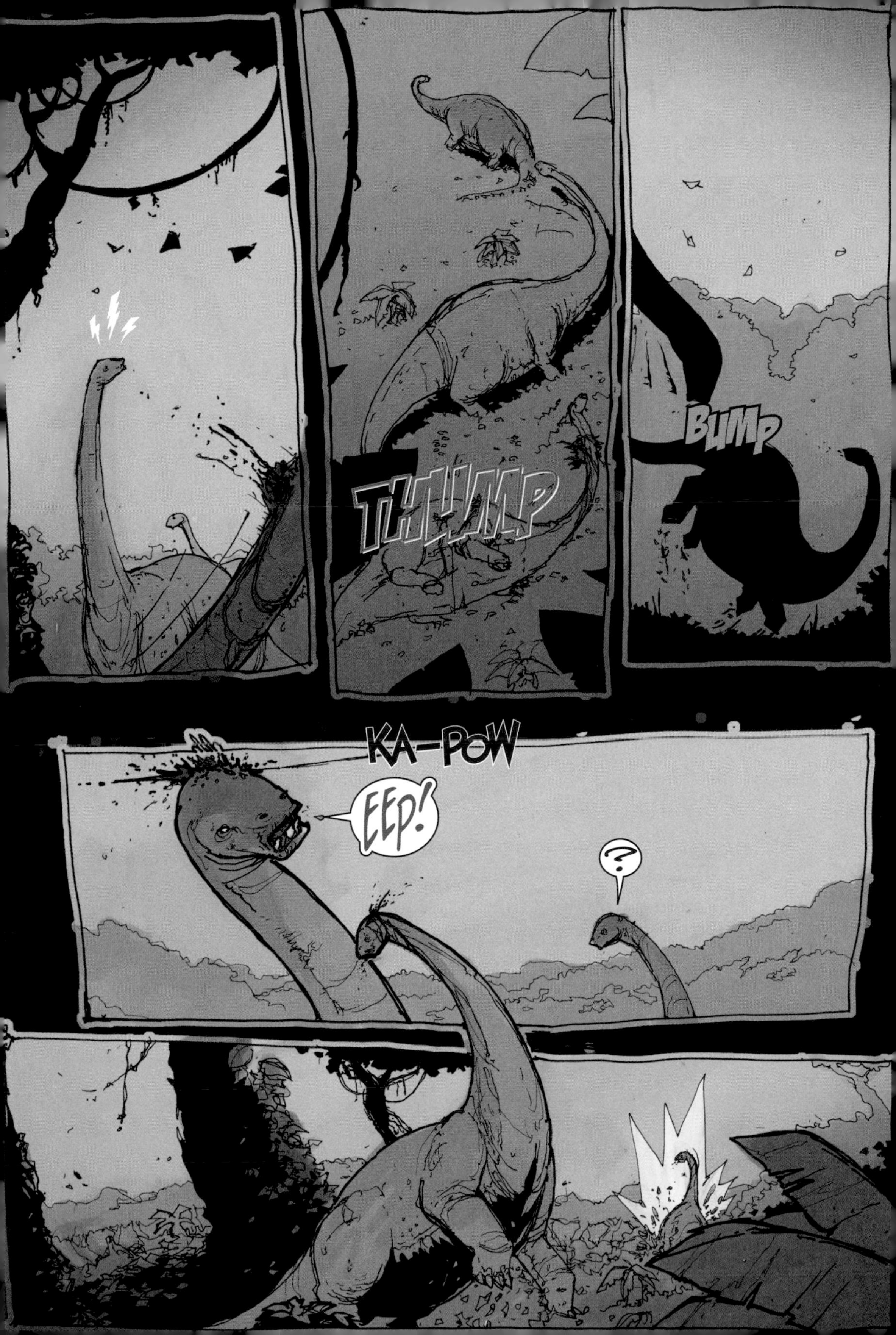
THUMP
BUMP
KA-POW
EEP!
?

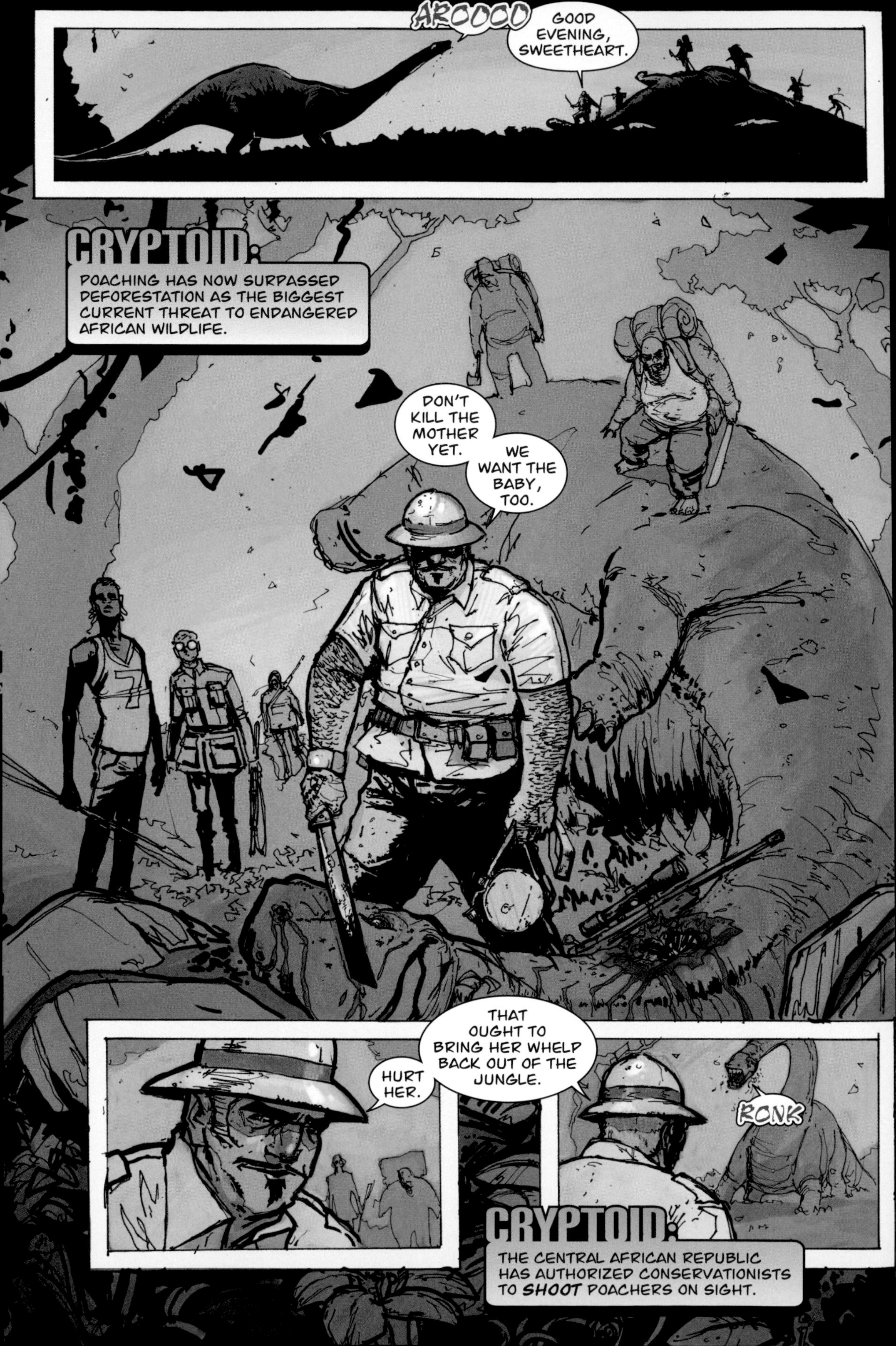
AROOOO
GOOD EVENING, SWEETHEART.
CRYPTOID:
POACHING HAS NOW SURPASSED DEFORESTATION AS THE BIGGEST CURRENT THREAT TO ENDANGERED AFRICAN WILDLIFE.
DON'T KILL THE MOTHER YET.
WE WANT THE BABY, TOO.
HURT HER.
THAT OUGHT TO BRING HER WHELP BACK OUT OF THE JUNGLE.
RONK
CRYPTOID:
THE CENTRAL AFRICAN REPUBLIC HAS AUTHORIZED CONSERVATIONISTS TO SHOOT POACHERS ON SIGHT.

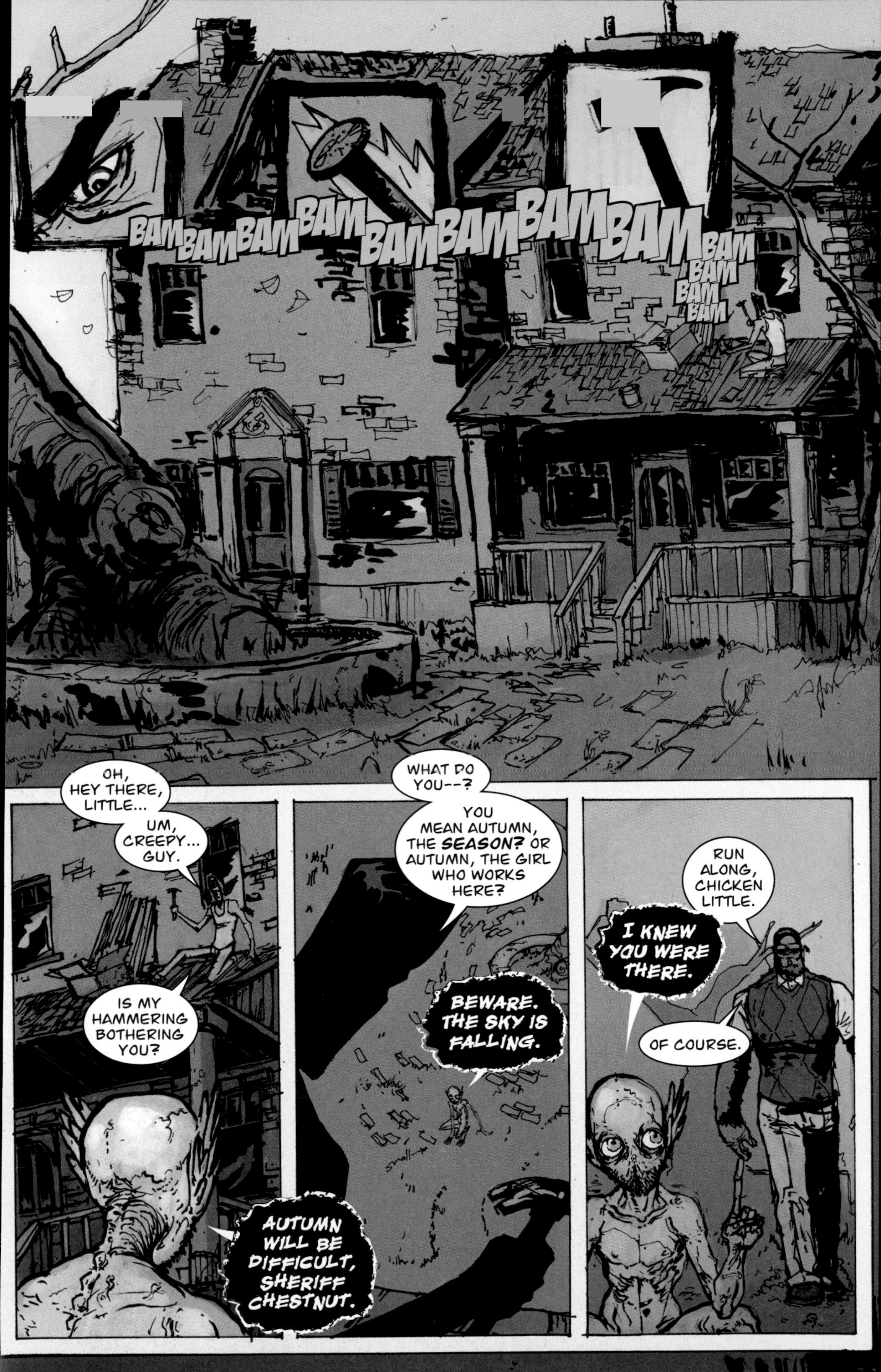
BAM BAM BAM BAM BAM BAM BAM BAM BAM BAM BAM BAM
OH, HEY THERE, LITTLE...
UM, CREEPY... GUY.
IS MY HAMMERING BOTHERING YOU?
AUTUMN WILL BE DIFFICULT, SHERIFF CHESTNUT.
WHAT DO YOU--?
YOU MEAN AUTUMN, THE SEASON? OR AUTUMN, THE GIRL WHO WORKS HERE?
BEWARE. THE SKY IS FALLING.
RUN ALONG, CHICKEN LITTLE.
I KNEW YOU WERE THERE.
OF COURSE.

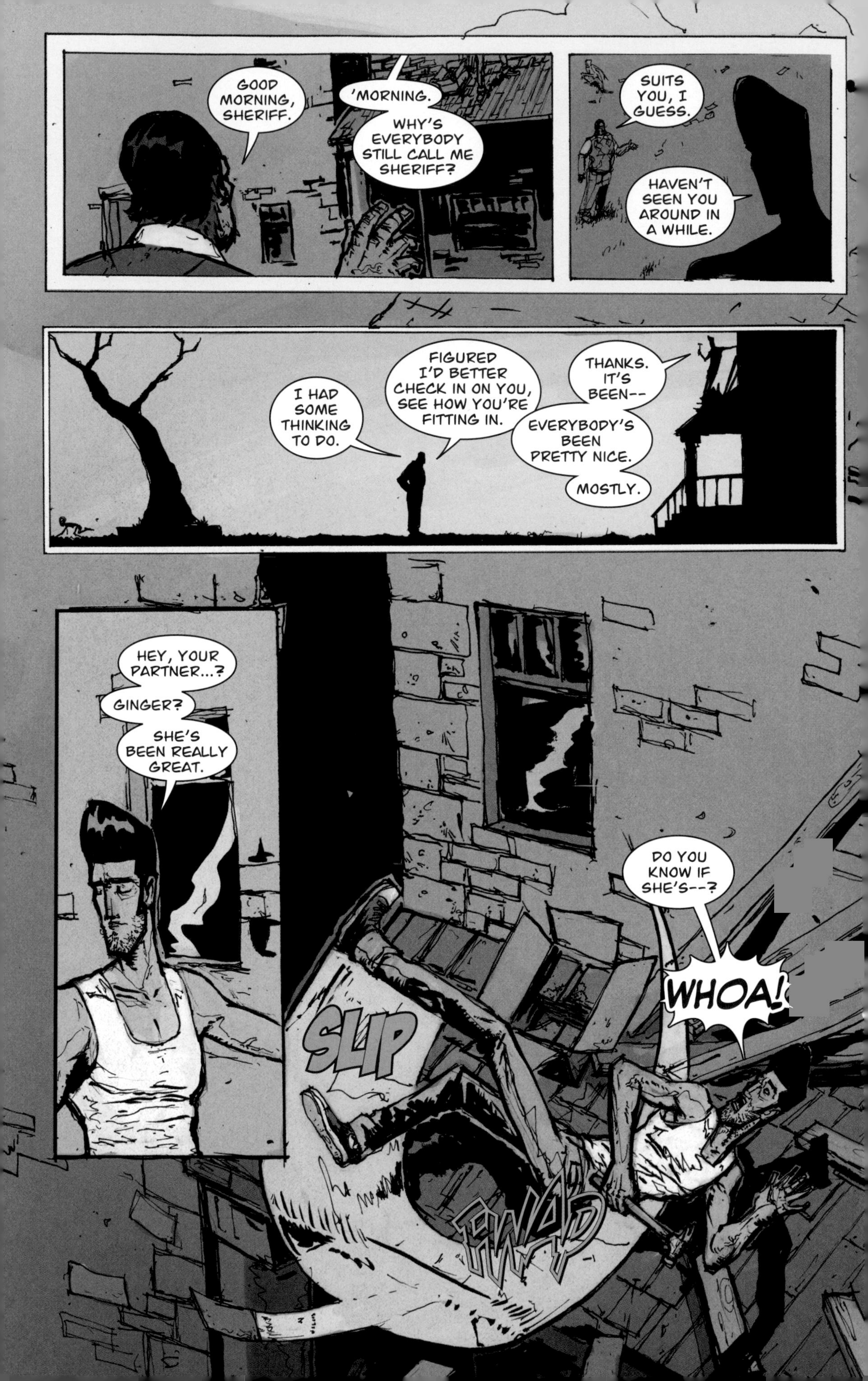
GOOD MORNING, SHERIFF.
'MORNING.
WHY'S EVERYBODY STILL CALL ME SHERIFF?
SUITS YOU, I GUESS.
HAVEN'T SEEN YOU AROUND IN A WHILE.
I HAD SOME THINKING TO DO.
FIGURED I'D BETTER CHECK IN ON YOU, SEE HOW YOU'RE FITTING IN.
THANKS. IT'S BEEN--
EVERYBODY'S BEEN PRETTY NICE.
MOSTLY.
HEY, YOUR PARTNER...?
GINGER?
SHE'S BEEN REALLY GREAT.
DO YOU KNOW IF SHE'S--?
WHOA!
SLIP
FWAP

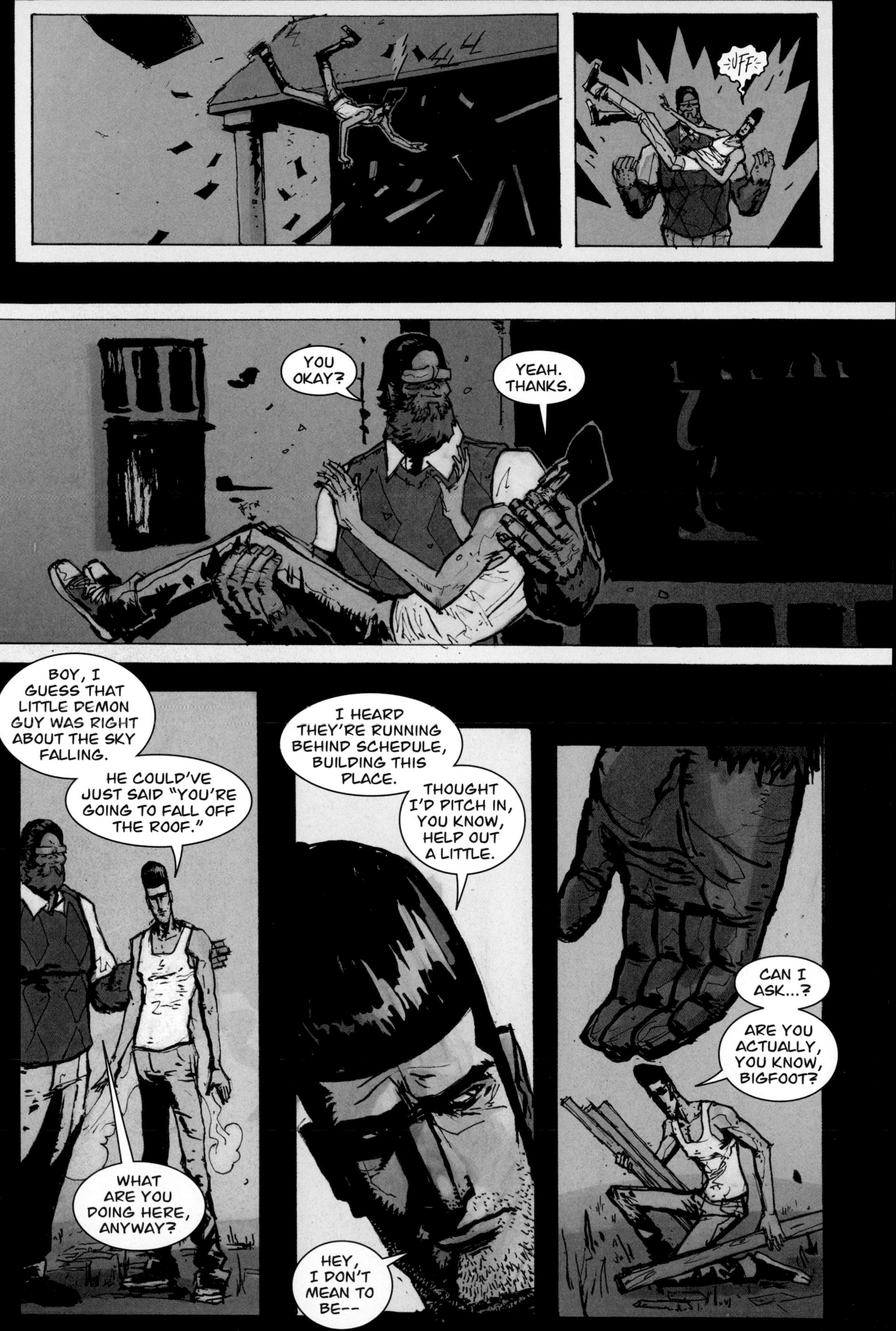
UFF
YOU OKAY?
YEAH. THANKS.
BOY, I GUESS THAT LITTLE DEMON GUY WAS RIGHT ABOUT THE SKY FALLING.
HE COULD'VE JUST SAID "YOU'RE GOING TO FALL OFF THE ROOF."
WHAT ARE YOU DOING HERE, ANYWAY?
I HEARD THEY'RE RUNNING BEHIND SCHEDULE, BUILDING THIS PLACE.
THOUGHT I'D PITCH IN, YOU KNOW, HELP OUT A LITTLE.
HEY, I DON'T MEAN TO BE--
CAN I ASK...?
ARE YOU ACTUALLY, YOU KNOW, BIGFOOT?

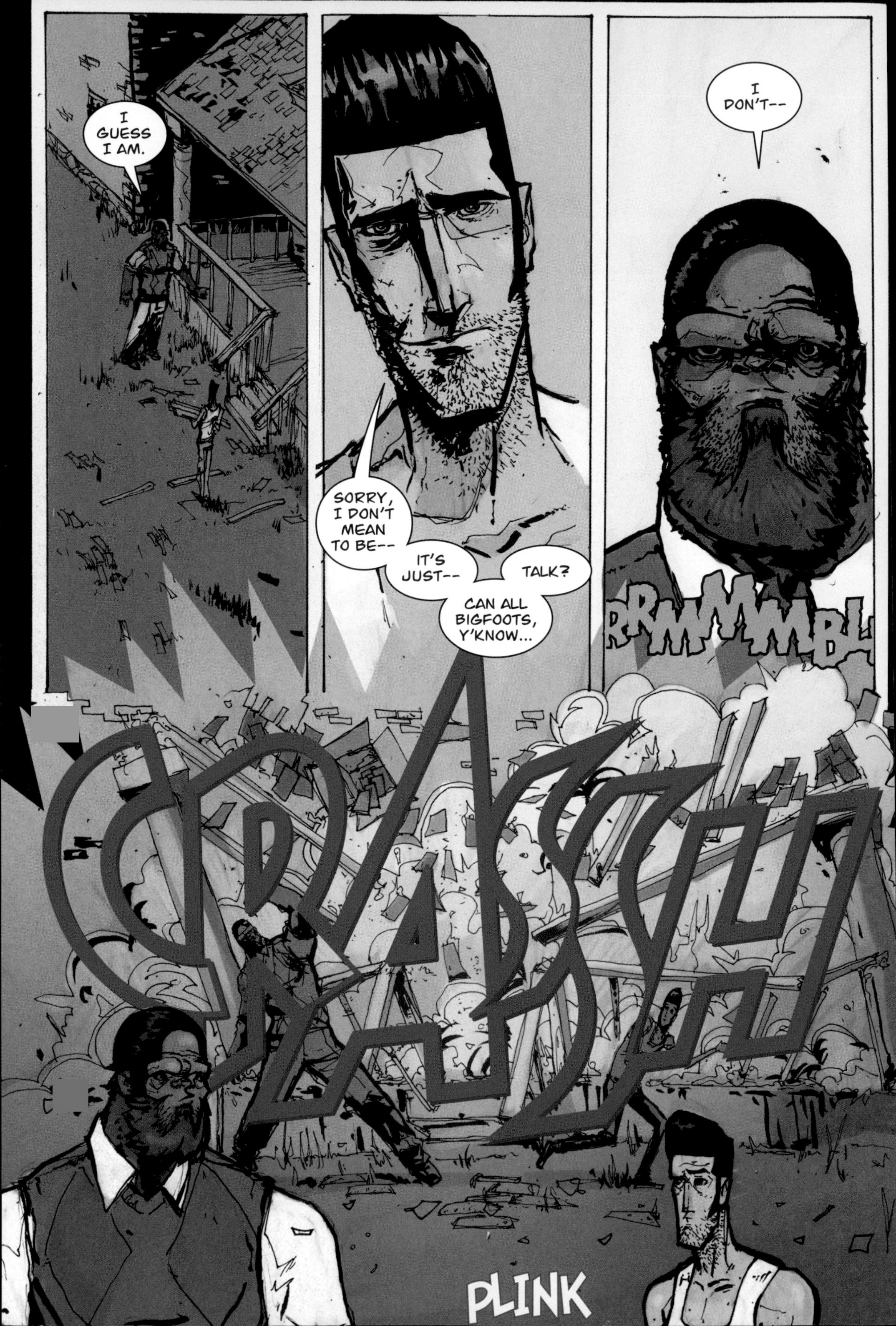
I GUESS I AM.
SORRY, I DON'T MEAN TO BE--
IT'S JUST--
CAN ALL BIGFOOTS, Y'KNOW...
TALK?
I DON'T--
CRASH
PLINK

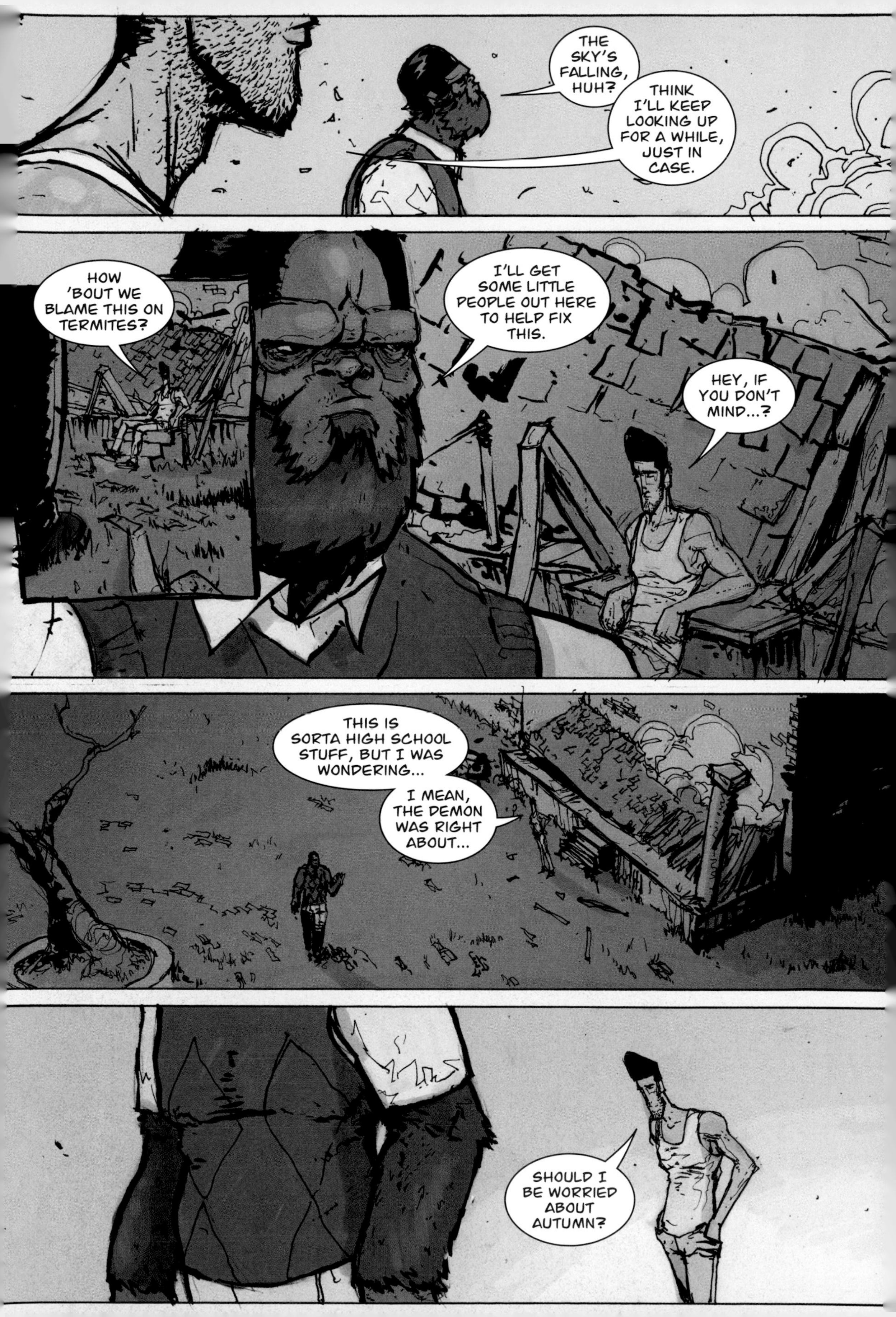
THE SKY'S FALLING, HUH?
THINK I'LL KEEP LOOKING UP FOR A WHILE, JUST IN CASE.
HOW 'BOUT WE BLAME THIS ON TERMITES?
I'LL GET SOME LITTLE PEOPLE OUT HERE TO HELP FIX THIS.
HEY, IF YOU DON'T MIND...?
THIS IS SORTA HIGH SCHOOL STUFF, BUT I WAS WONDERING...
I MEAN, THE DEMON WAS RIGHT ABOUT...
SHOULD I BE WORRIED ABOUT AUTUMN?

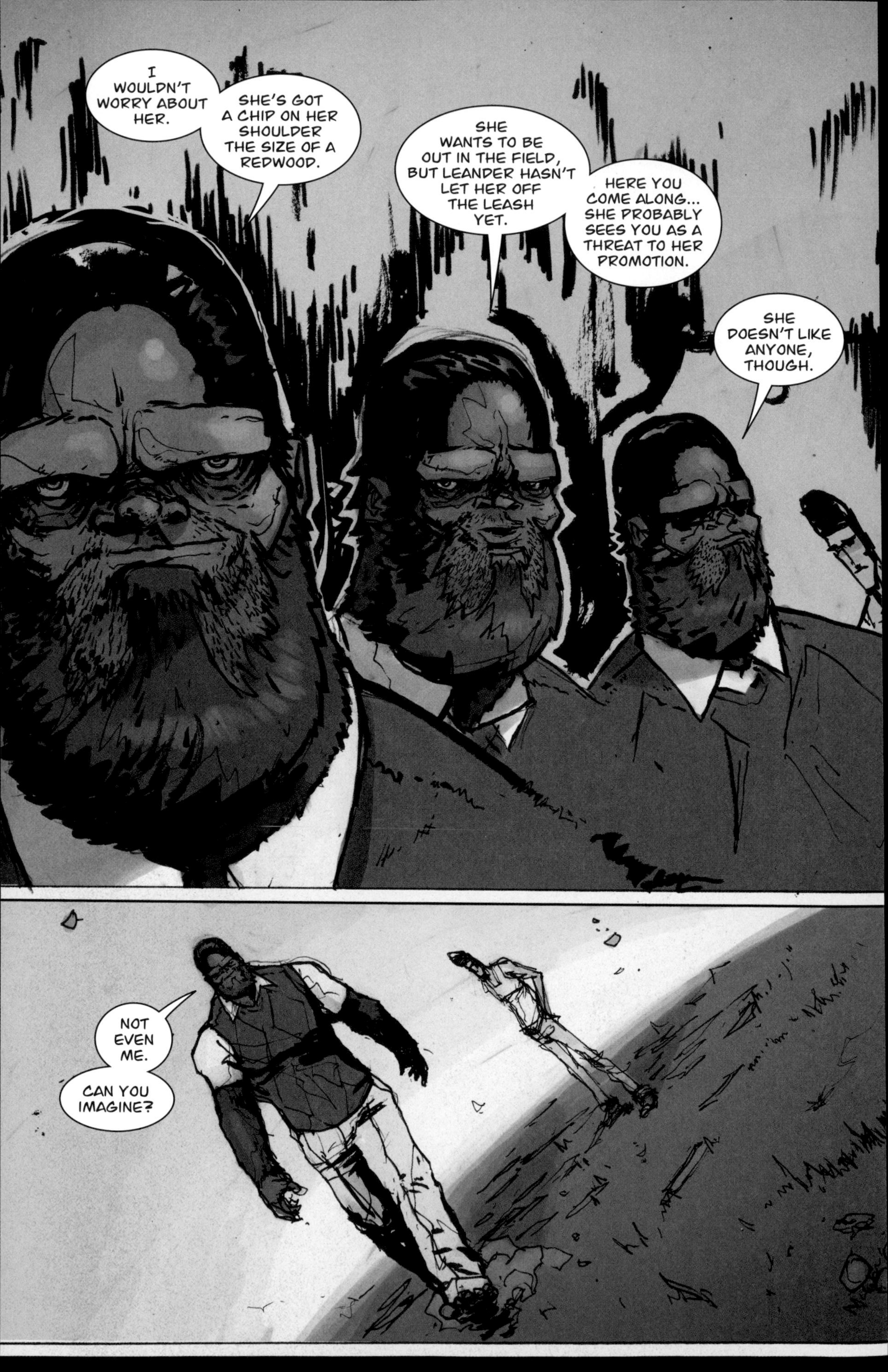
I WOULDN'T WORRY ABOUT HER.
SHE'S GOT A CHIP ON HER SHOULDER THE SIZE OF A REDWOOD.
SHE WANTS TO BE OUT IN THE FIELD, BUT LEANDER HASN'T LET HER OFF THE LEASH YET.
HERE YOU COME ALONG... SHE PROBABLY SEES YOU AS A THREAT TO HER PROMOTION.
SHE DOESN'T LIKE ANYONE, THOUGH.
NOT EVEN ME.
CAN YOU IMAGINE?

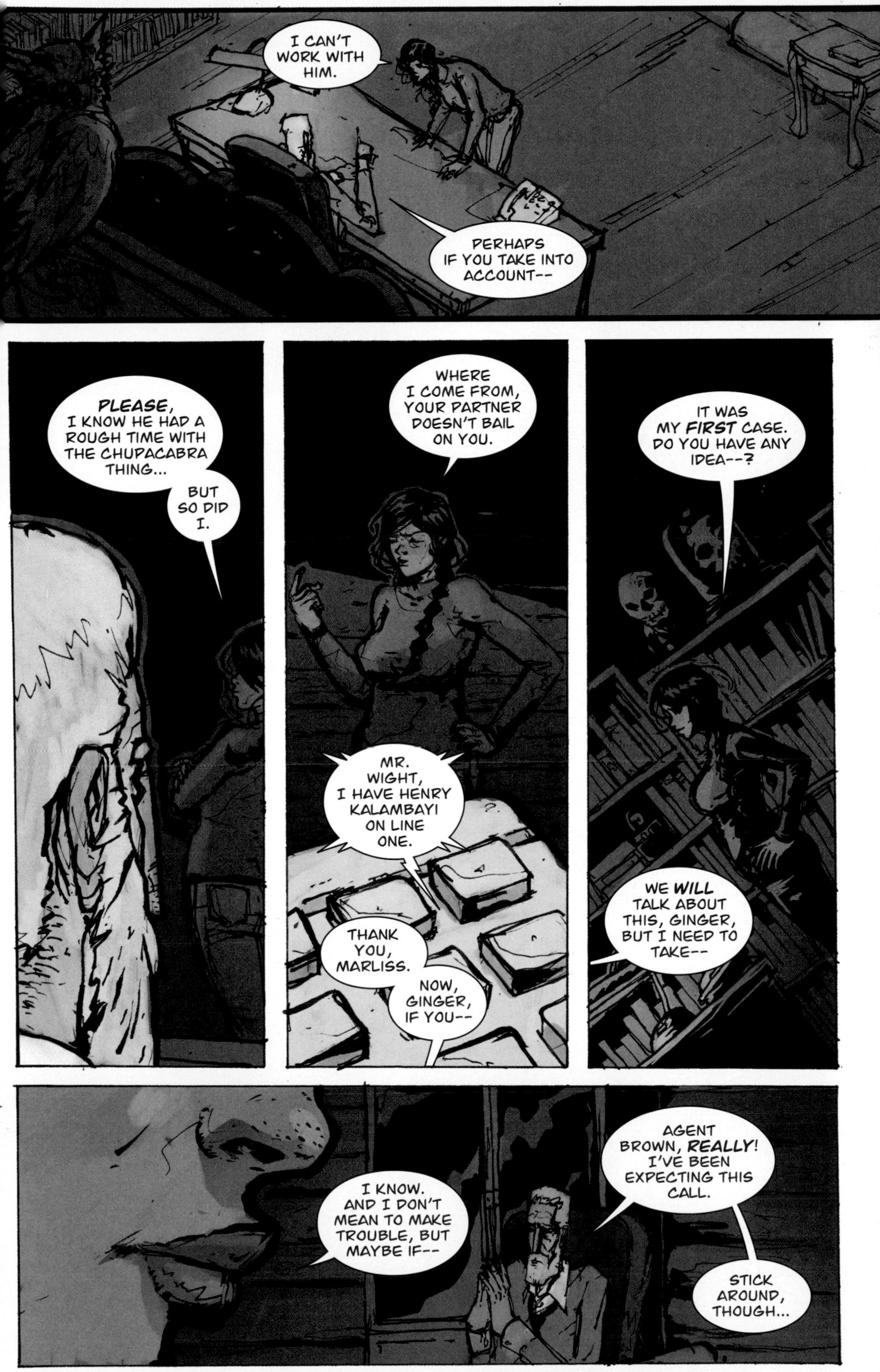

I CAN'T WORK WITH HIM.
PERHAPS IF YOU TAKE INTO ACCOUNT--
PLEASE, I KNOW HE HAD A ROUGH TIME WITH THE CHUPACABRA THING...
BUT SO DID I.
WHERE I COME FROM, YOUR PARTNER DOESN'T BAIL ON YOU.
MR. WIGHT, I HAVE HENRY KALAMBAYI ON LINE ONE.
THANK YOU, MARLISS.
NOW, GINGER, IF YOU--
IT WAS MY FIRST CASE. DO YOU HAVE ANY IDEA--?
WE WILL TALK ABOUT THIS, GINGER, BUT I NEED TO TAKE--
AGENT BROWN, REALLY! I'VE BEEN EXPECTING THIS CALL.
I KNOW. AND I DON'T MEAN TO MAKE TROUBLE, BUT MAYBE IF--
STICK AROUND, THOUGH...

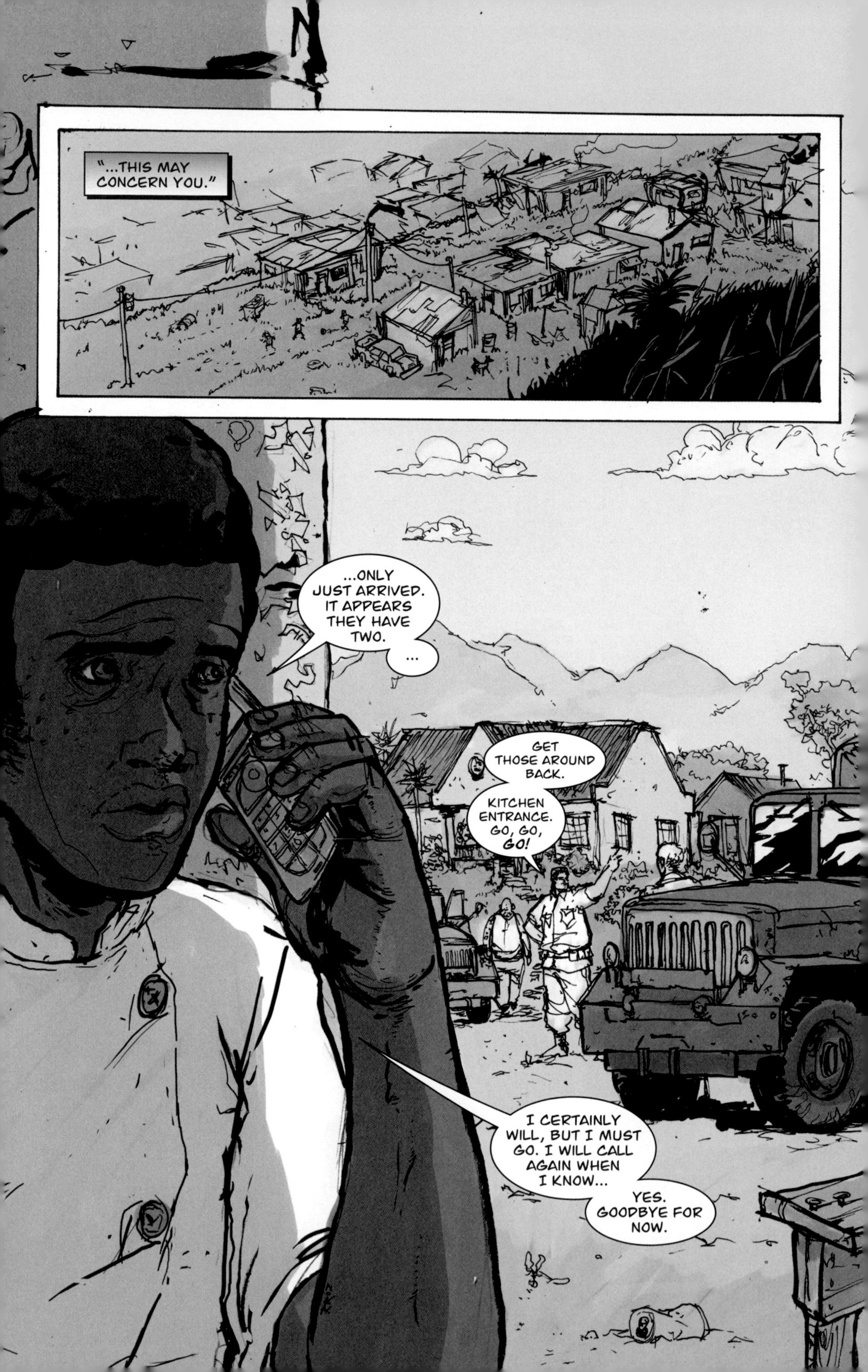
"...THIS MAY CONCERN YOU."
...ONLY JUST ARRIVED. IT APPEARS THEY HAVE TWO.
...
GET THOSE AROUND BACK.
KITCHEN ENTRANCE. GO, GO, GO!
I CERTAINLY WILL, BUT I MUST GO. I WILL CALL AGAIN WHEN I KNOW...
YES. GOODBYE FOR NOW.

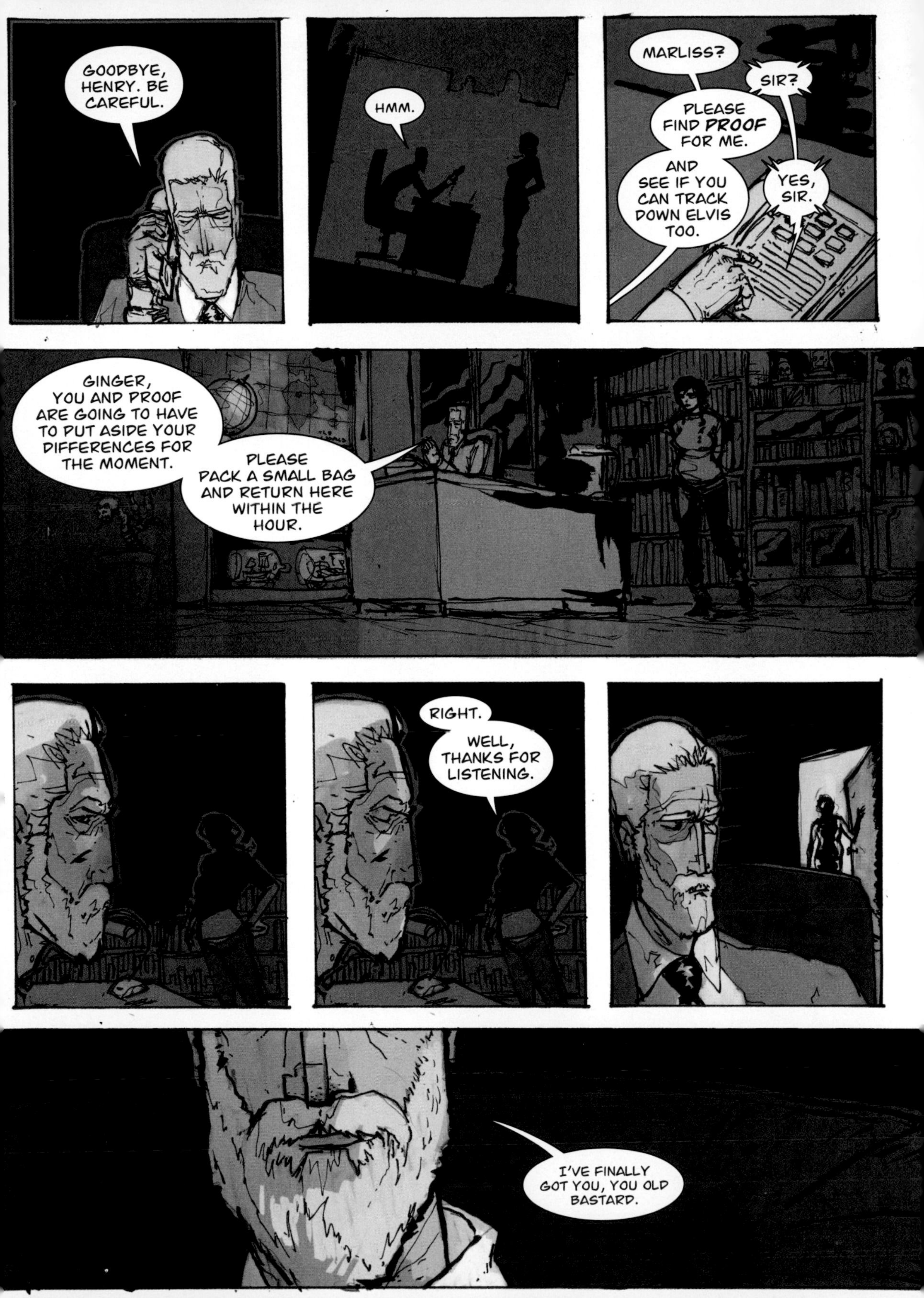
GOODBYE, HENRY. BE CAREFUL.
HMM.
MARLISS?
SIR?
PLEASE FIND PROOF FOR ME.
AND SEE IF YOU CAN TRACK DOWN ELVIS TOO.
YES, SIR.
GINGER, YOU AND PROOF ARE GOING TO HAVE TO PUT ASIDE YOUR DIFFERENCES FOR THE MOMENT.
PLEASE PACK A SMALL BAG AND RETURN HERE WITHIN THE HOUR.
RIGHT.
WELL, THANKS FOR LISTENING.
I'VE FINALLY GOT YOU, YOU OLD BASTARD.

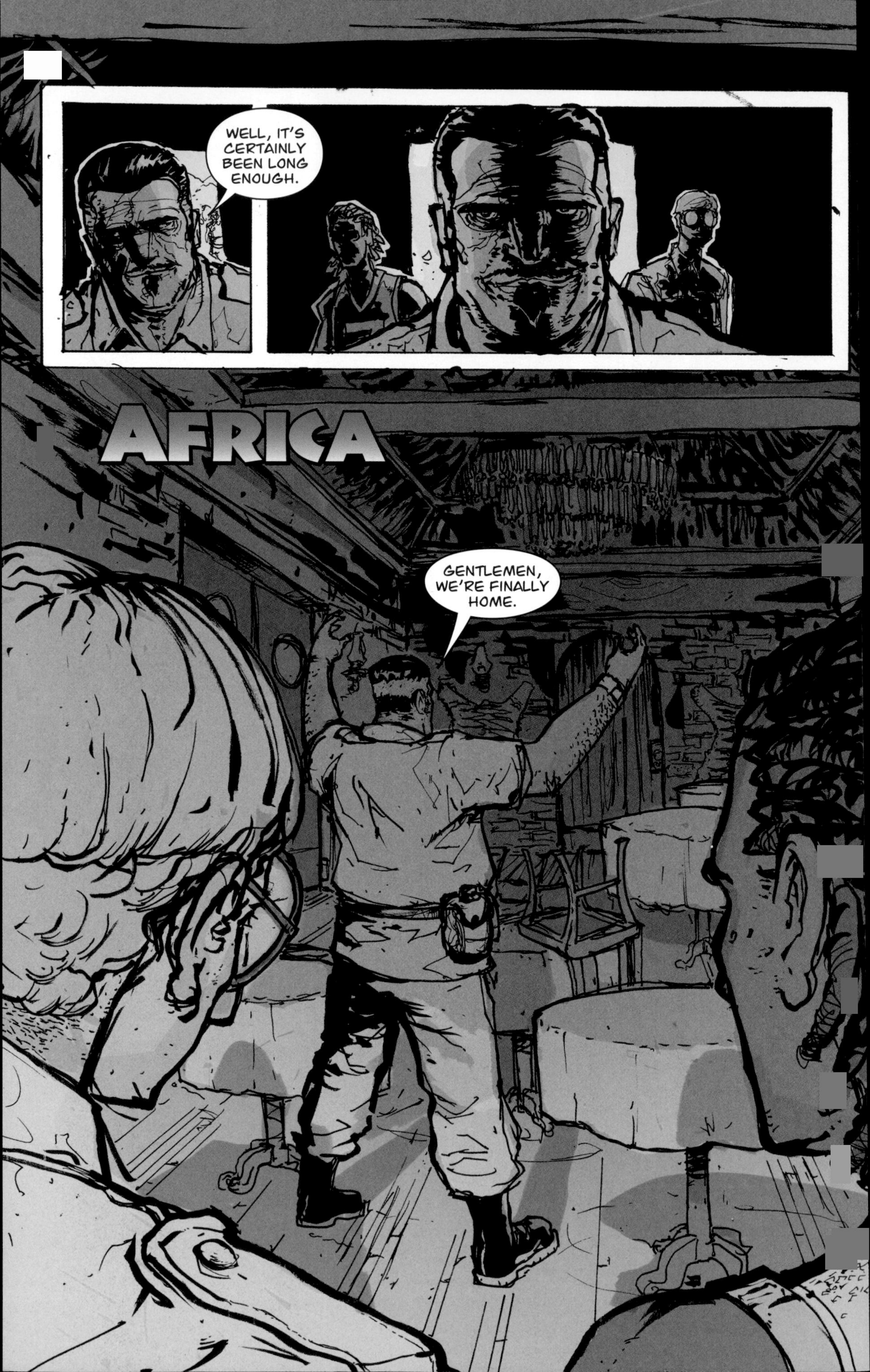
WELL, IT'S CERTAINLY BEEN LONG ENOUGH.
AFRICA
GENTLEMEN, WE'RE FINALLY HOME.

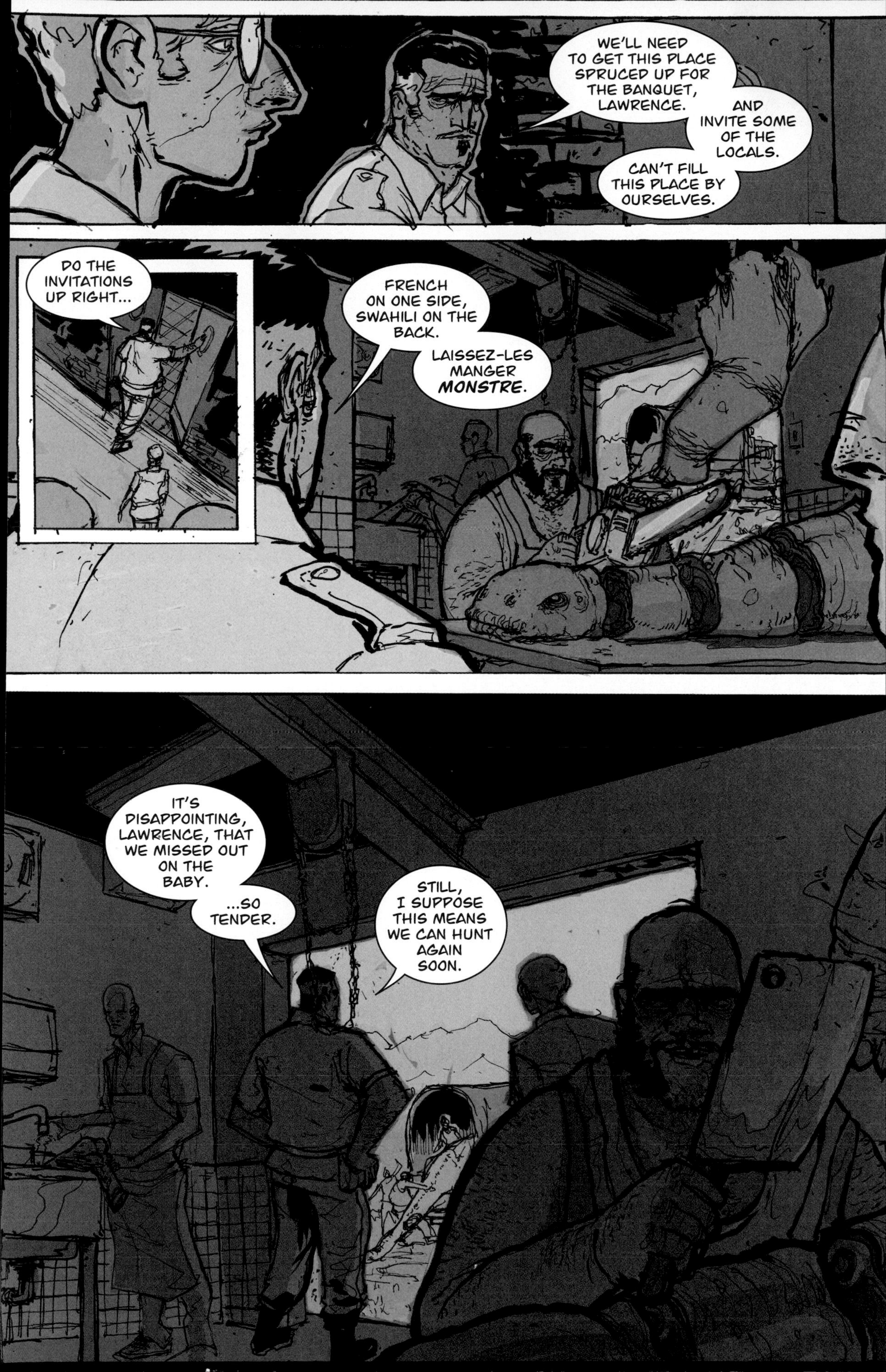
WE'LL NEED TO GET THIS PLACE SPRUCED UP FOR THE BANQUET, LAWRENCE.
AND INVITE SOME OF THE LOCALS.
CAN'T FILL THIS PLACE BY OURSELVES.
DO THE INVITATIONS UP RIGHT...
FRENCH ON ONE SIDE, SWAHILI ON THE BACK.
LAISSEZ-LES MANGER *MONSTRE*.
IT'S DISAPPOINTING, LAWRENCE, THAT WE MISSED OUT ON THE BABY.
...SO TENDER.
STILL, I SUPPOSE THIS MEANS WE CAN HUNT AGAIN SOON.

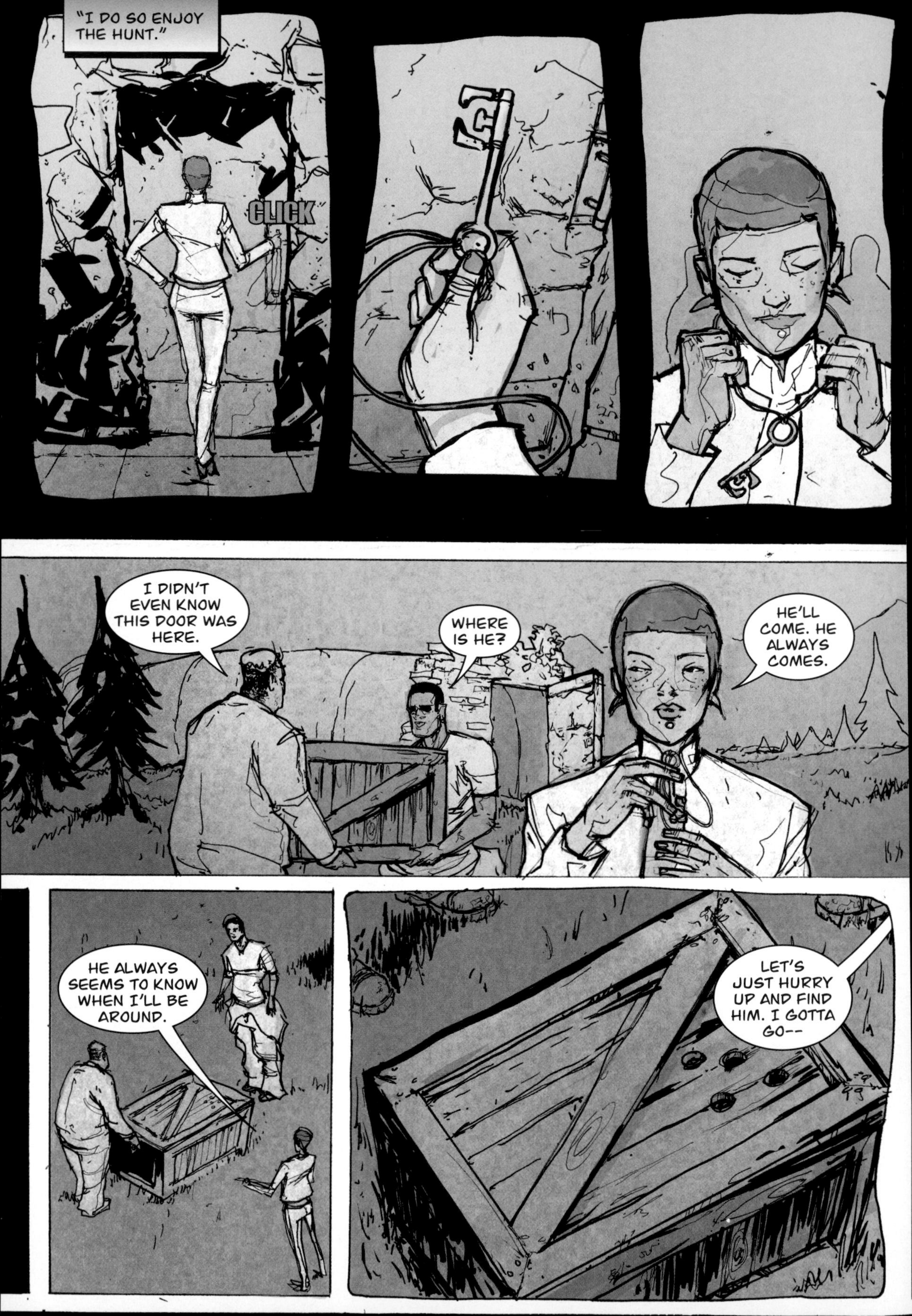
"I DO SO ENJOY THE HUNT."
CLICK
I DIDN'T EVEN KNOW THIS DOOR WAS HERE.
WHERE IS HE?
HE'LL COME. HE ALWAYS COMES.
HE ALWAYS SEEMS TO KNOW WHEN I'LL BE AROUND.
LET'S JUST HURRY UP AND FIND HIM. I GOTTA GO--

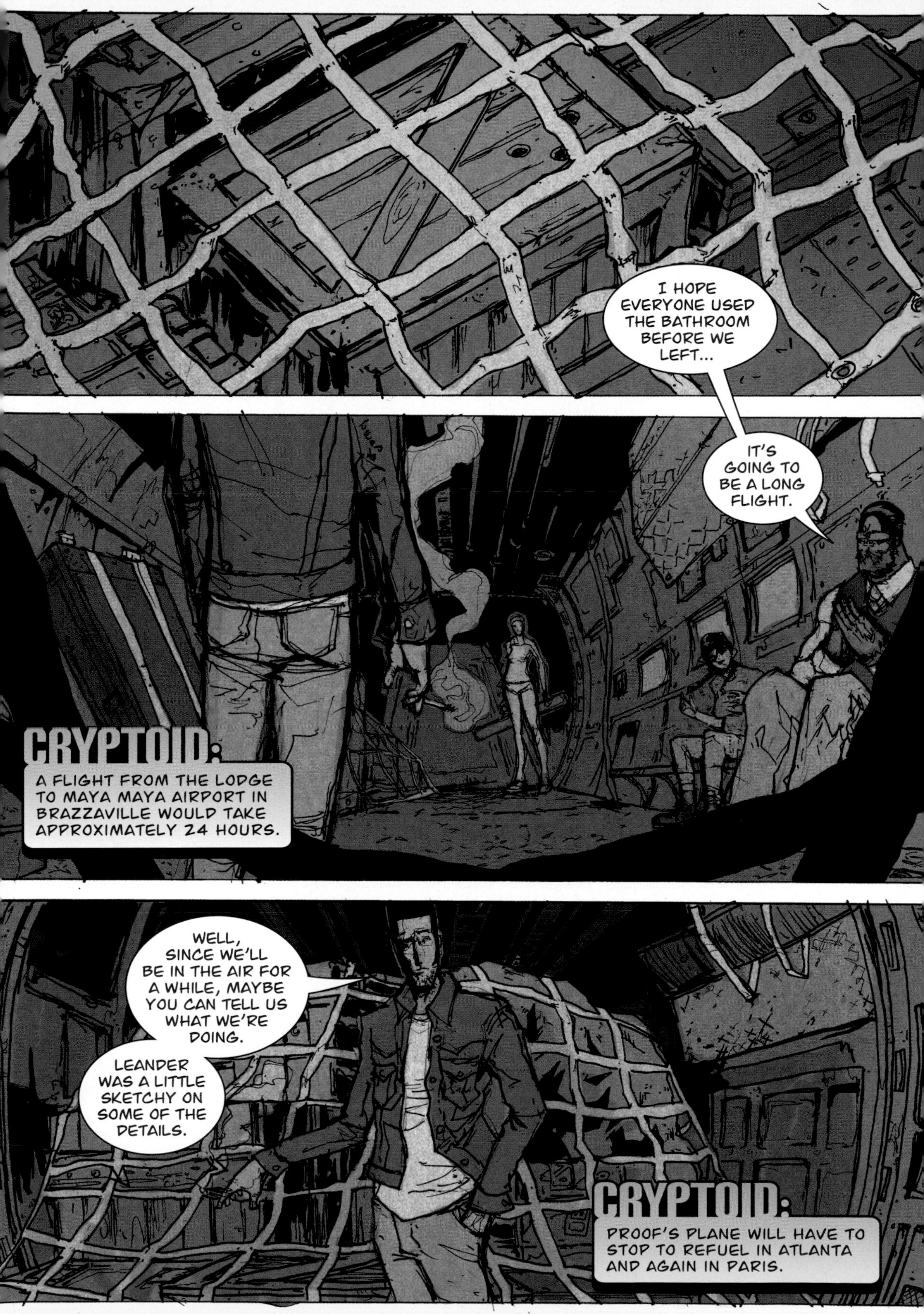
I HOPE EVERYONE USED THE BATHROOM BEFORE WE LEFT...
IT'S GOING TO BE A LONG FLIGHT.
CRYPTOID:
A FLIGHT FROM THE LODGE TO MAYA MAYA AIRPORT IN BRAZZAVILLE WOULD TAKE APPROXIMATELY 24 HOURS.
WELL, SINCE WE'LL BE IN THE AIR FOR A WHILE, MAYBE YOU CAN TELL US WHAT WE'RE DOING.
LEANDER WAS A LITTLE SKETCHY ON SOME OF THE DETAILS.
CRYPTOID:
PROOF'S PLANE WILL HAVE TO STOP TO REFUEL IN ATLANTA AND AGAIN IN PARIS.

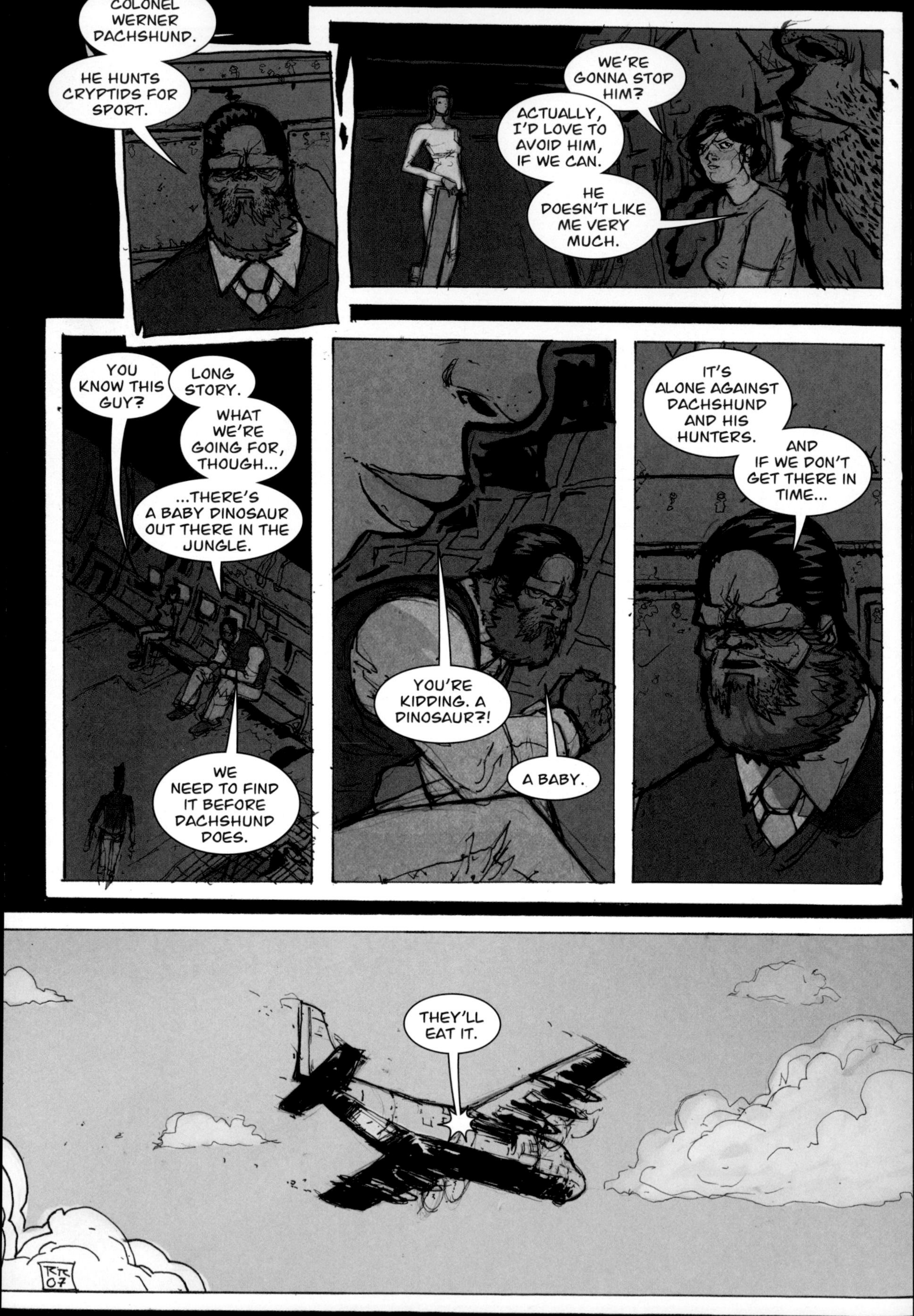
COLONEL WERNER DACHSHUND.
HE HUNTS CRYPTIDS FOR SPORT.
WE'RE GONNA STOP HIM?
ACTUALLY, I'D LOVE TO AVOID HIM, IF WE CAN.
HE DOESN'T LIKE ME VERY MUCH.
YOU KNOW THIS GUY?
LONG STORY.
WHAT WE'RE GOING FOR, THOUGH...
...THERE'S A BABY DINOSAUR OUT THERE IN THE JUNGLE.
WE NEED TO FIND IT BEFORE DACHSHUND DOES.
YOU'RE KIDDING. A DINOSAUR?!
A BABY.
IT'S ALONE AGAINST DACHSHUND AND HIS HUNTERS.
AND IF WE DON'T GET THERE IN TIME...
THEY'LL EAT IT.
RK 07

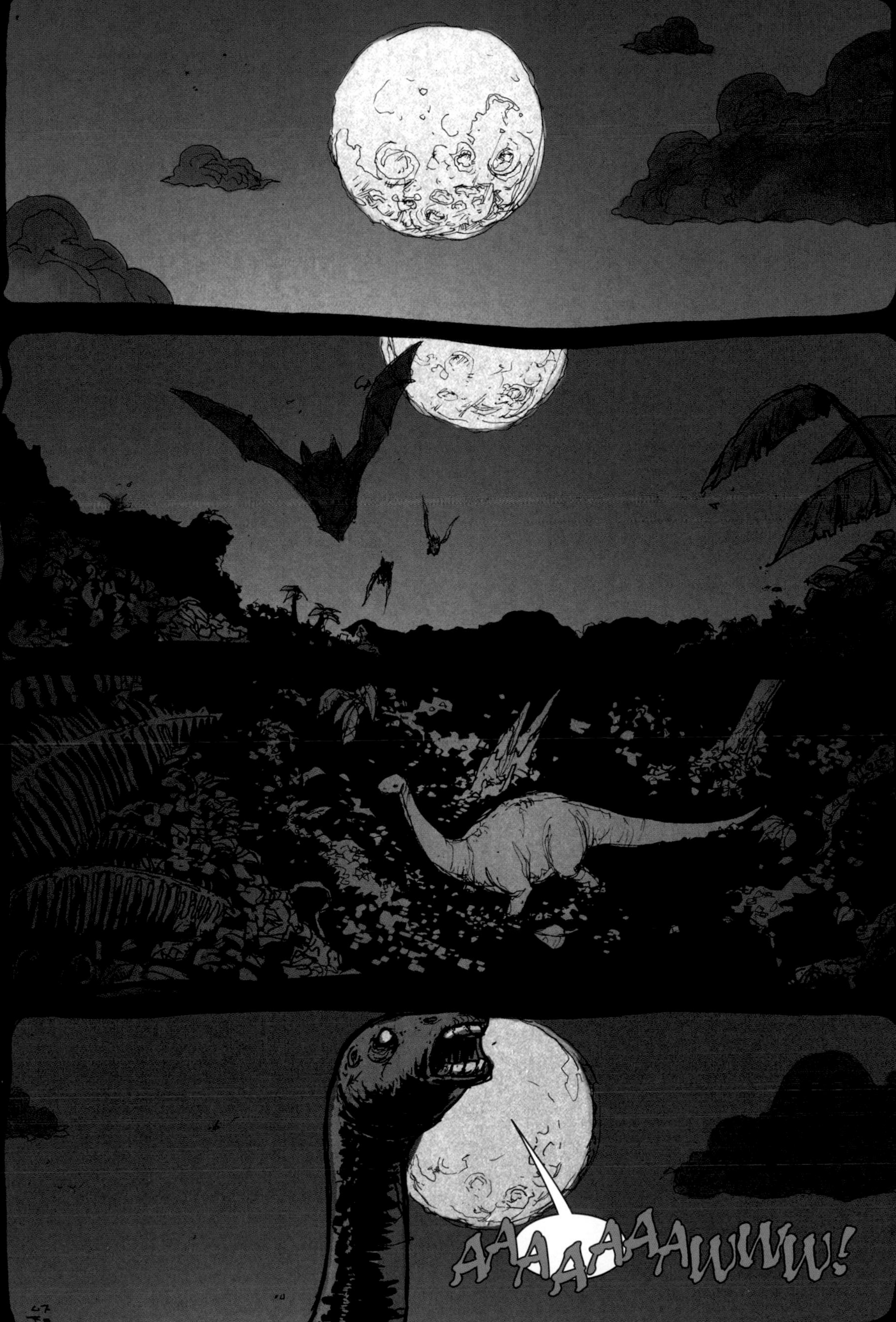
AAAAAAAAWWWW!

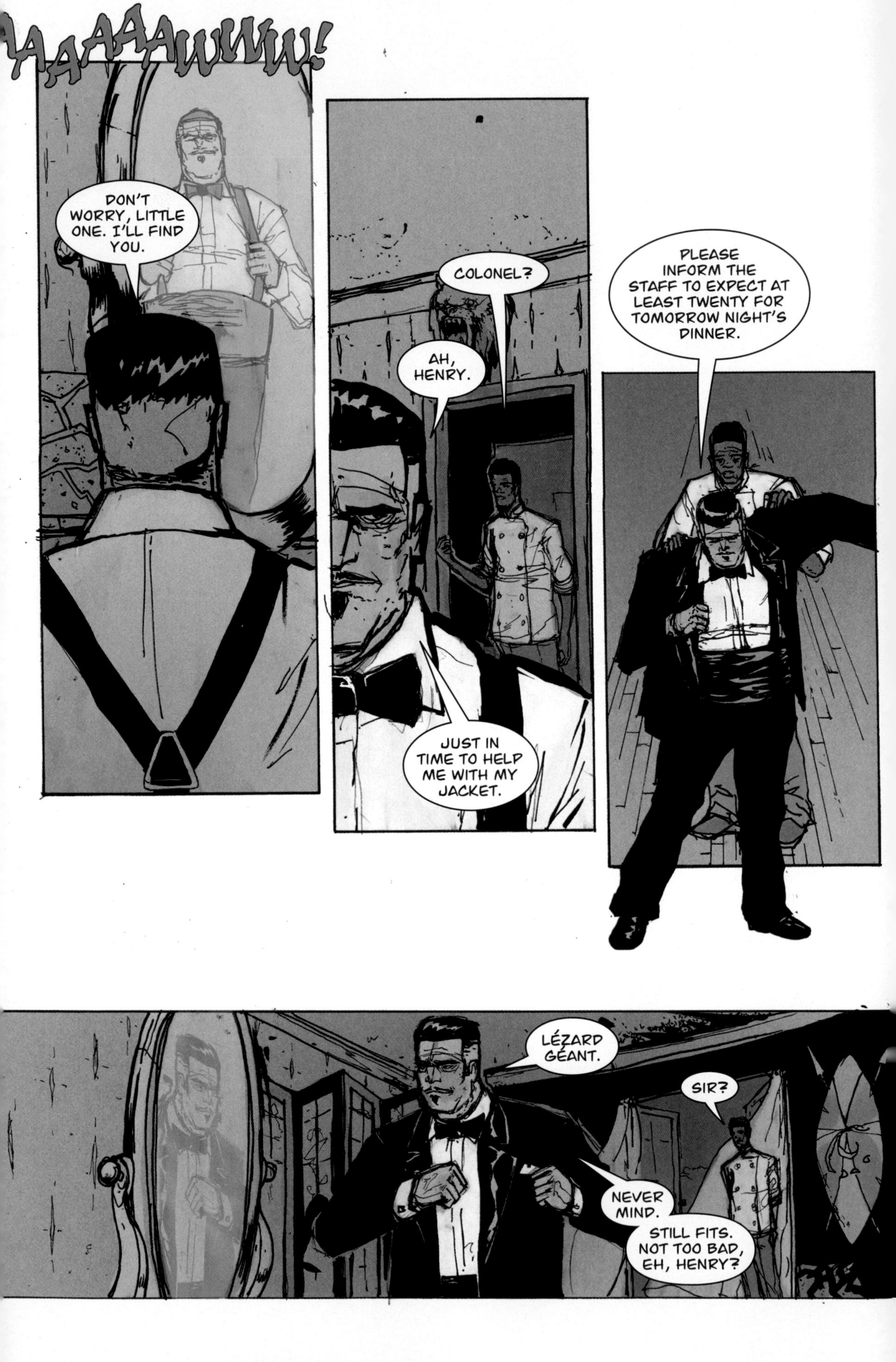
AAAAAWWWW!
DON'T WORRY, LITTLE ONE. I'LL FIND YOU.
COLONEL?
AH, HENRY.
JUST IN TIME TO HELP ME WITH MY JACKET.
PLEASE INFORM THE STAFF TO EXPECT AT LEAST TWENTY FOR TOMORROW NIGHT'S DINNER.
LÉZARD GÉANT.
SIR?
NEVER MIND.
STILL FITS. NOT TOO BAD, EH, HENRY?

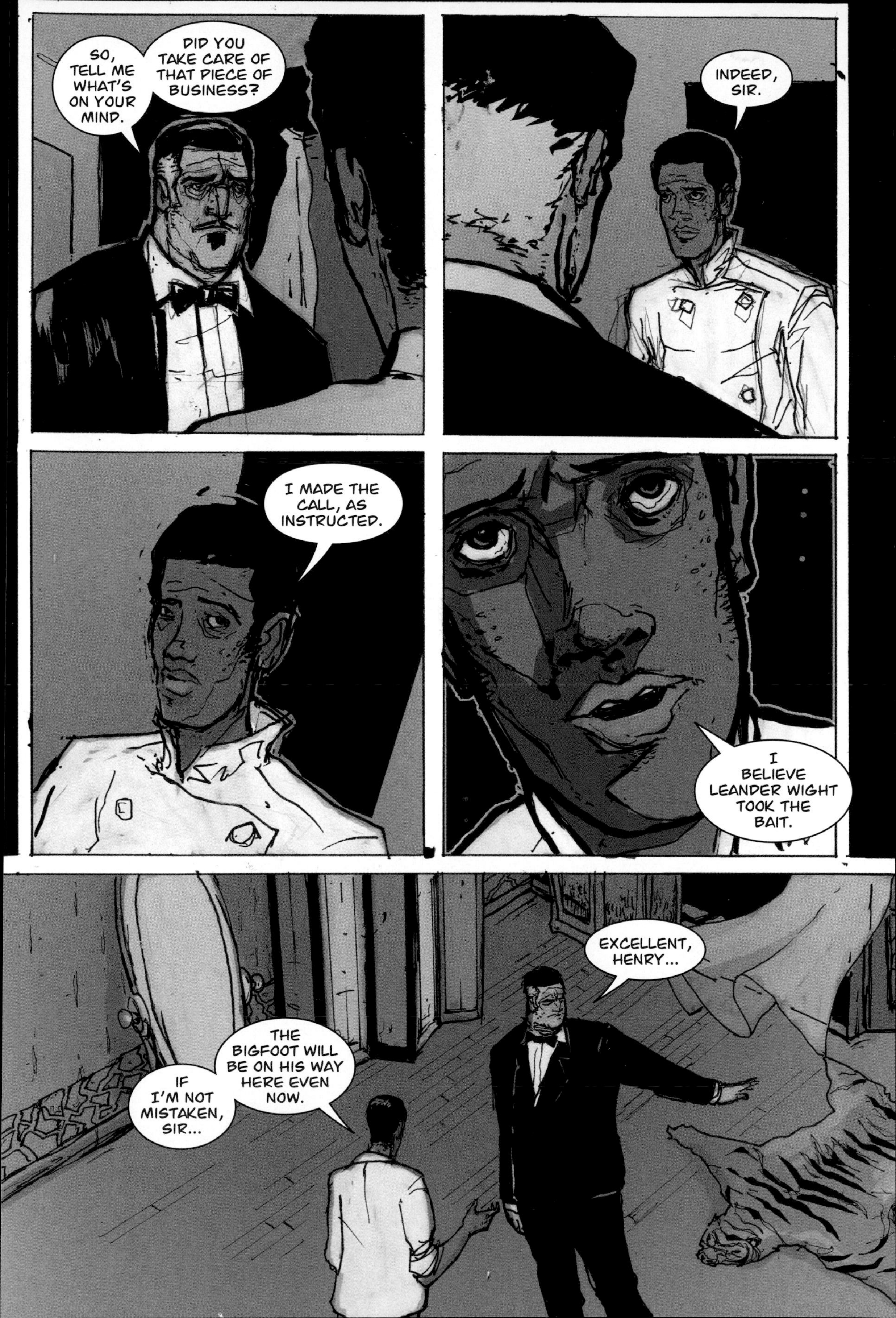
SO, TELL ME WHAT'S ON YOUR MIND.
DID YOU TAKE CARE OF THAT PIECE OF BUSINESS?
INDEED, SIR.
I MADE THE CALL, AS INSTRUCTED.
I BELIEVE LEANDER WIGHT TOOK THE BAIT.
EXCELLENT, HENRY...
THE BIGFOOT WILL BE ON HIS WAY HERE EVEN NOW.
IF I'M NOT MISTAKEN, SIR...

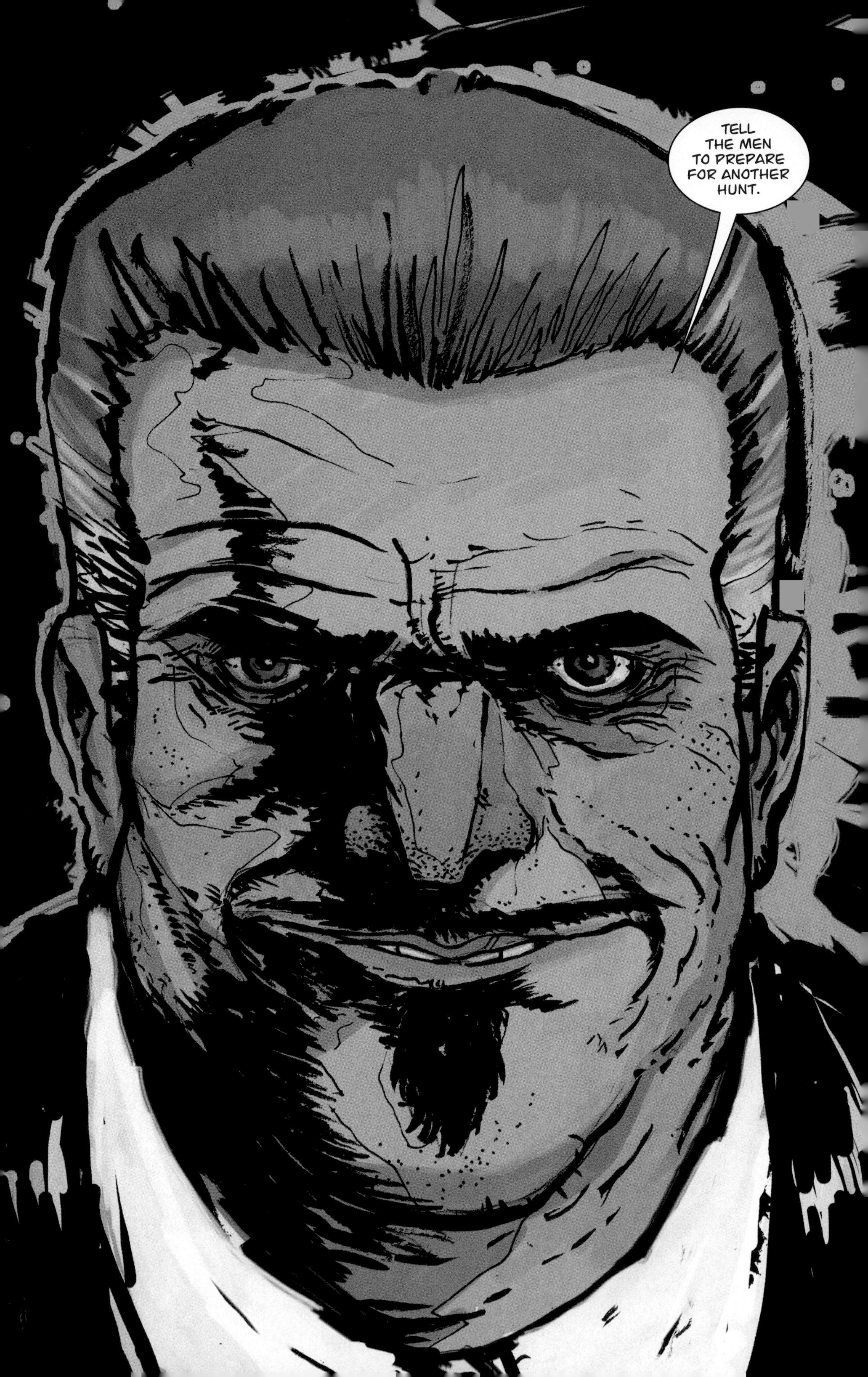
TELL THE MEN TO PREPARE FOR ANOTHER HUNT.

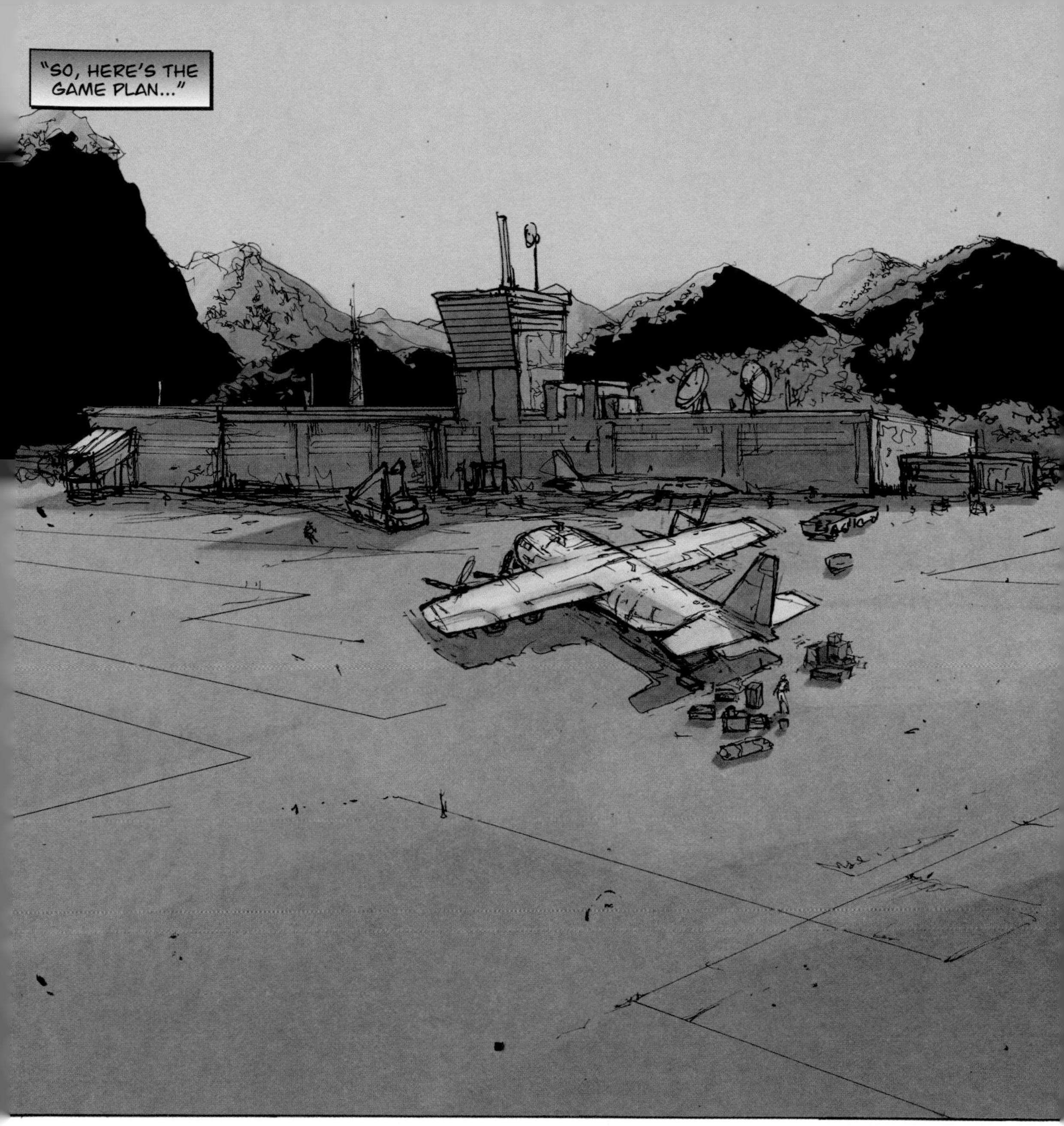
"SO, HERE'S THE GAME PLAN..."

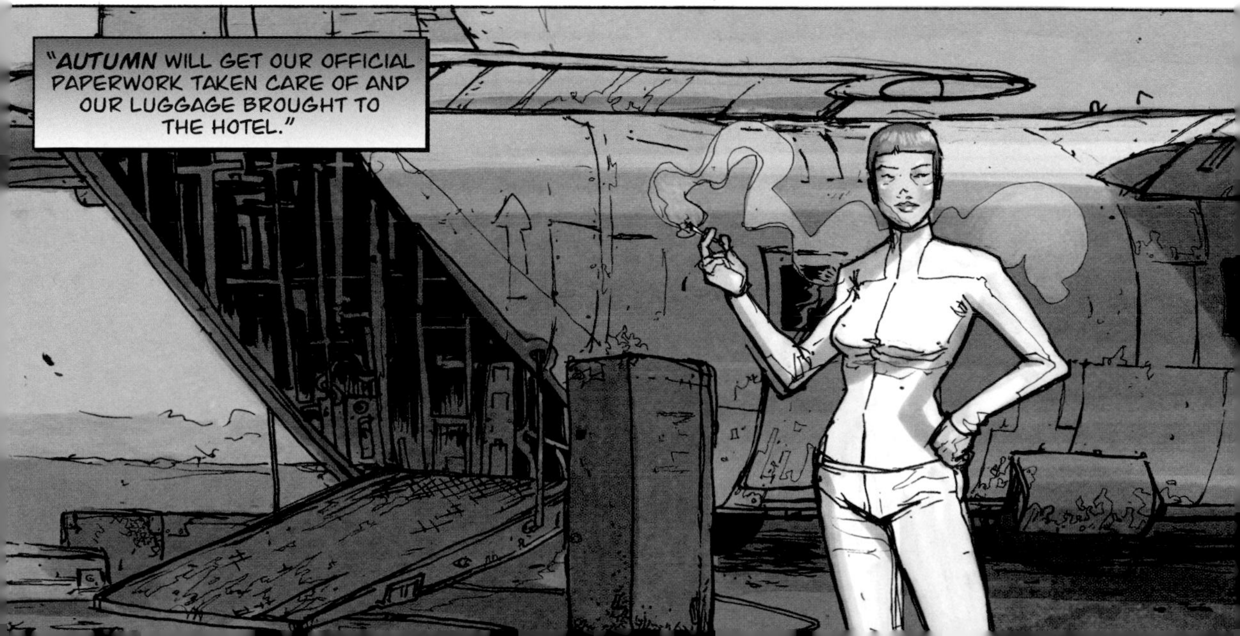
"AUTUMN WILL GET OUR OFFICIAL PAPERWORK TAKEN CARE OF AND OUR LUGGAGE BROUGHT TO THE HOTEL."

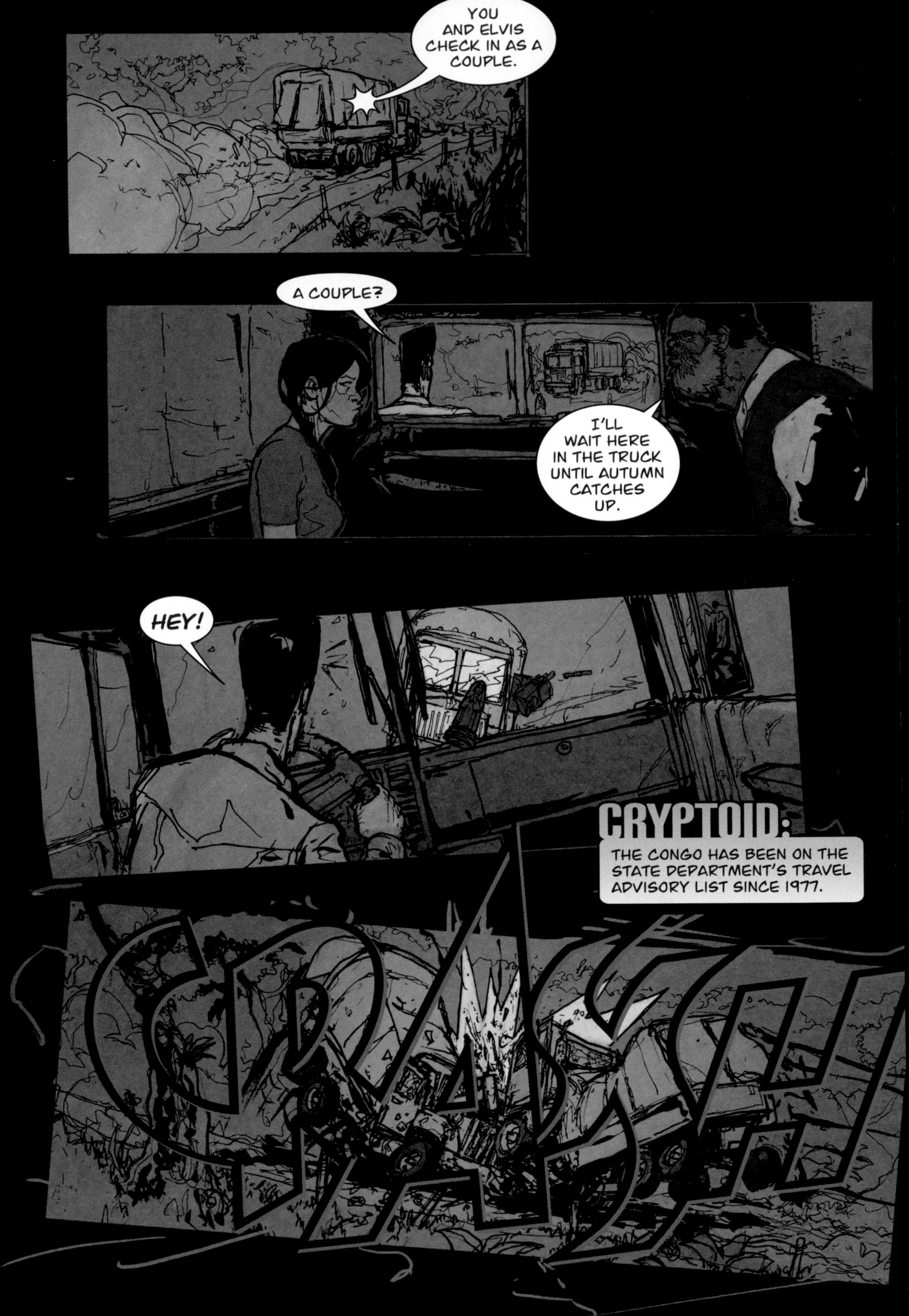
YOU AND ELVIS CHECK IN AS A COUPLE.
A COUPLE?
I'LL WAIT HERE IN THE TRUCK UNTIL AUTUMN CATCHES UP.
HEY!
CRYPTOID:
THE CONGO HAS BEEN ON THE STATE DEPARTMENT'S TRAVEL ADVISORY LIST SINCE 1977.
CRASH!

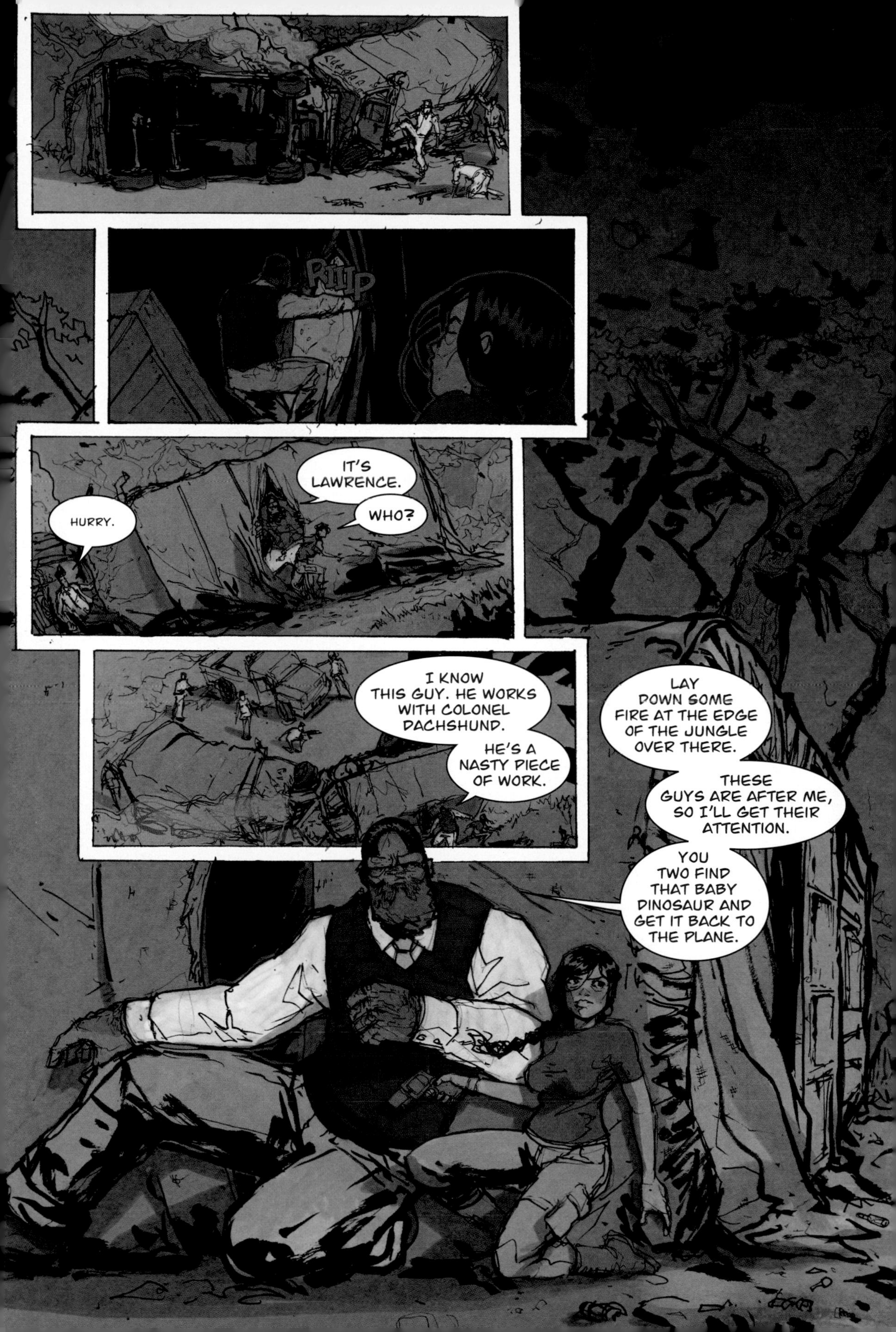
RIIIP
IT'S LAWRENCE.
WHO?
HURRY.
I KNOW THIS GUY. HE WORKS WITH COLONEL DACHSHUND.
HE'S A NASTY PIECE OF WORK.
LAY DOWN SOME FIRE AT THE EDGE OF THE JUNGLE OVER THERE.
THESE GUYS ARE AFTER ME, SO I'LL GET THEIR ATTENTION.
YOU TWO FIND THAT BABY DINOSAUR AND GET IT BACK TO THE PLANE.

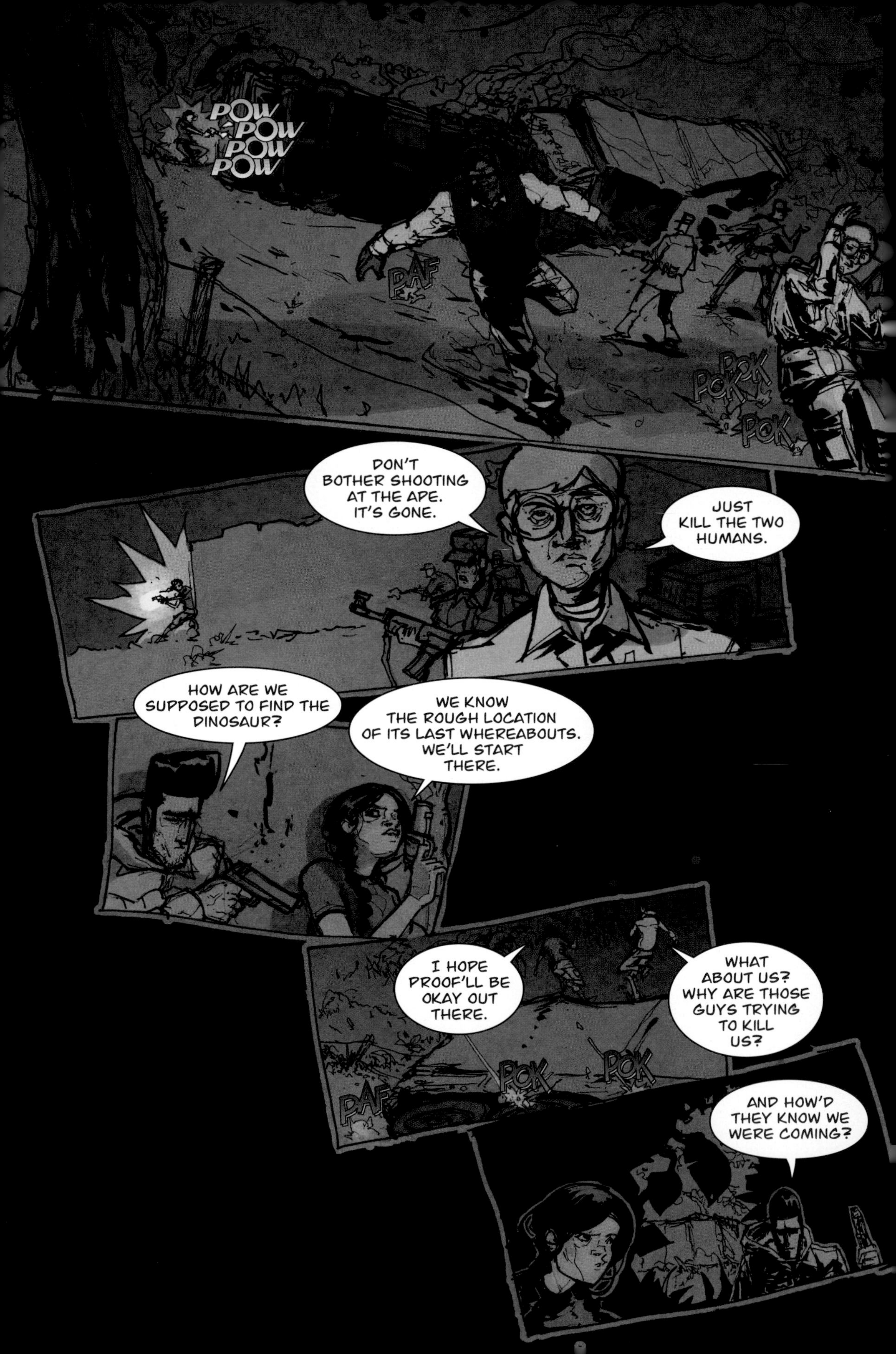
POW POW POW POW
PAF
POK POK POK POK
DON'T BOTHER SHOOTING AT THE APE. IT'S GONE.
JUST KILL THE TWO HUMANS.
HOW ARE WE SUPPOSED TO FIND THE DINOSAUR?
WE KNOW THE ROUGH LOCATION OF ITS LAST WHEREABOUTS. WE'LL START THERE.
I HOPE PROOF'LL BE OKAY OUT THERE.
WHAT ABOUT US? WHY ARE THOSE GUYS TRYING TO KILL US?
PAF
POK
POK
AND HOW'D THEY KNOW WE WERE COMING?

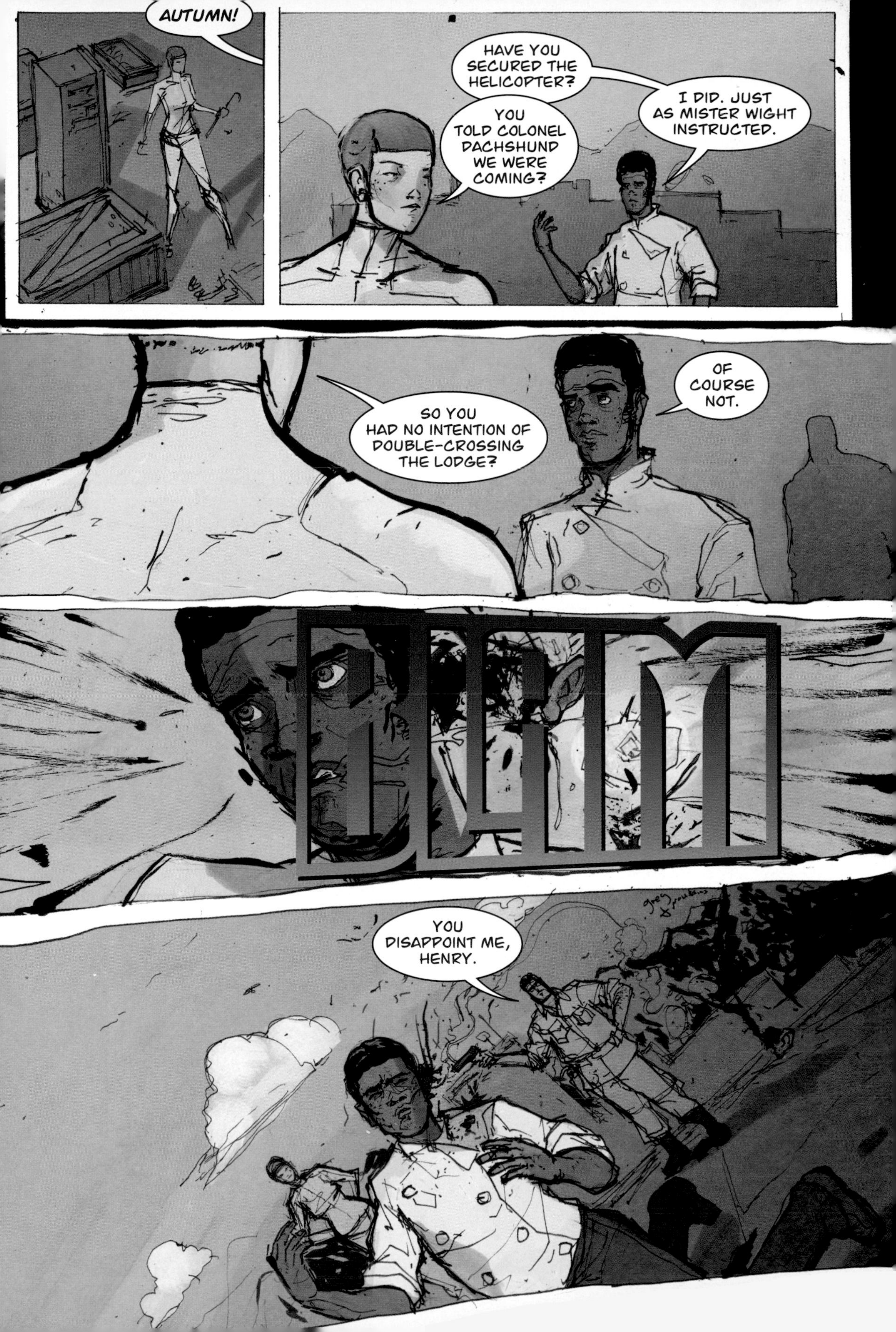
AUTUMN!
HAVE YOU SECURED THE HELICOPTER?
I DID. JUST AS MISTER WIGHT INSTRUCTED.
YOU TOLD COLONEL DACHSHUND WE WERE COMING?
SO YOU HAD NO INTENTION OF DOUBLE-CROSSING THE LODGE?
OF COURSE NOT.
YOU DISAPPOINT ME, HENRY.

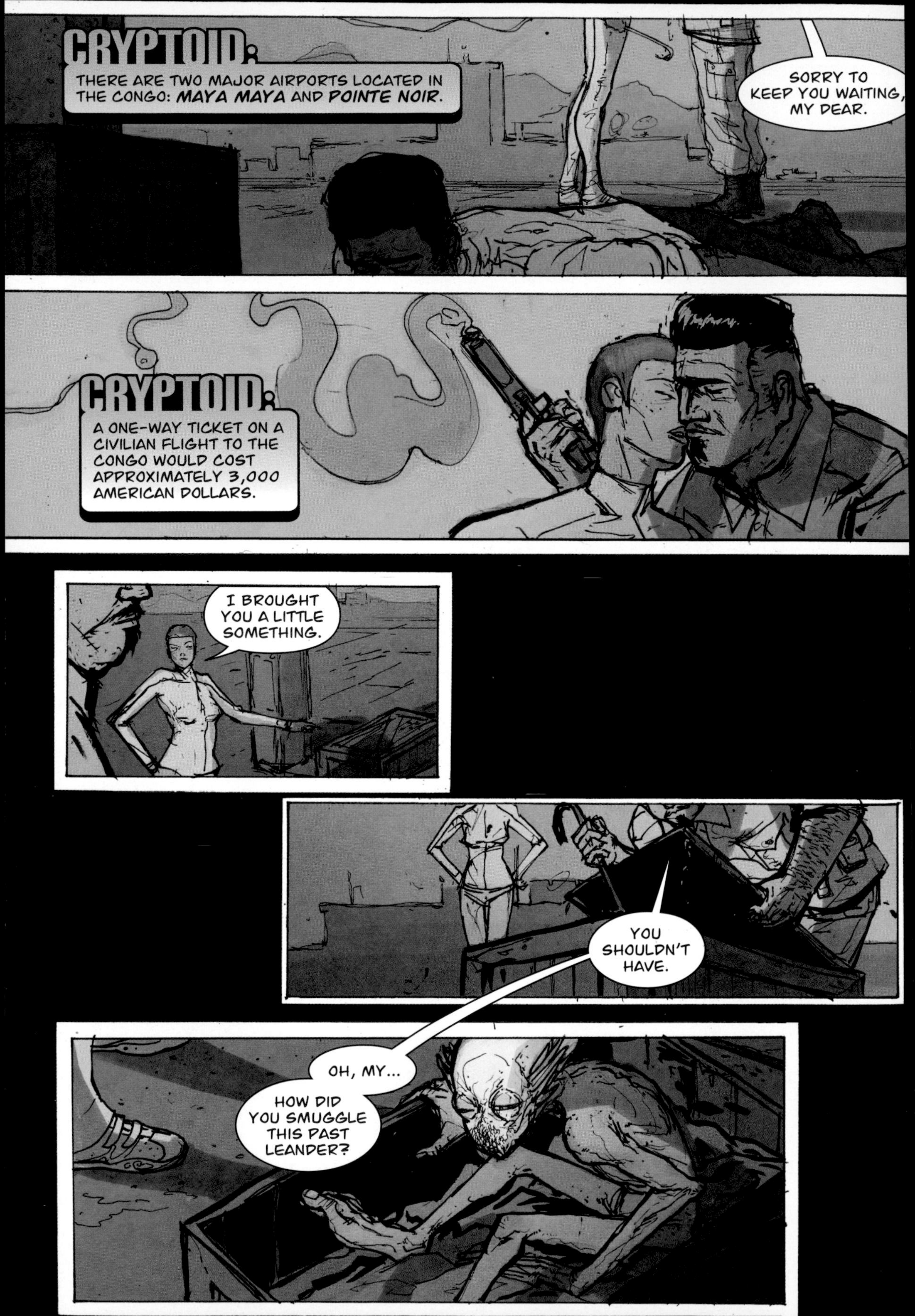
CRYPTOID:
THERE ARE TWO MAJOR AIRPORTS LOCATED IN THE CONGO: *MAYA MAYA* AND *POINTE NOIR*.
SORRY TO KEEP YOU WAITING, MY DEAR.
CRYPTOID:
A ONE-WAY TICKET ON A CIVILIAN FLIGHT TO THE CONGO WOULD COST APPROXIMATELY 3,000 AMERICAN DOLLARS.
I BROUGHT YOU A LITTLE SOMETHING.
YOU SHOULDN'T HAVE.
OH, MY...
HOW DID YOU SMUGGLE THIS PAST LEANDER?

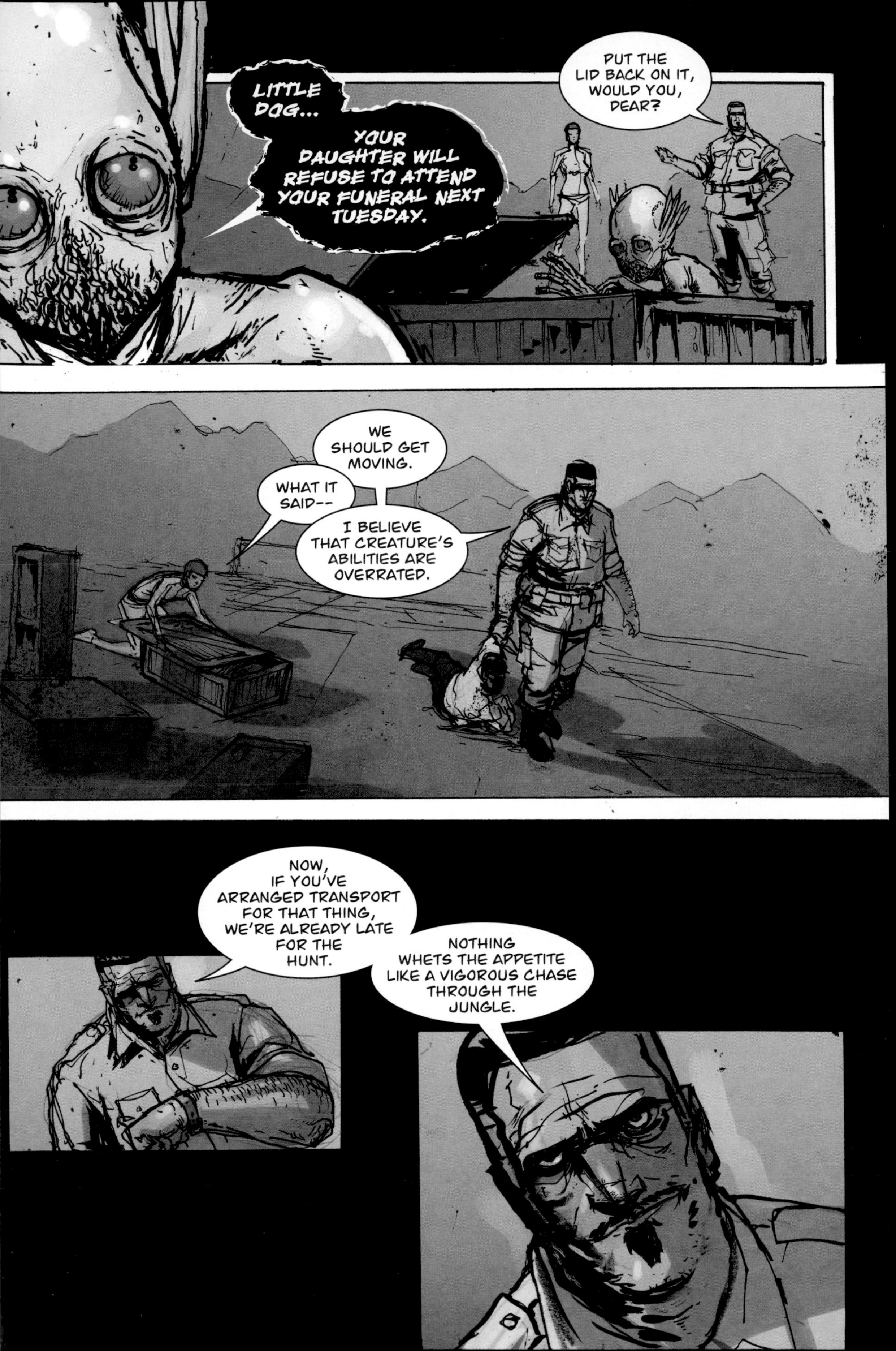
LITTLE DOG...
YOUR DAUGHTER WILL REFUSE TO ATTEND YOUR FUNERAL NEXT TUESDAY.
PUT THE LID BACK ON IT, WOULD YOU, DEAR?
WE SHOULD GET MOVING.
WHAT IT SAID--
I BELIEVE THAT CREATURE'S ABILITIES ARE OVERRATED.
NOW, IF YOU'VE ARRANGED TRANSPORT FOR THAT THING, WE'RE ALREADY LATE FOR THE HUNT.
NOTHING WHETS THE APPETITE LIKE A VIGOROUS CHASE THROUGH THE JUNGLE.

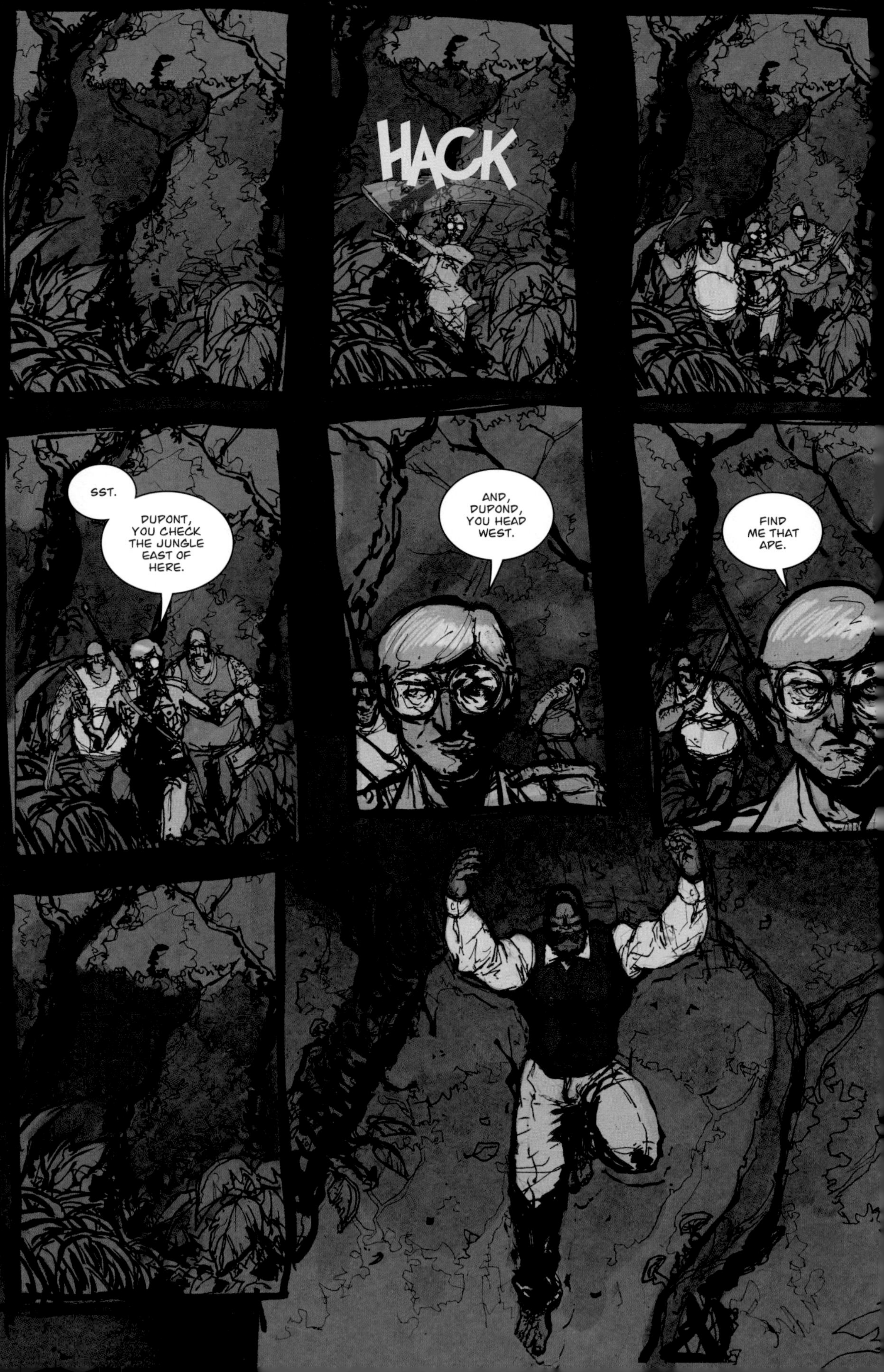
HACK
SST.
DUPONT, YOU CHECK THE JUNGLE EAST OF HERE.
AND, DUPOND, YOU HEAD WEST.
FIND ME THAT APE.

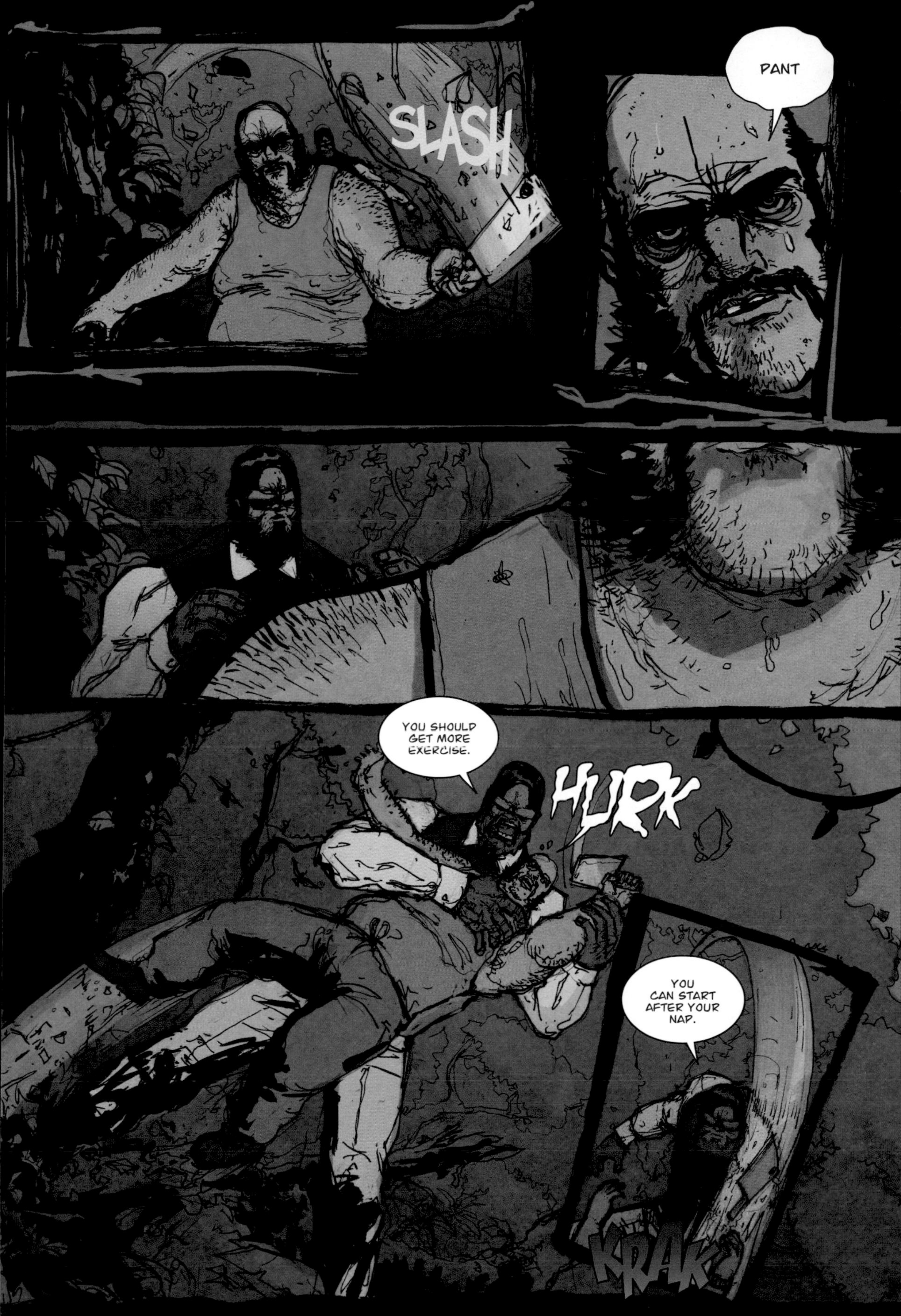
SLASH
PANT
YOU SHOULD GET MORE EXERCISE.
HURK
YOU CAN START AFTER YOUR NAP.
KRAK

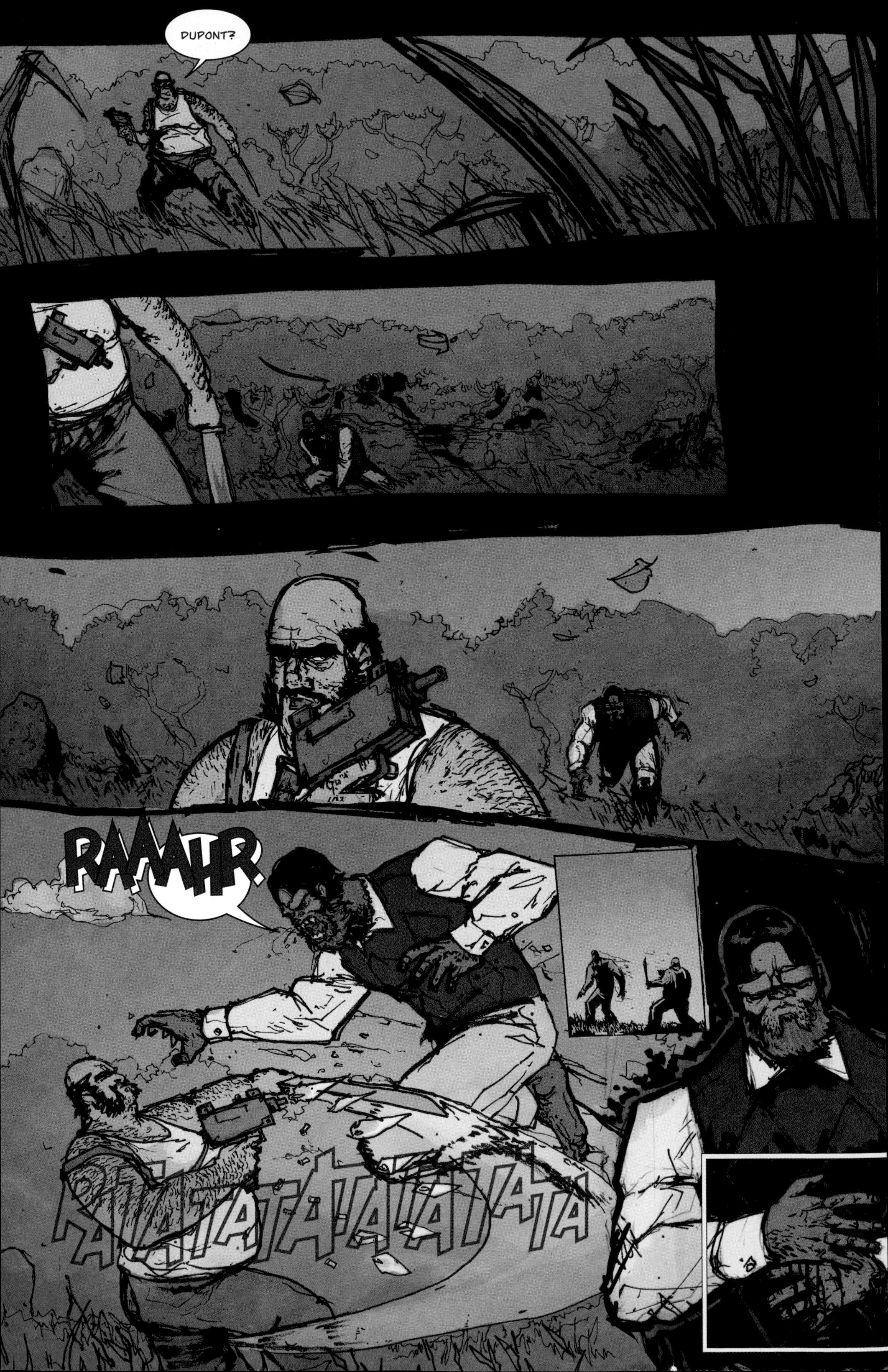
DUPONT?
RAAAHR.
RATATATATATATATA

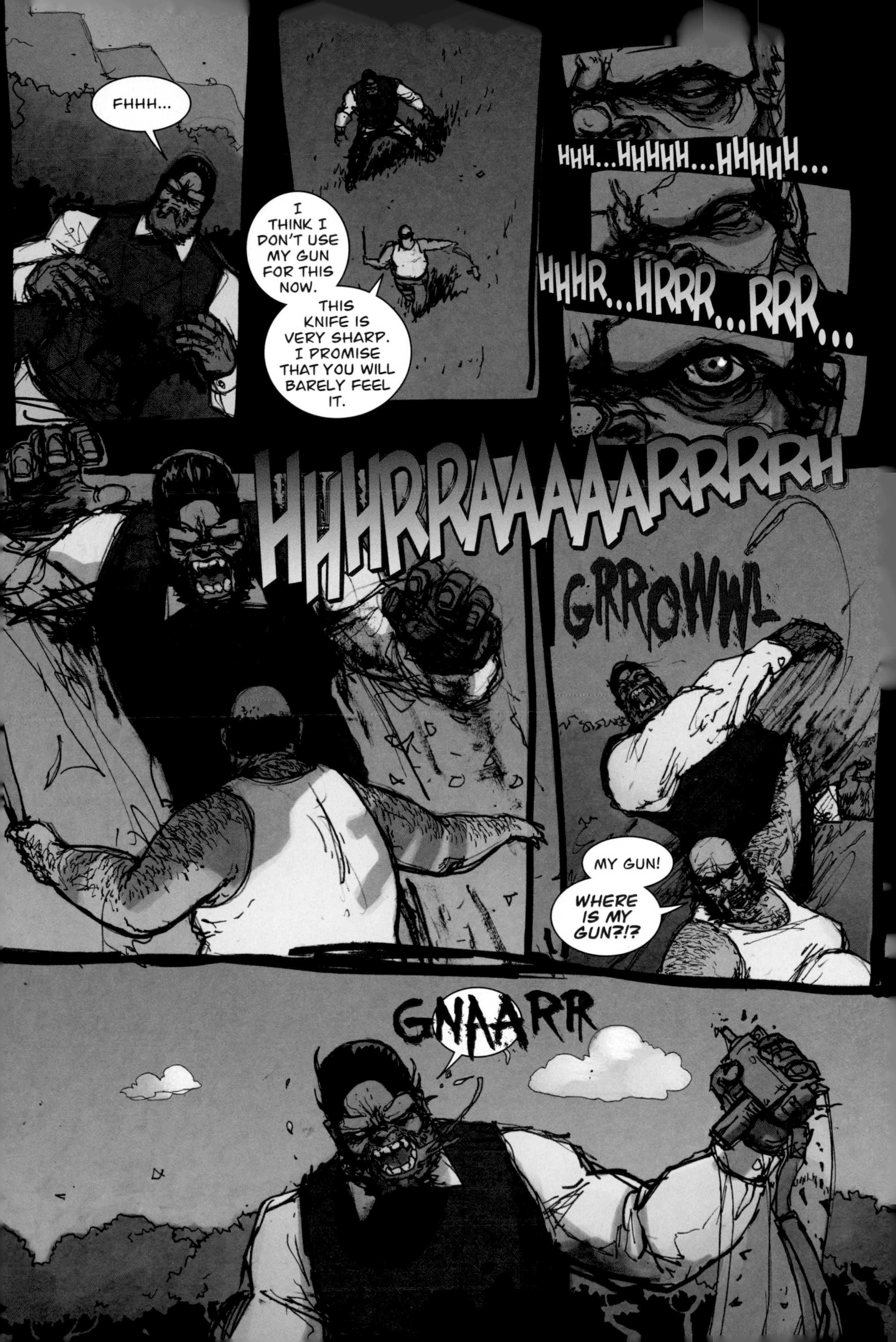
FHHH...
I THINK I DON'T USE MY GUN FOR THIS NOW.
THIS KNIFE IS VERY SHARP. I PROMISE THAT YOU WILL BARELY FEEL IT.
HHH...HHHHH...HHHHH...
HHHR...HRRR...RRR...
HHHRAAAAAARRRRH
GRROWWL
MY GUN!
WHERE IS MY GUN?!?
GNAARR

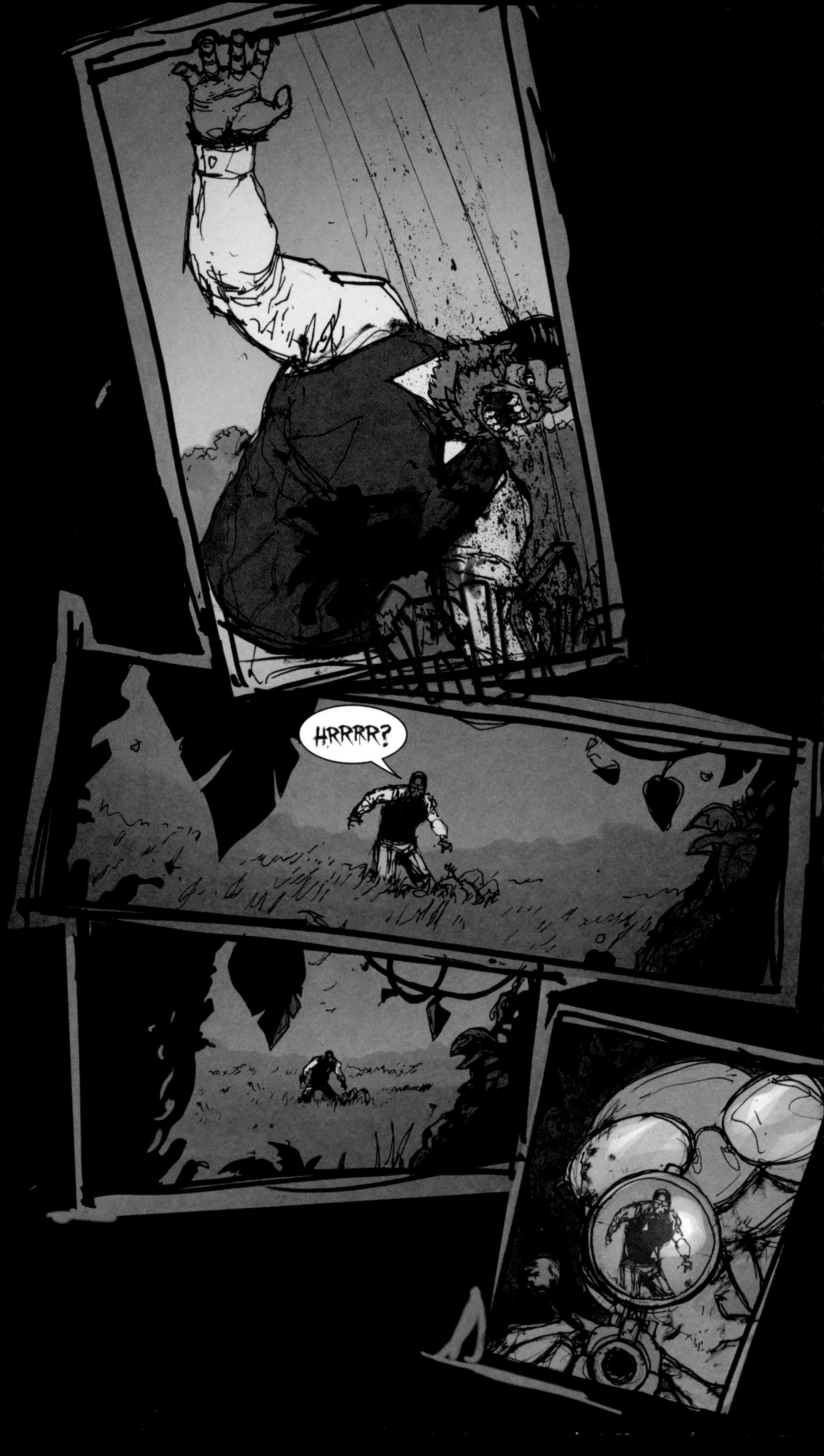
HRRRR?

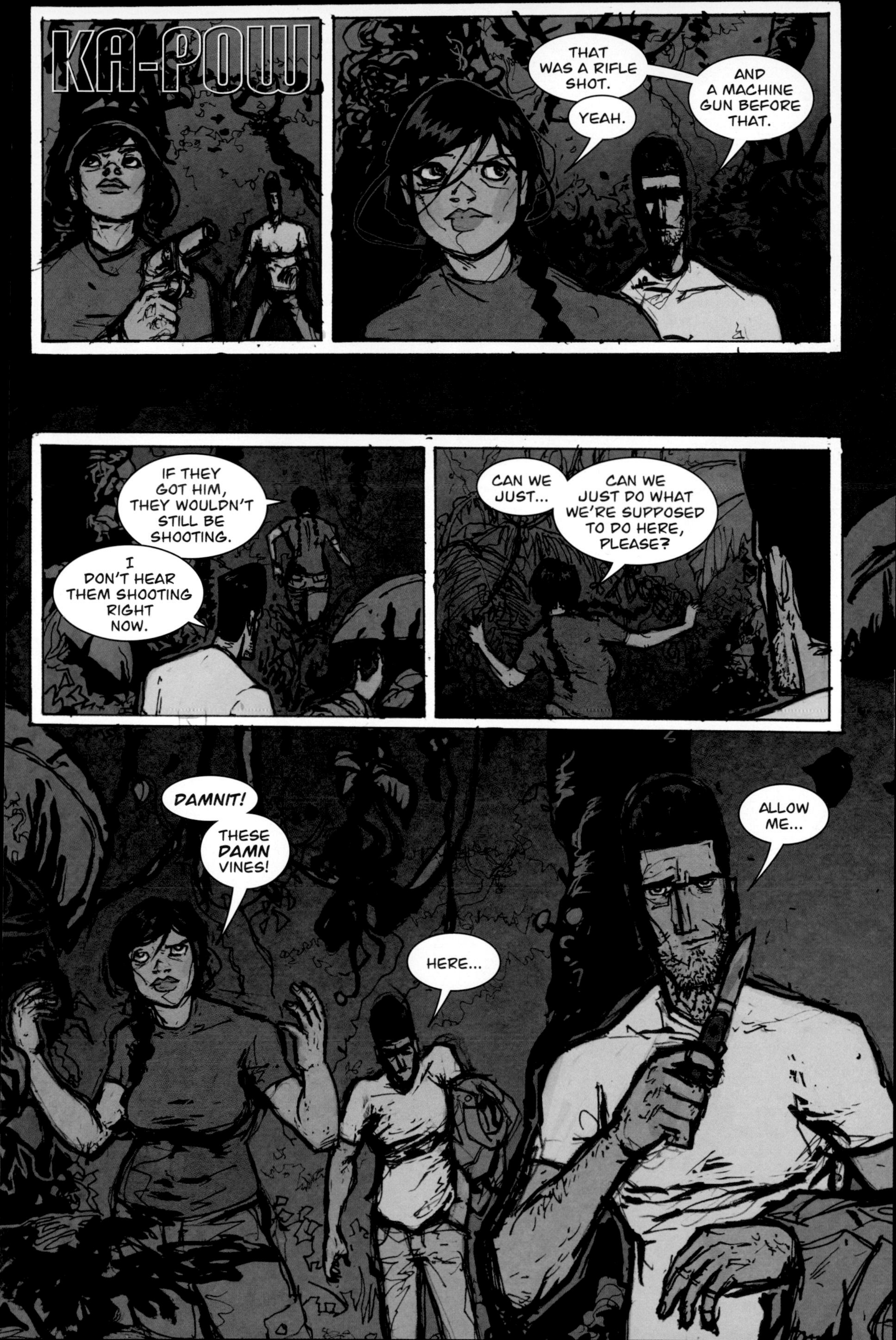
KA-POW
THAT WAS A RIFLE SHOT.
YEAH.
AND A MACHINE GUN BEFORE THAT.
IF THEY GOT HIM, THEY WOULDN'T STILL BE SHOOTING.
I DON'T HEAR THEM SHOOTING RIGHT NOW.
CAN WE JUST...
CAN WE JUST DO WHAT WE'RE SUPPOSED TO DO HERE, PLEASE?
DAMNIT!
THESE DAMN VINES!
HERE...
ALLOW ME...

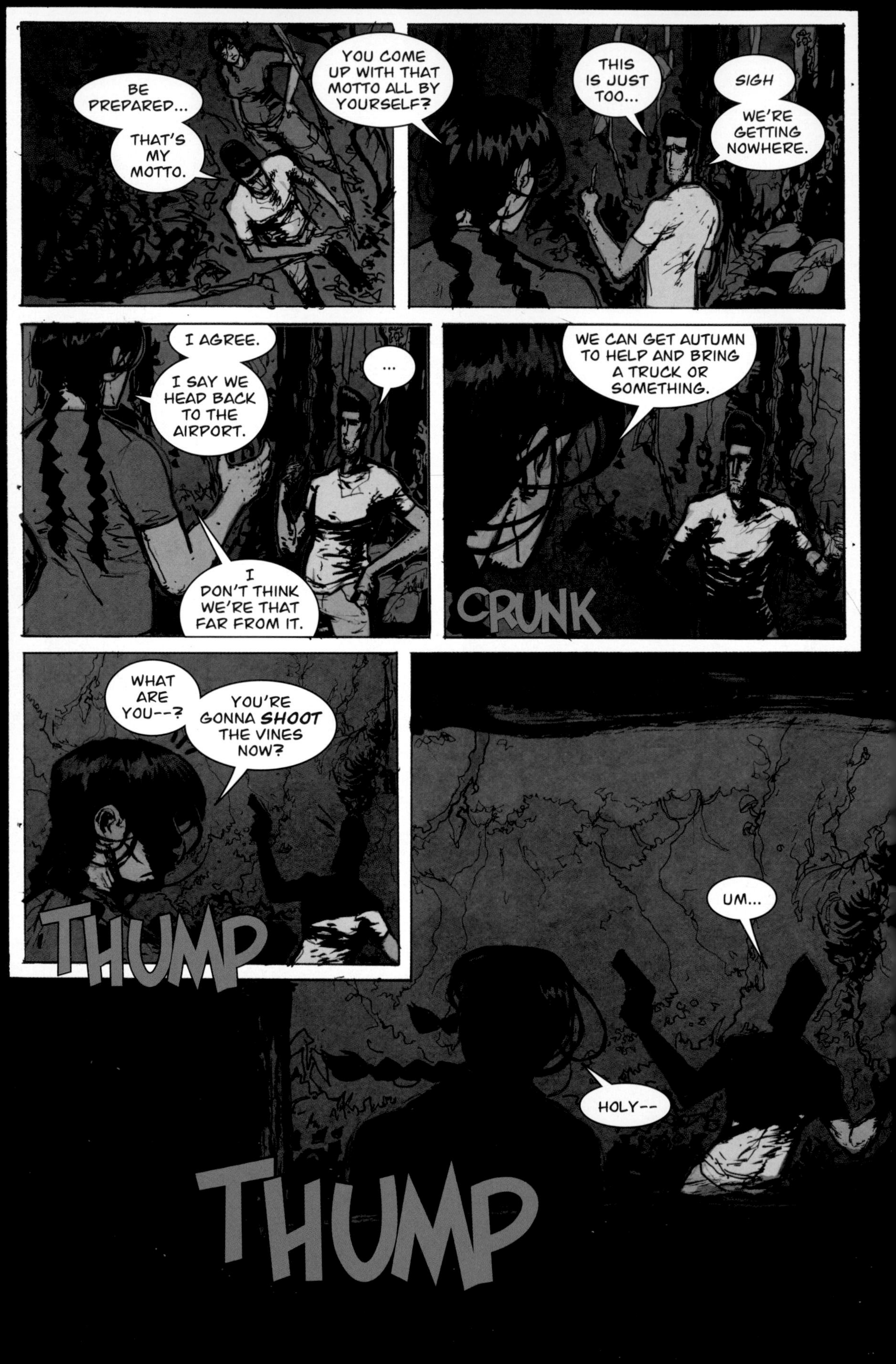
BE PREPARED...
THAT'S MY MOTTO.
YOU COME UP WITH THAT MOTTO ALL BY YOURSELF?
THIS IS JUST TOO...
SIGH
WE'RE GETTING NOWHERE.
I AGREE.
I SAY WE HEAD BACK TO THE AIRPORT.
...
I DON'T THINK WE'RE THAT FAR FROM IT.
WE CAN GET AUTUMN TO HELP AND BRING A TRUCK OR SOMETHING.
CRUNK
WHAT ARE YOU--?
YOU'RE GONNA SHOOT THE VINES NOW?
THUMP
UM...
HOLY--
THUMP

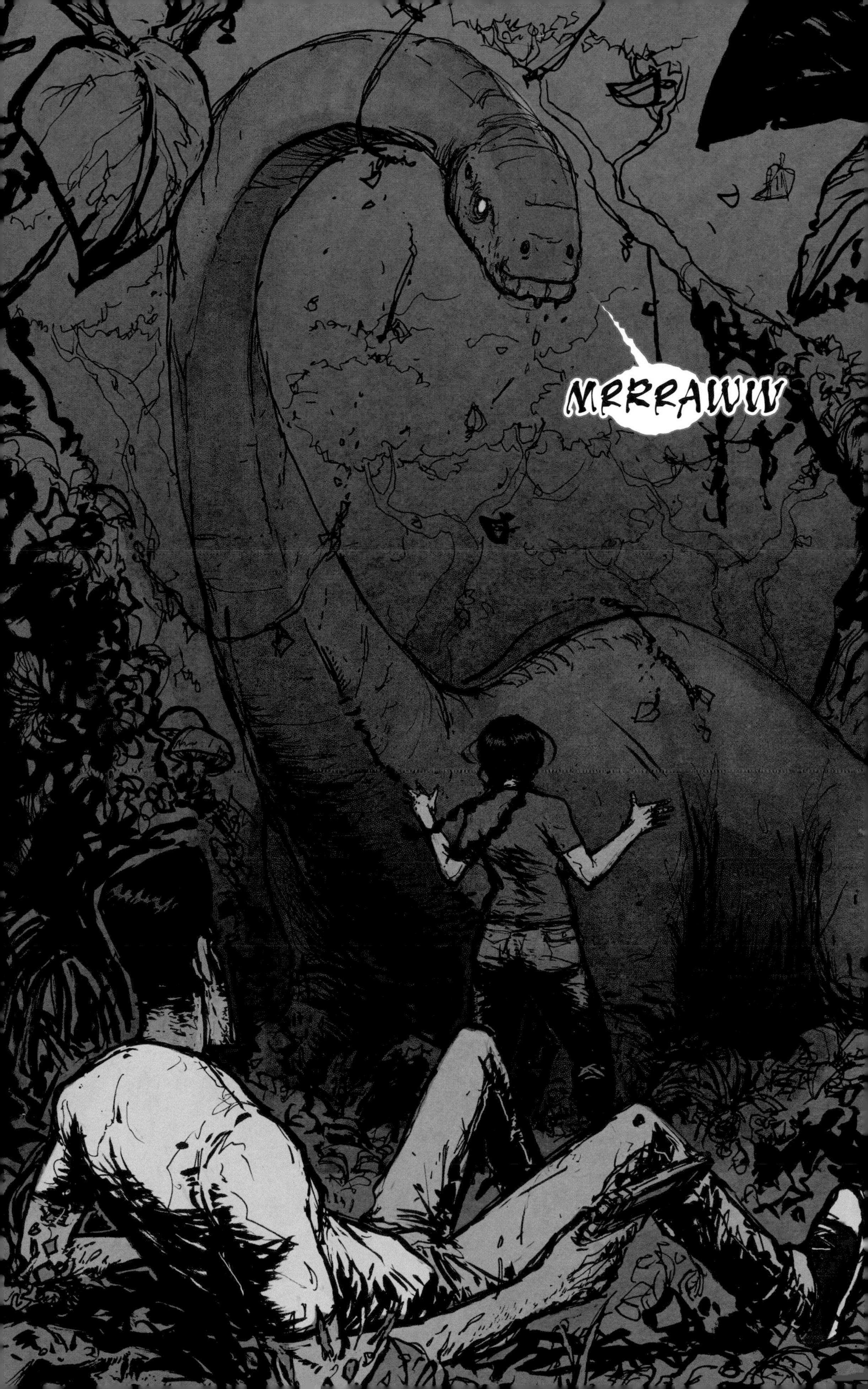
MRRRAWW

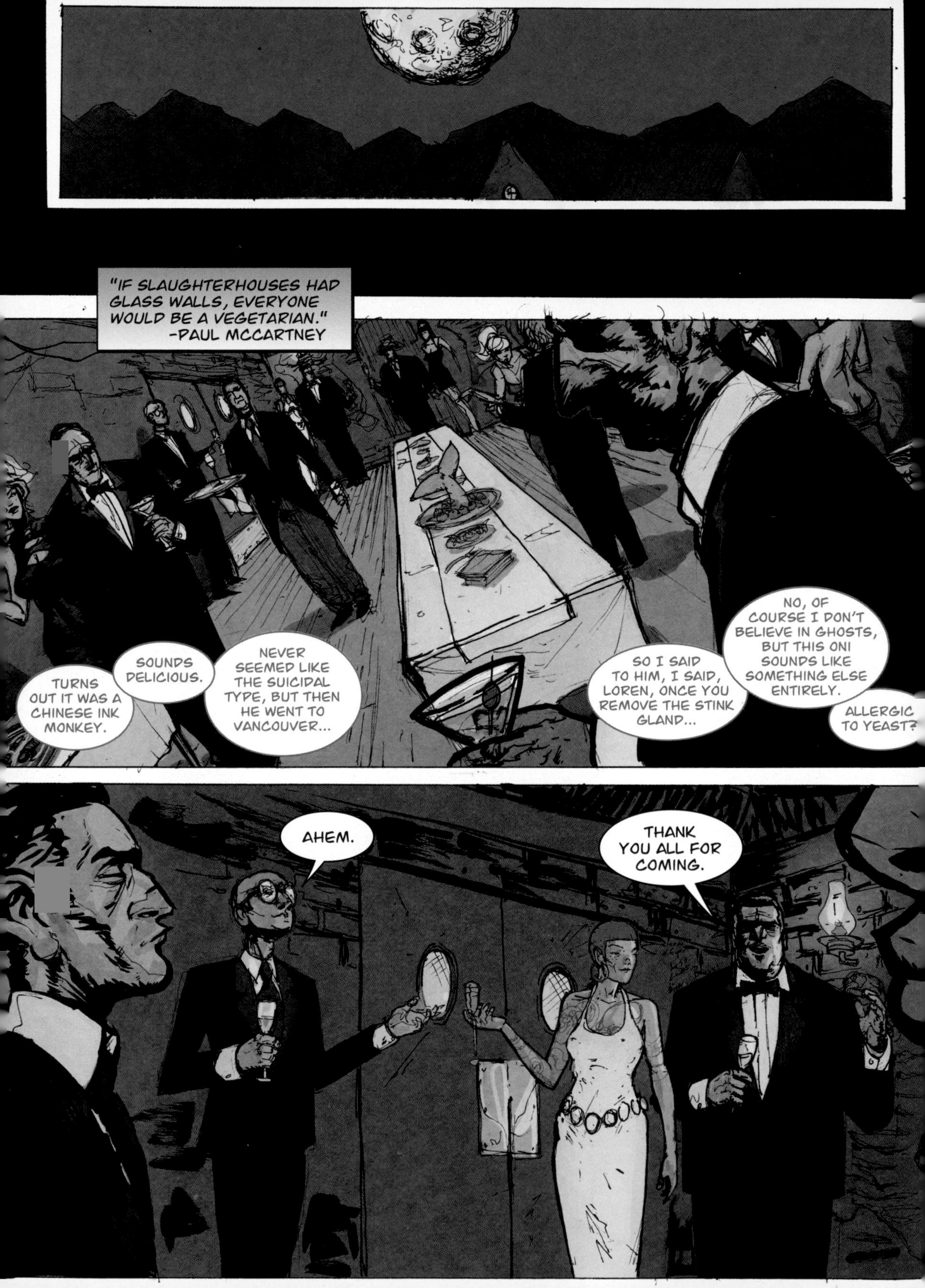
"IF SLAUGHTERHOUSES HAD GLASS WALLS, EVERYONE WOULD BE A VEGETARIAN." -PAUL MCCARTNEY
TURNS OUT IT WAS A CHINESE INK MONKEY.
SOUNDS DELICIOUS.
NEVER SEEMED LIKE THE SUICIDAL TYPE, BUT THEN HE WENT TO VANCOUVER...
SO I SAID TO HIM, I SAID, LOREN, ONCE YOU REMOVE THE STINK GLAND...
NO, OF COURSE I DON'T BELIEVE IN GHOSTS, BUT THIS ONI SOUNDS LIKE SOMETHING ELSE ENTIRELY.
ALLERGIC TO YEAST?
AHEM.
THANK YOU ALL FOR COMING.

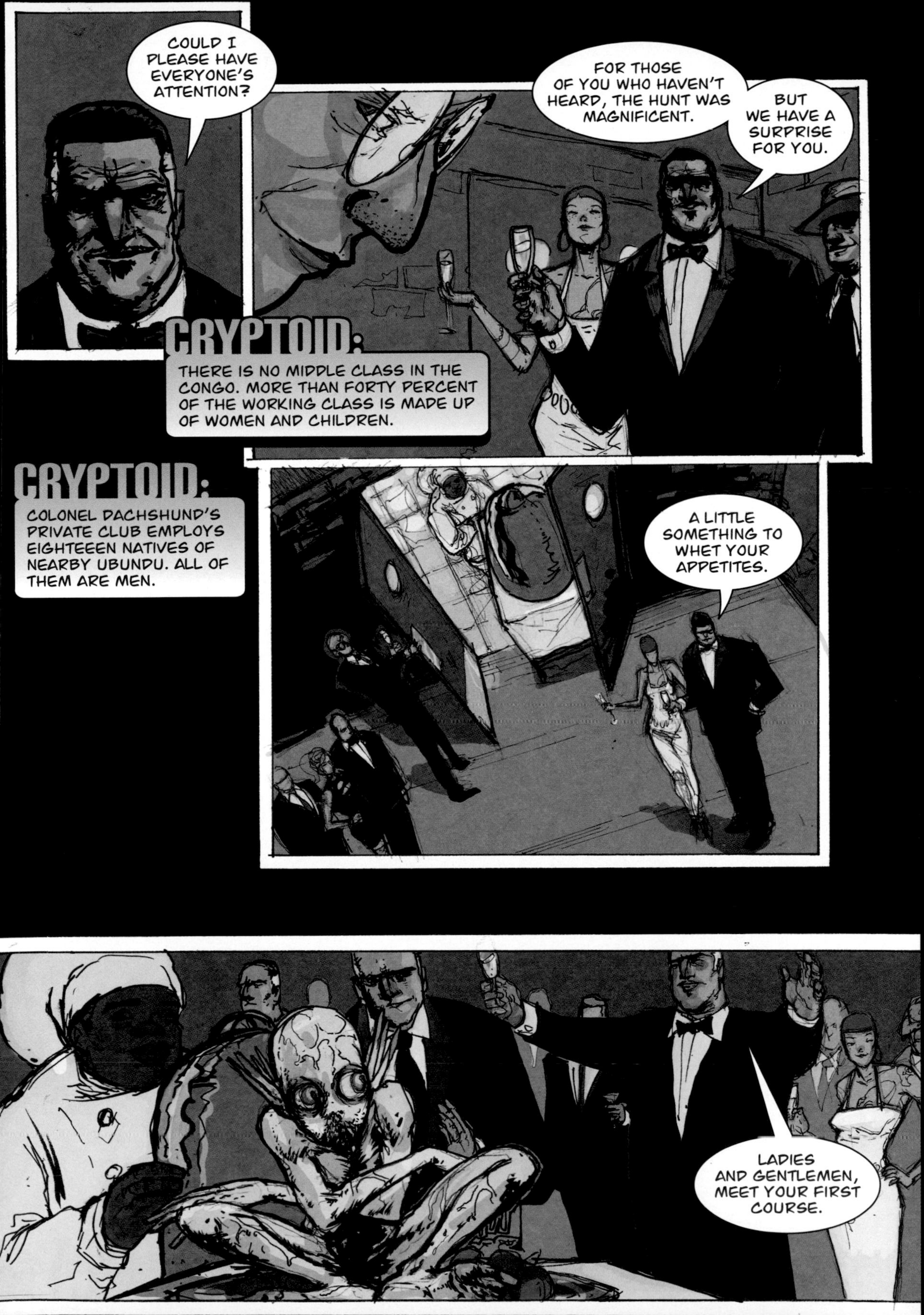
COULD I PLEASE HAVE EVERYONE'S ATTENTION?
FOR THOSE OF YOU WHO HAVEN'T HEARD, THE HUNT WAS MAGNIFICENT.
BUT WE HAVE A SURPRISE FOR YOU.
CRYPTOID:
THERE IS NO MIDDLE CLASS IN THE CONGO. MORE THAN FORTY PERCENT OF THE WORKING CLASS IS MADE UP OF WOMEN AND CHILDREN.
CRYPTOID:
COLONEL DACHSHUND'S PRIVATE CLUB EMPLOYS EIGHTEEEN NATIVES OF NEARBY UBUNDU. ALL OF THEM ARE MEN.
A LITTLE SOMETHING TO WHET YOUR APPETITES.
LADIES AND GENTLEMEN, MEET YOUR FIRST COURSE.

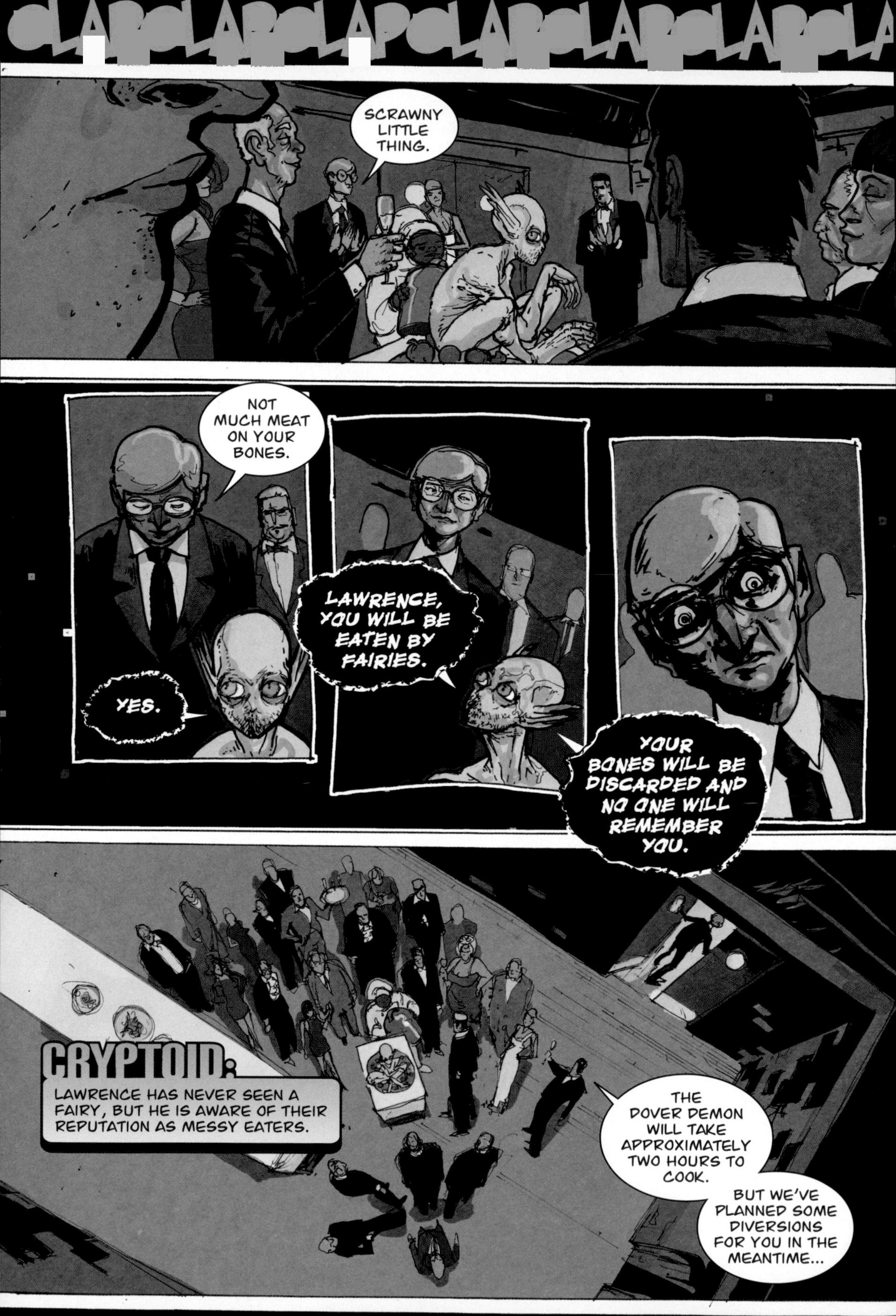
CLAPCLAPCLAPCLAPCLAPCLA
SCRAWNY LITTLE THING.
NOT MUCH MEAT ON YOUR BONES.
YES.
LAWRENCE, YOU WILL BE EATEN BY FAIRIES.
YOUR BONES WILL BE DISCARDED AND NO ONE WILL REMEMBER YOU.
CRYPTOID:
LAWRENCE HAS NEVER SEEN A FAIRY, BUT HE IS AWARE OF THEIR REPUTATION AS MESSY EATERS.
THE DOVER DEMON WILL TAKE APPROXIMATELY TWO HOURS TO COOK.
BUT WE'VE PLANNED SOME DIVERSIONS FOR YOU IN THE MEANTIME...

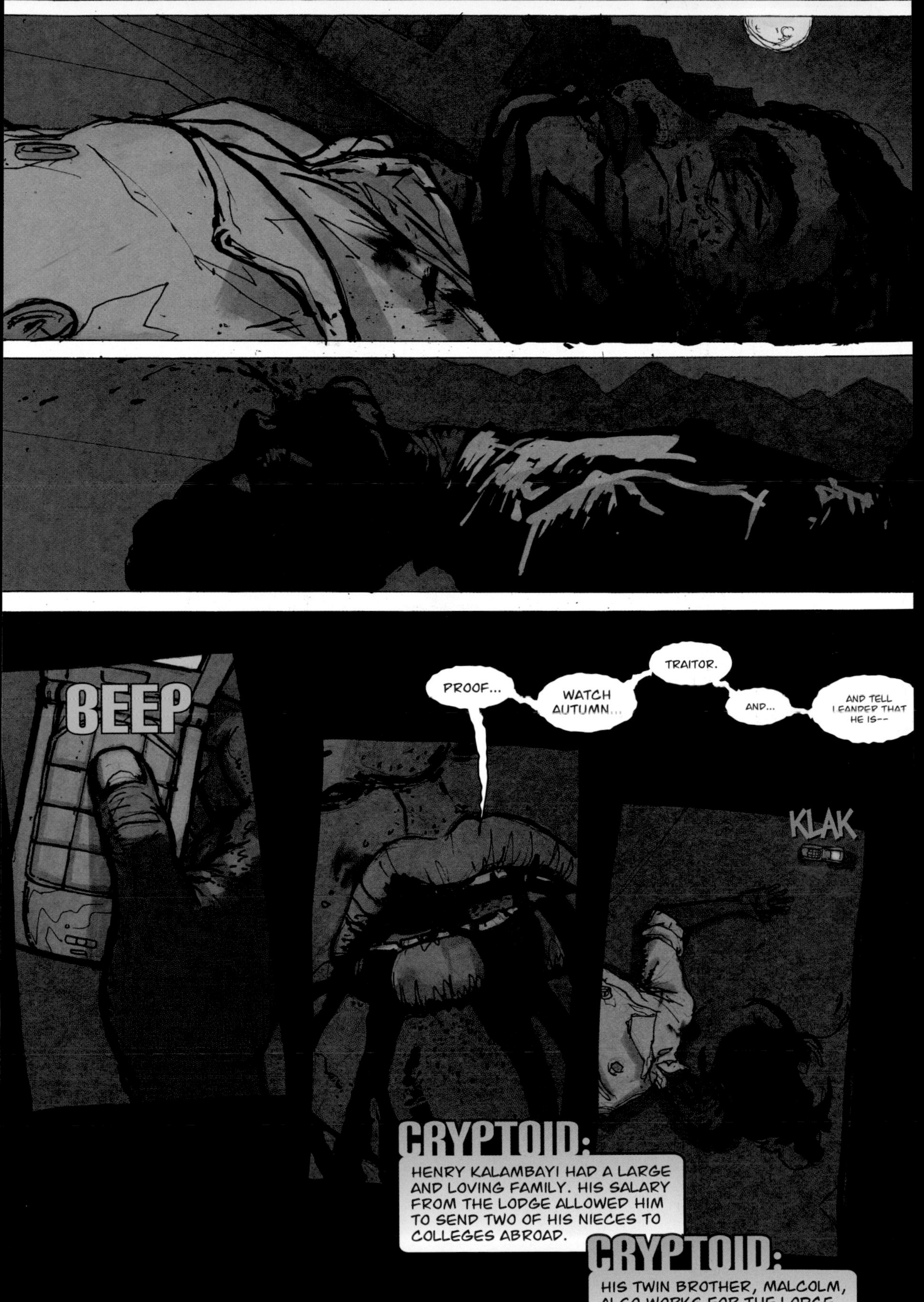
BEEP
PROOF...
WATCH AUTUMN...
TRAITOR.
AND...
AND TELL LEANDER THAT HE IS--
KLAK
CRYPTOID:
HENRY KALAMBAYI HAD A LARGE AND LOVING FAMILY. HIS SALARY FROM THE LODGE ALLOWED HIM TO SEND TWO OF HIS NIECES TO COLLEGES ABROAD.
CRYPTOID:
HIS TWIN BROTHER, MALCOLM,

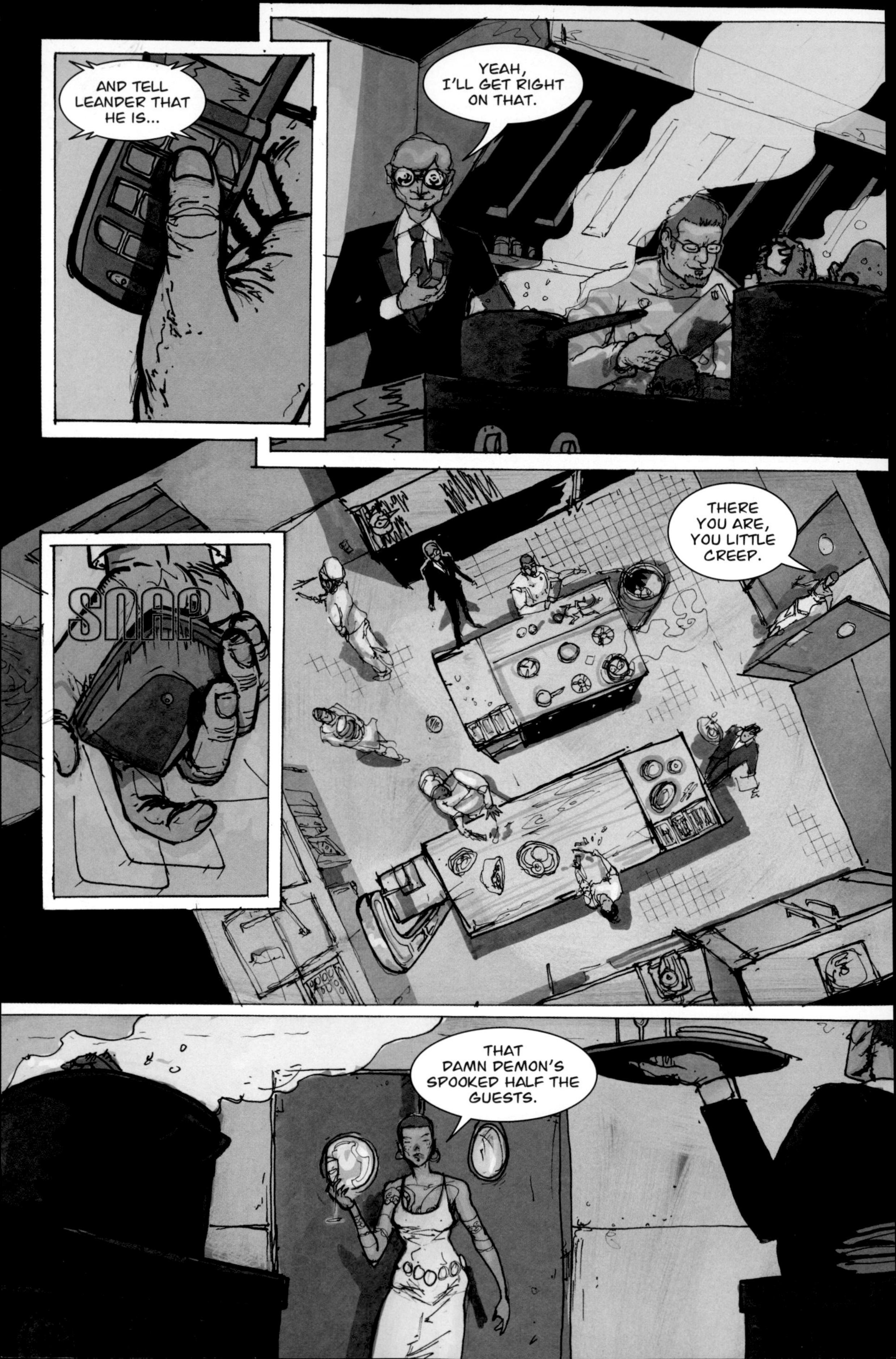
AND TELL LEANDER THAT HE IS...
YEAH, I'LL GET RIGHT ON THAT.
SNAP
THERE YOU ARE, YOU LITTLE CREEP.
THAT DAMN DEMON'S SPOOKED HALF THE GUESTS.

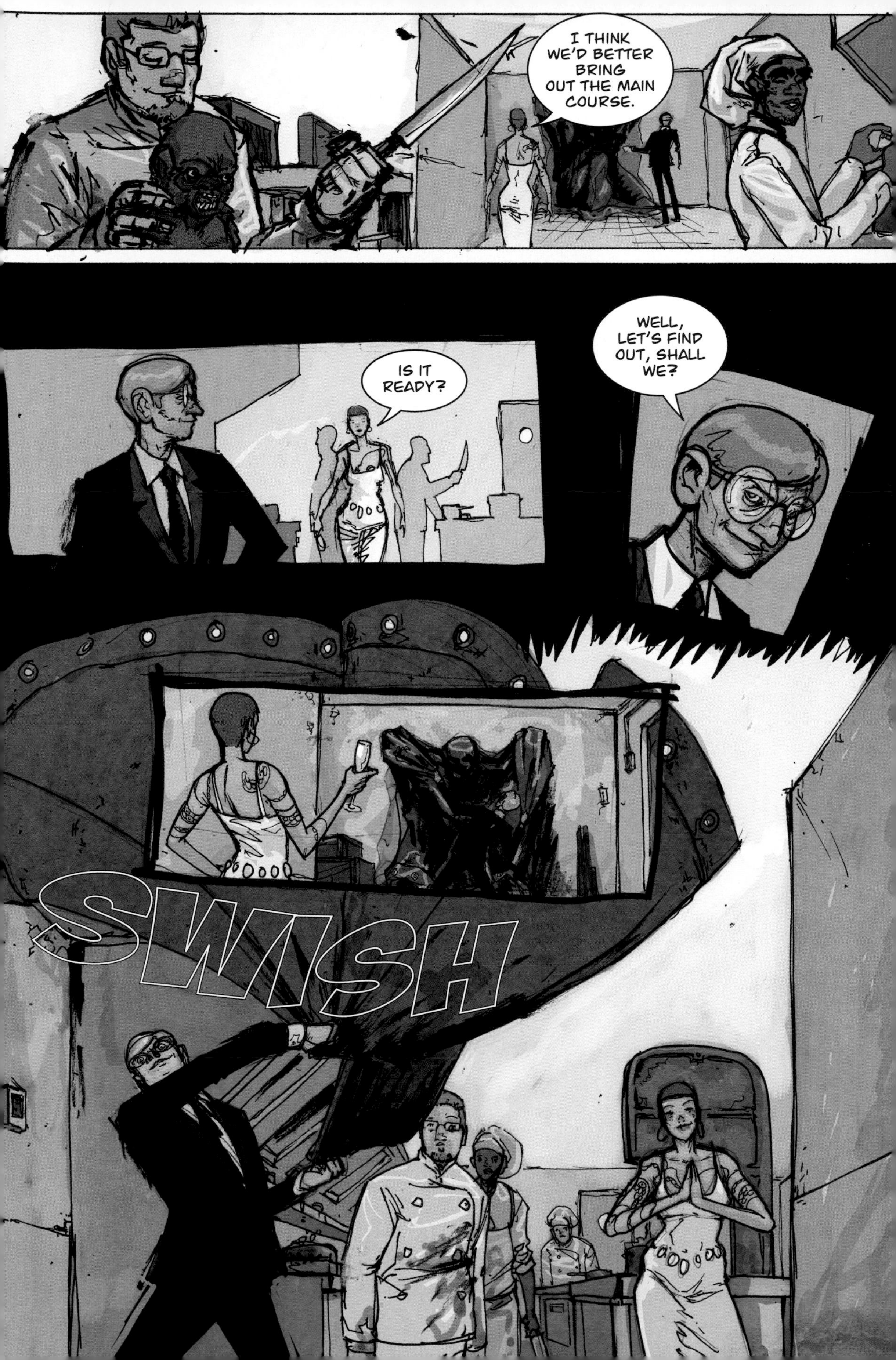
I THINK WE'D BETTER BRING OUT THE MAIN COURSE.
IS IT READY?
WELL, LET'S FIND OUT, SHALL WE?
SWISH

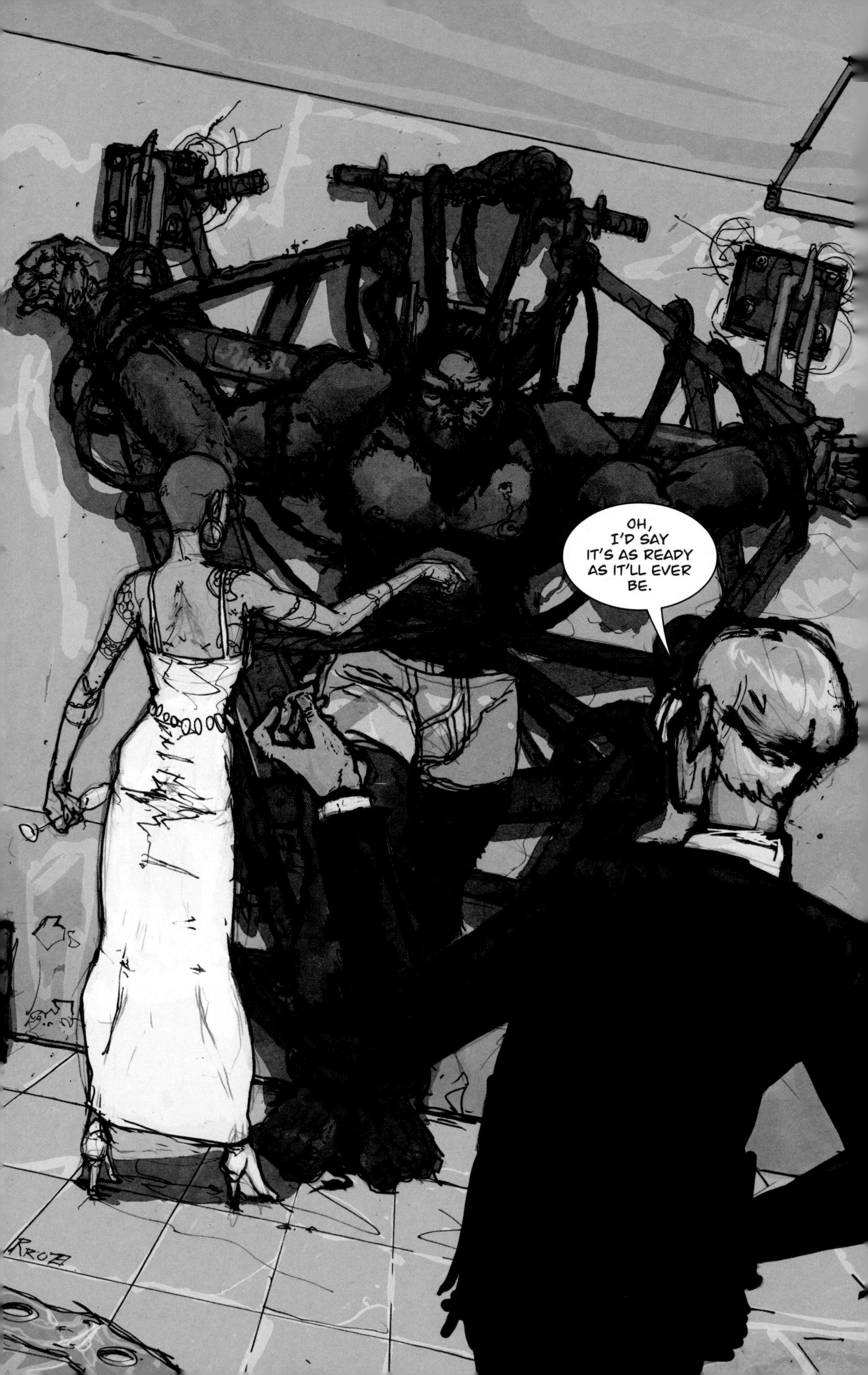
OH, I'D SAY IT'S AS READY AS IT'LL EVER BE.
RROZ

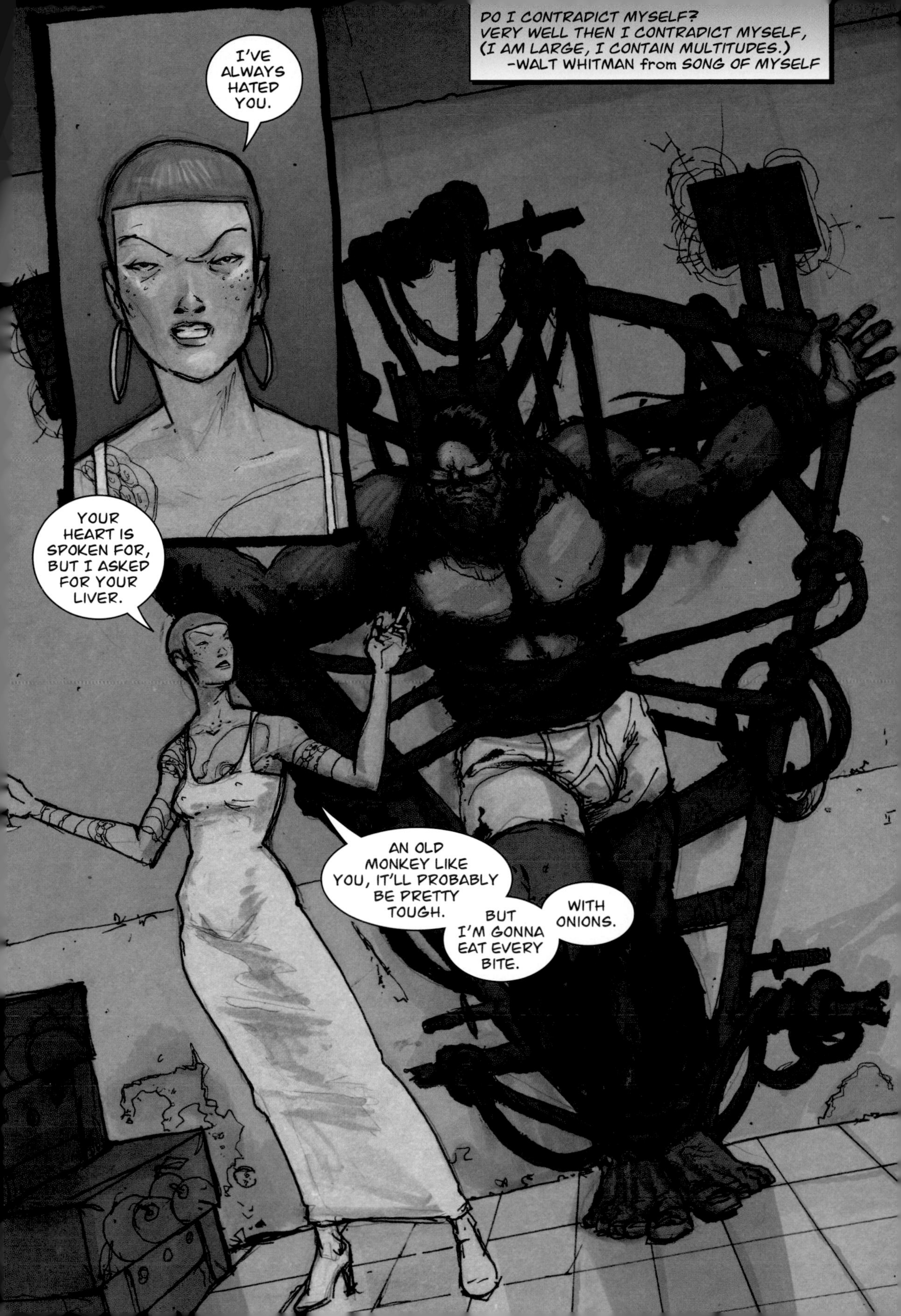
DO I CONTRADICT MYSELF? VERY WELL THEN I CONTRADICT MYSELF, (I AM LARGE, I CONTAIN MULTITUDES.) -WALT WHITMAN from SONG OF MYSELF
I'VE ALWAYS HATED YOU.
YOUR HEART IS SPOKEN FOR, BUT I ASKED FOR YOUR LIVER.
AN OLD MONKEY LIKE YOU, IT'LL PROBABLY BE PRETTY TOUGH.
BUT I'M GONNA EAT EVERY BITE.
WITH ONIONS.

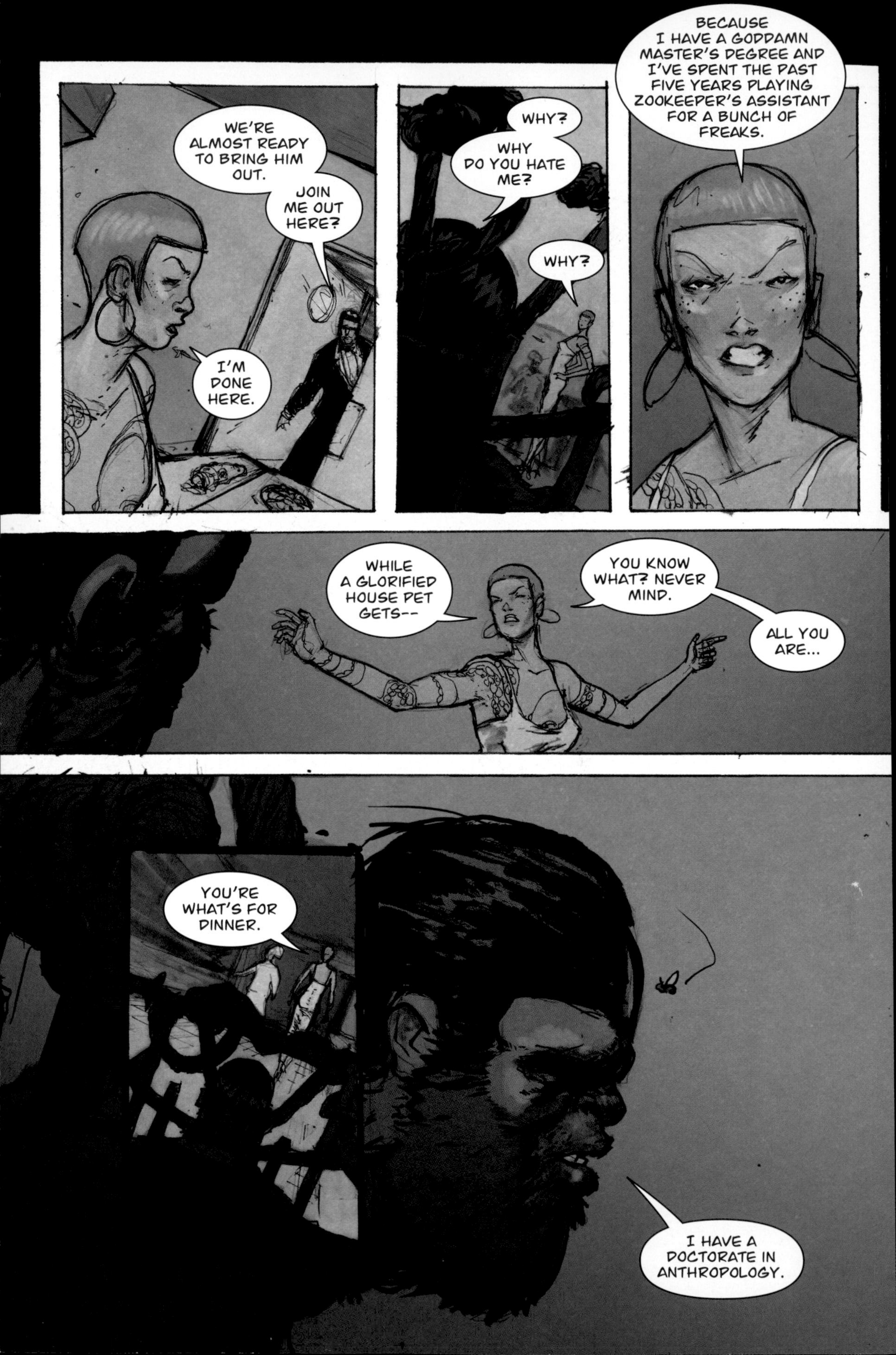
WE'RE ALMOST READY TO BRING HIM OUT.
JOIN ME OUT HERE?
I'M DONE HERE.
WHY?
WHY DO YOU HATE ME?
WHY?
BECAUSE I HAVE A GODDAMN MASTER'S DEGREE AND I'VE SPENT THE PAST FIVE YEARS PLAYING ZOOKEEPER'S ASSISTANT FOR A BUNCH OF FREAKS.
WHILE A GLORIFIED HOUSE PET GETS--
YOU KNOW WHAT? NEVER MIND.
ALL YOU ARE...
YOU'RE WHAT'S FOR DINNER.
I HAVE A DOCTORATE IN ANTHROPOLOGY.

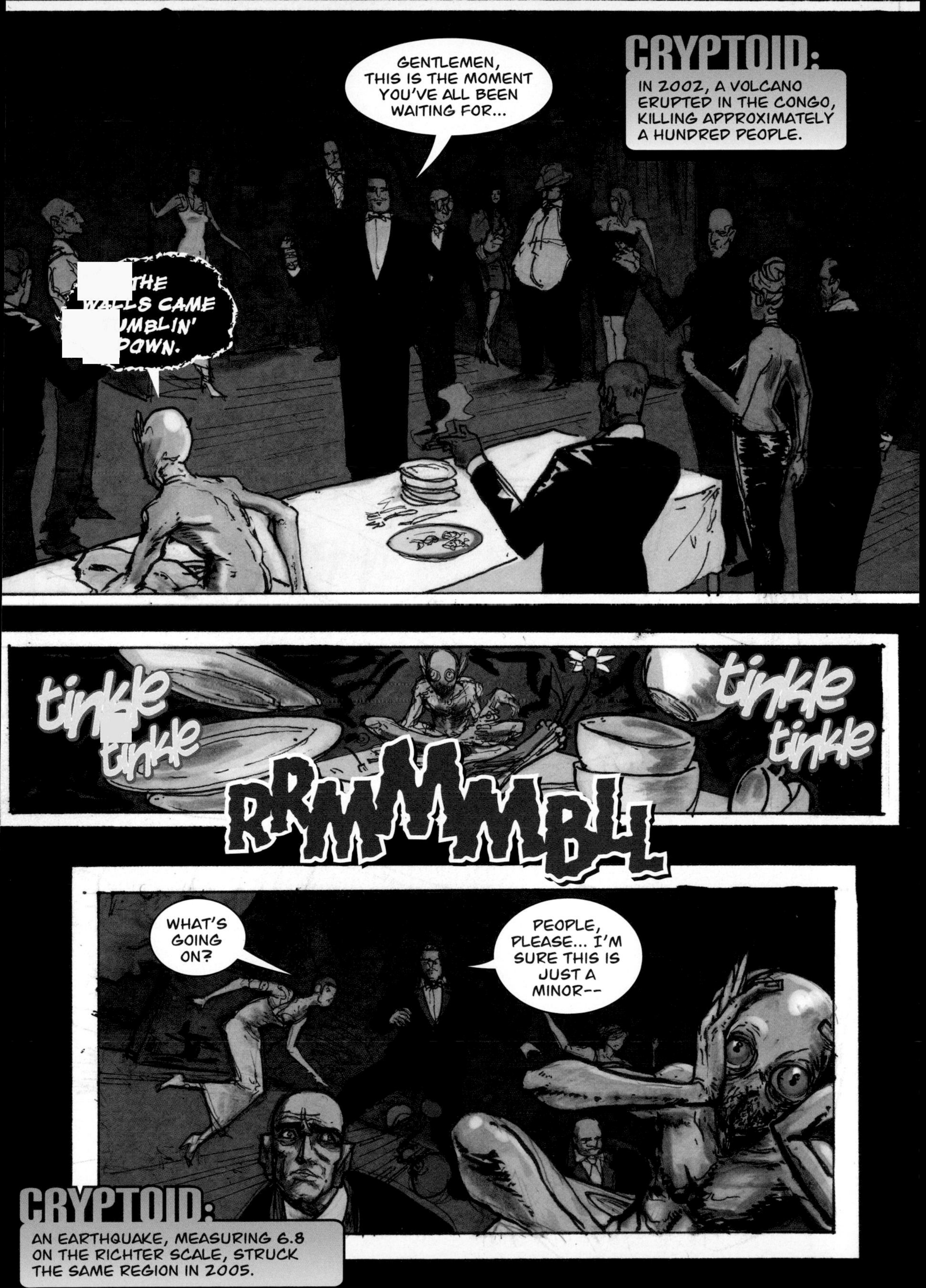
CRYPTOID:
IN 2002, A VOLCANO ERUPTED IN THE CONGO, KILLING APPROXIMATELY A HUNDRED PEOPLE.
GENTLEMEN, THIS IS THE MOMENT YOU'VE ALL BEEN WAITING FOR...
THE ALLS CAME UMBLIN' OWN.
tinkle tinkle
tinkle tinkle
RRMMMBLL
WHAT'S GOING ON?
PEOPLE, PLEASE... I'M SURE THIS IS JUST A MINOR--
CRYPTOID:
AN EARTHQUAKE, MEASURING 6.8 ON THE RICHTER SCALE, STRUCK THE SAME REGION IN 2005.

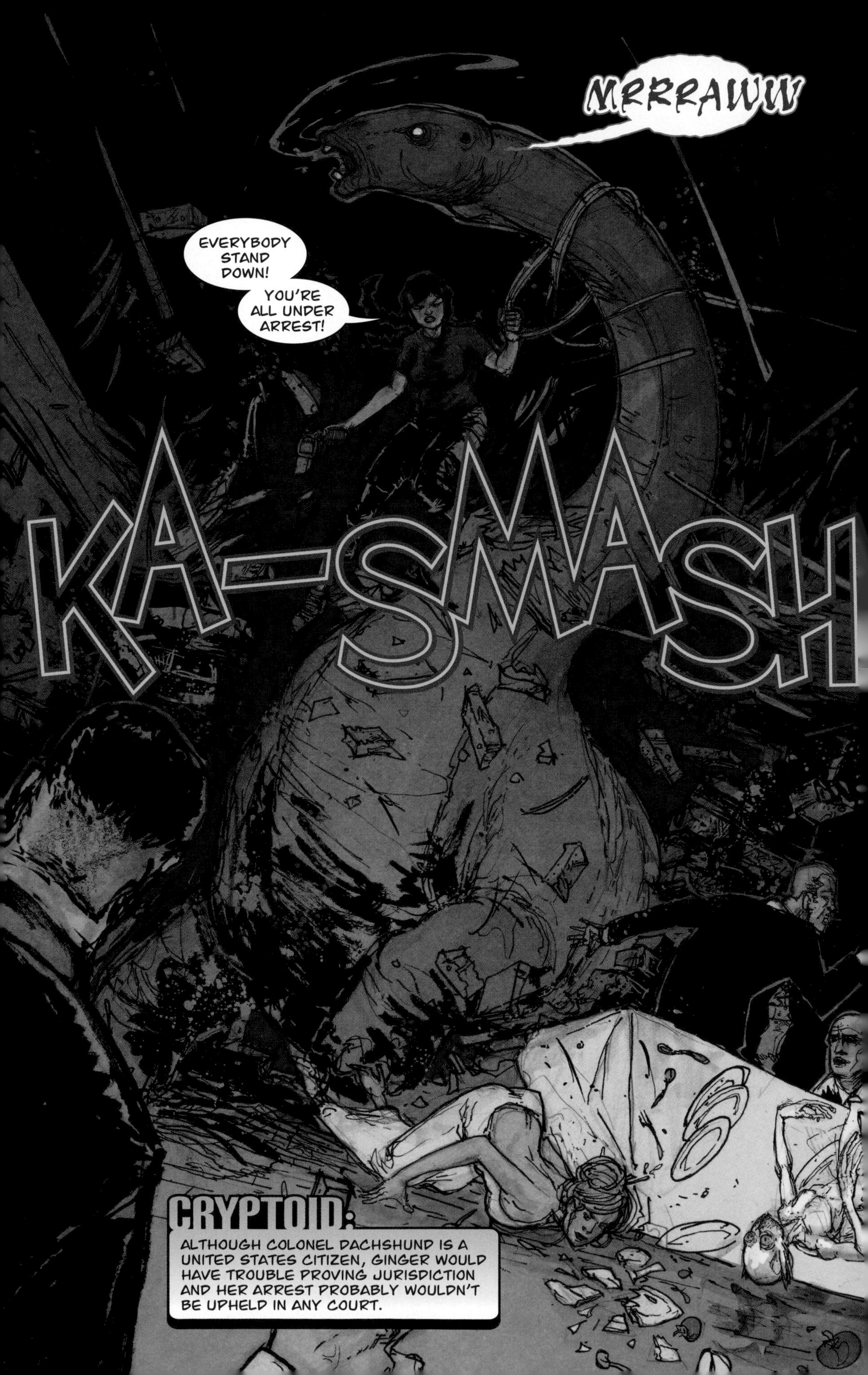
MRRRAWW
EVERYBODY STAND DOWN!
YOU'RE ALL UNDER ARREST!
KA-SMASH
CRYPTOID:
ALTHOUGH COLONEL DACHSHUND IS A UNITED STATES CITIZEN, GINGER WOULD HAVE TROUBLE PROVING JURISDICTION AND HER ARREST PROBABLY WOULDN'T BE UPHELD IN ANY COURT.

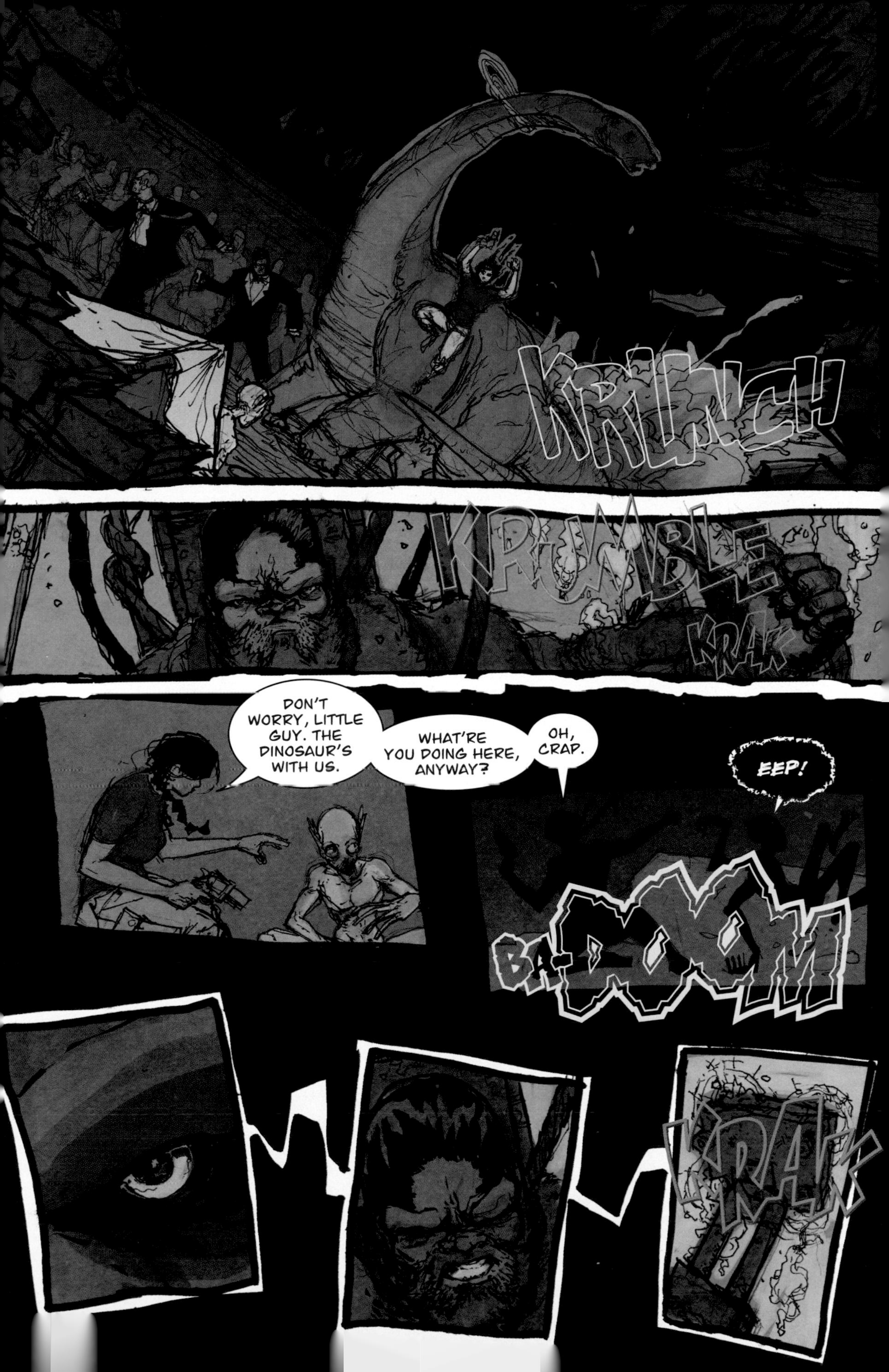
KRUNCH
KRUMBLE
KRAK
DON'T WORRY, LITTLE GUY. THE DINOSAUR'S WITH US.
WHAT'RE YOU DOING HERE, ANYWAY?
OH, CRAP.
EEP!
BA-DOOM
KRAK

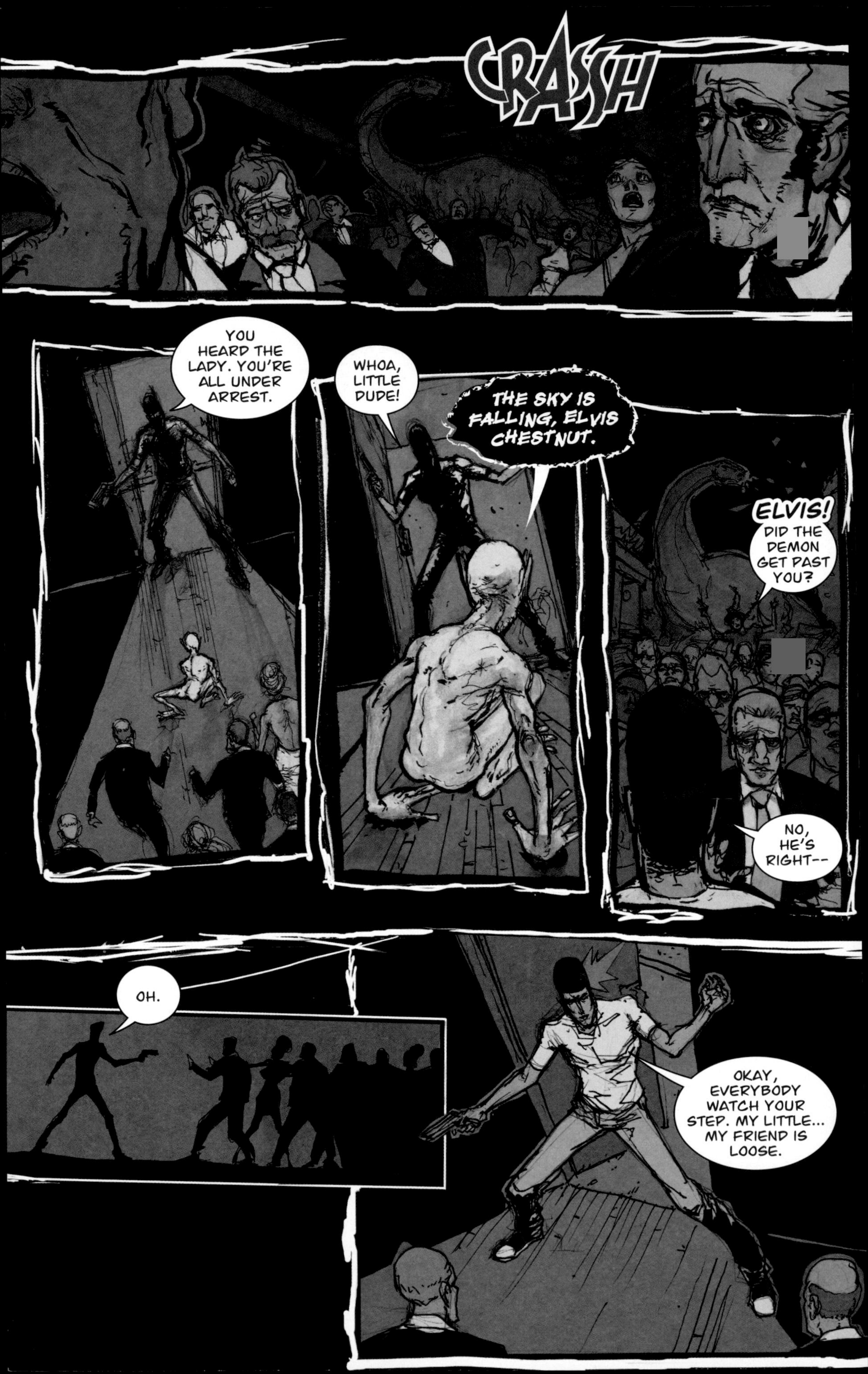
CRASSH
YOU HEARD THE LADY. YOU'RE ALL UNDER ARREST.
WHOA, LITTLE DUDE!
THE SKY IS FALLING, ELVIS CHESTNUT.
ELVIS! DID THE DEMON GET PAST YOU?
NO, HE'S RIGHT--
OH.
OKAY, EVERYBODY WATCH YOUR STEP. MY LITTLE... MY FRIEND IS LOOSE.

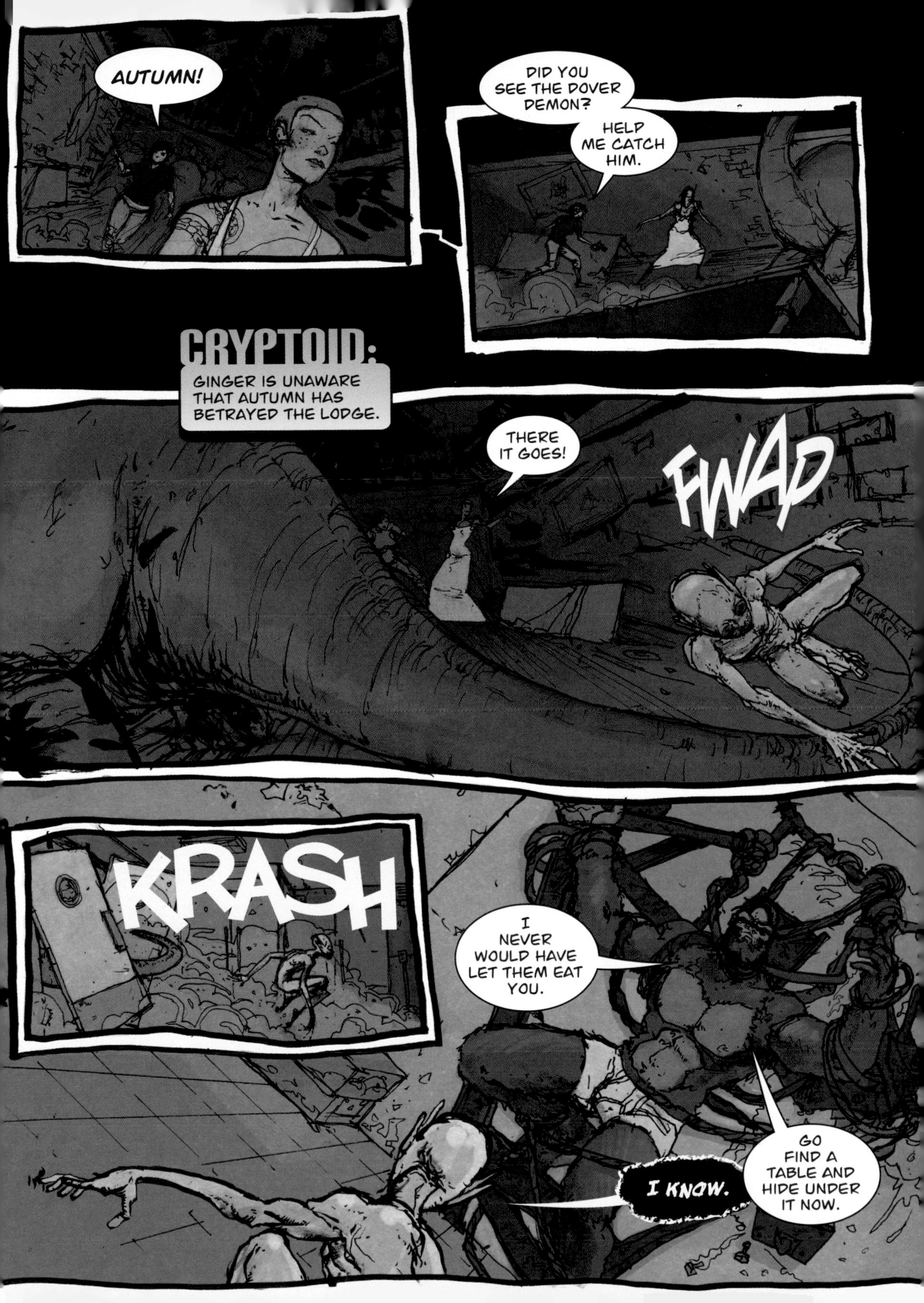

AUTUMN!
DID YOU SEE THE DOVER DEMON?
HELP ME CATCH HIM.
CRYPTOID:
GINGER IS UNAWARE THAT AUTUMN HAS BETRAYED THE LODGE.
THERE IT GOES!
FWAP
KRASH
I NEVER WOULD HAVE LET THEM EAT YOU.
GO FIND A TABLE AND HIDE UNDER IT NOW.
I KNOW.

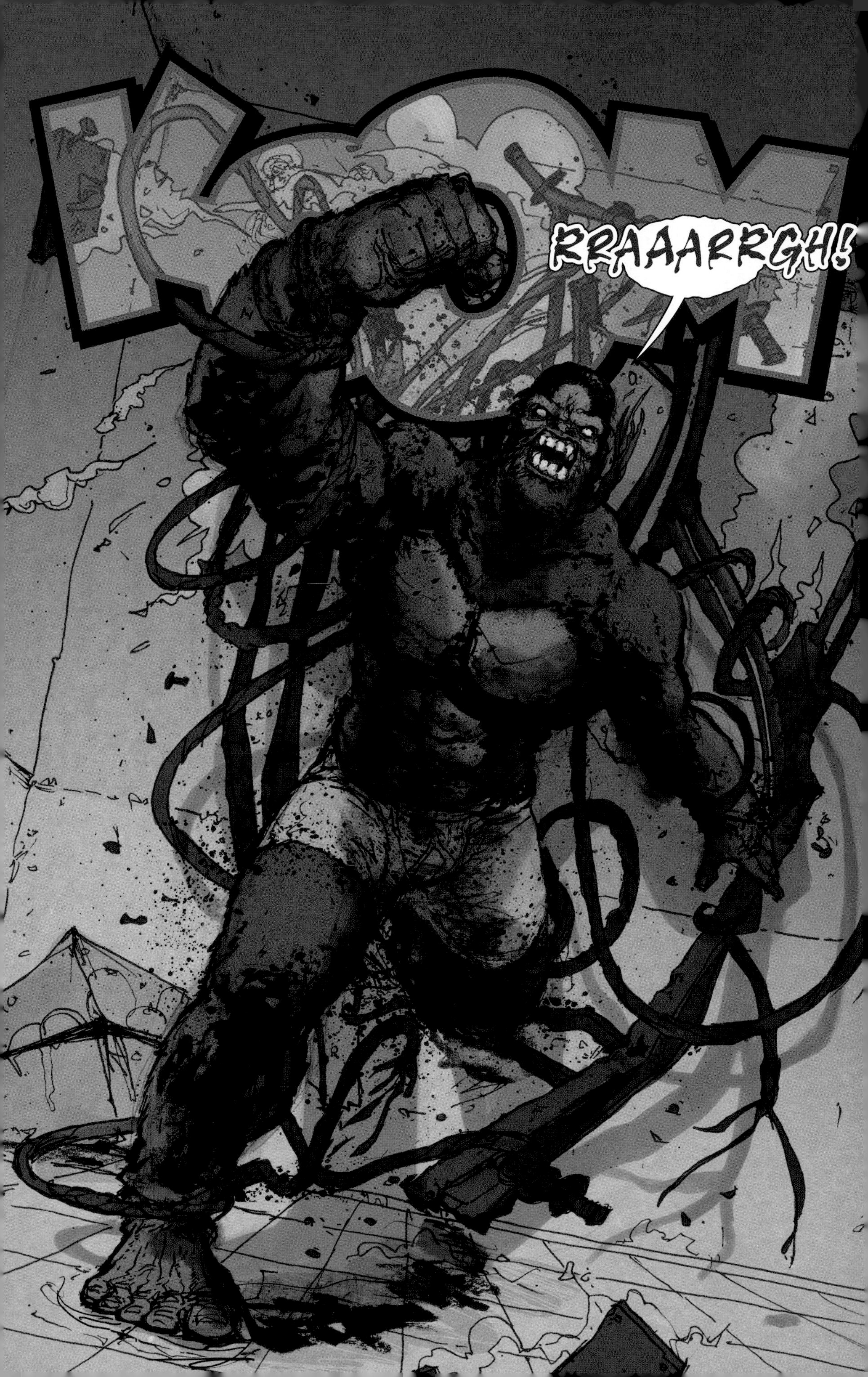
RRAAARRGH!

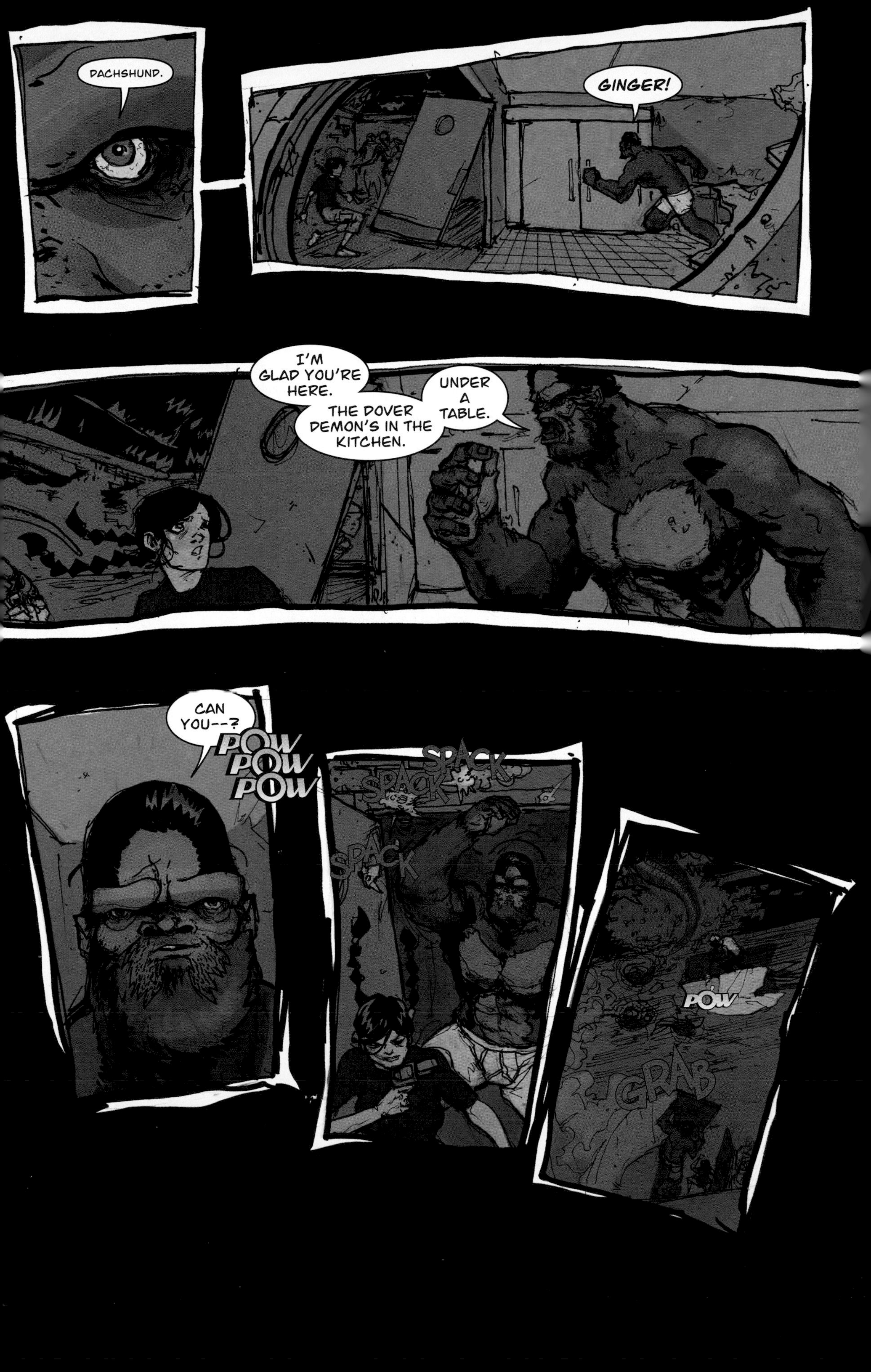
DACHSHUND.
GINGER!
I'M GLAD YOU'RE HERE.
THE DOVER DEMON'S IN THE KITCHEN.
UNDER A TABLE.
CAN YOU--?
POW POW POW
SPACK SPACK
SPACK
POW
GRAB

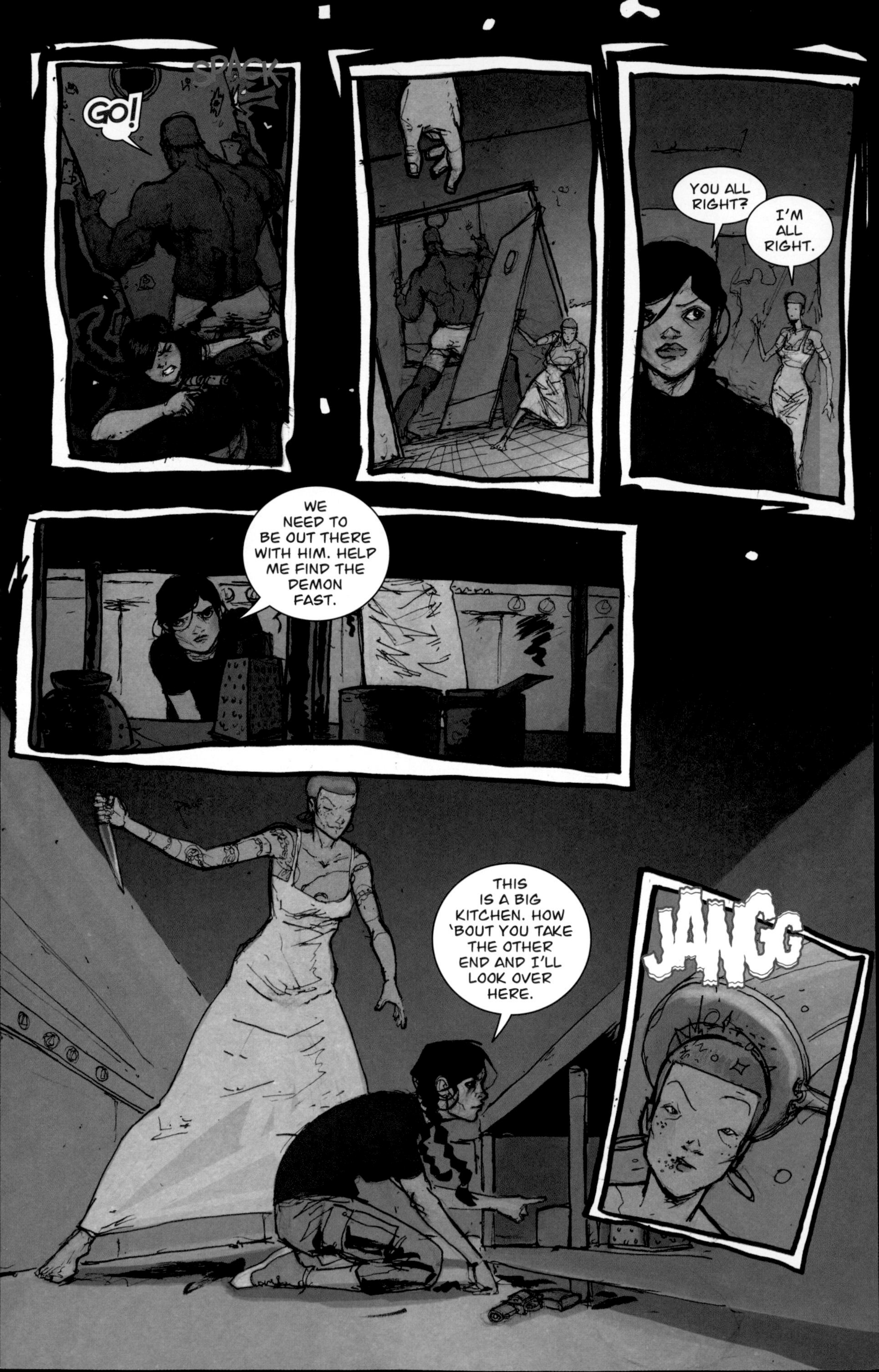
SPACK
GO!
YOU ALL RIGHT?
I'M ALL RIGHT.
WE NEED TO BE OUT THERE WITH HIM. HELP ME FIND THE DEMON FAST.
THIS IS A BIG KITCHEN. HOW 'BOUT YOU TAKE THE OTHER END AND I'LL LOOK OVER HERE.
JANGG

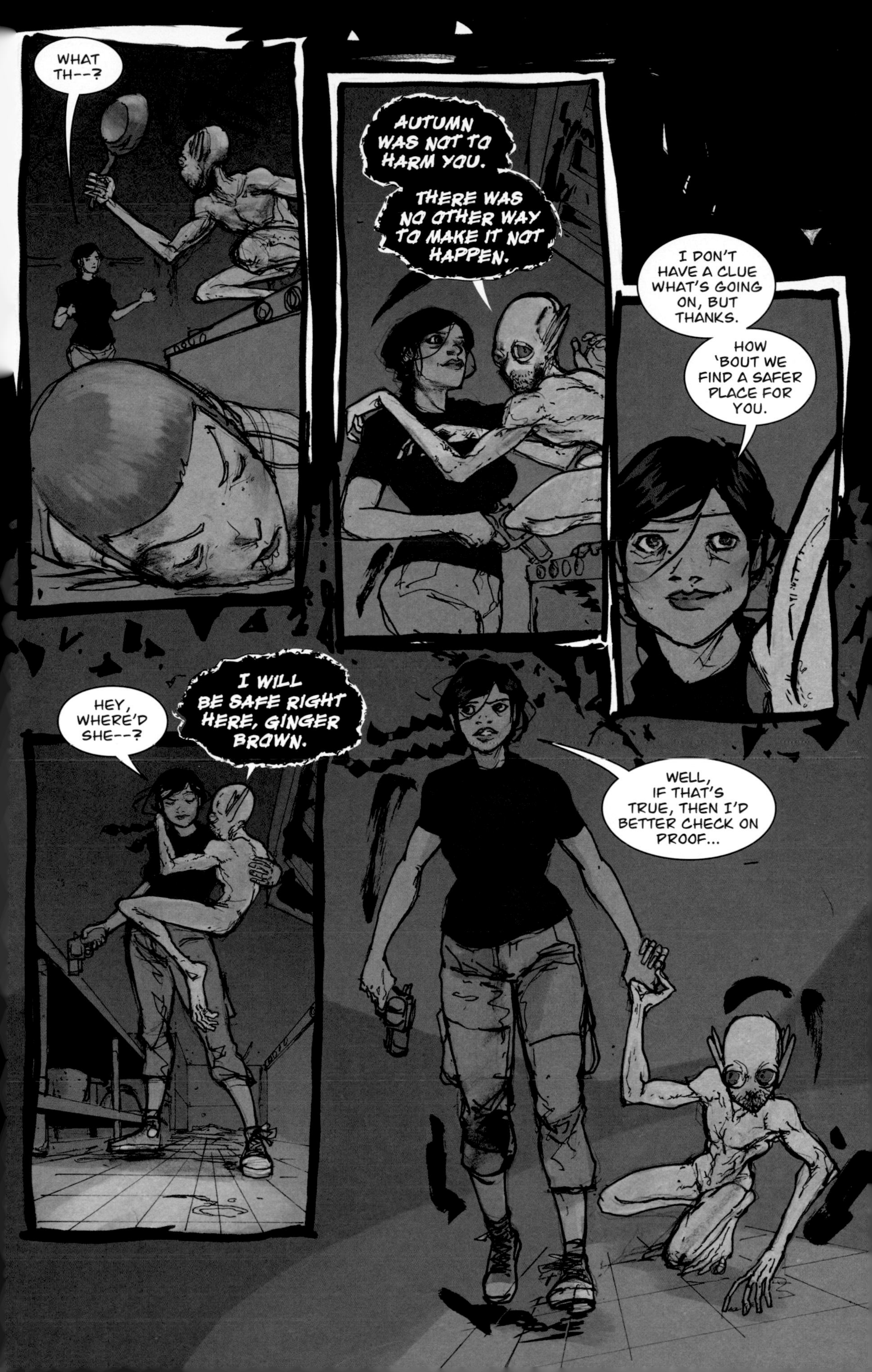
WHAT TH--?
AUTUMN WAS NOT TO HARM YOU.
THERE WAS NO OTHER WAY TO MAKE IT NOT HAPPEN.
I DON'T HAVE A CLUE WHAT'S GOING ON, BUT THANKS.
HOW 'BOUT WE FIND A SAFER PLACE FOR YOU.
HEY, WHERE'D SHE--?
I WILL BE SAFE RIGHT HERE, GINGER BROWN.
WELL, IF THAT'S TRUE, THEN I'D BETTER CHECK ON PROOF...

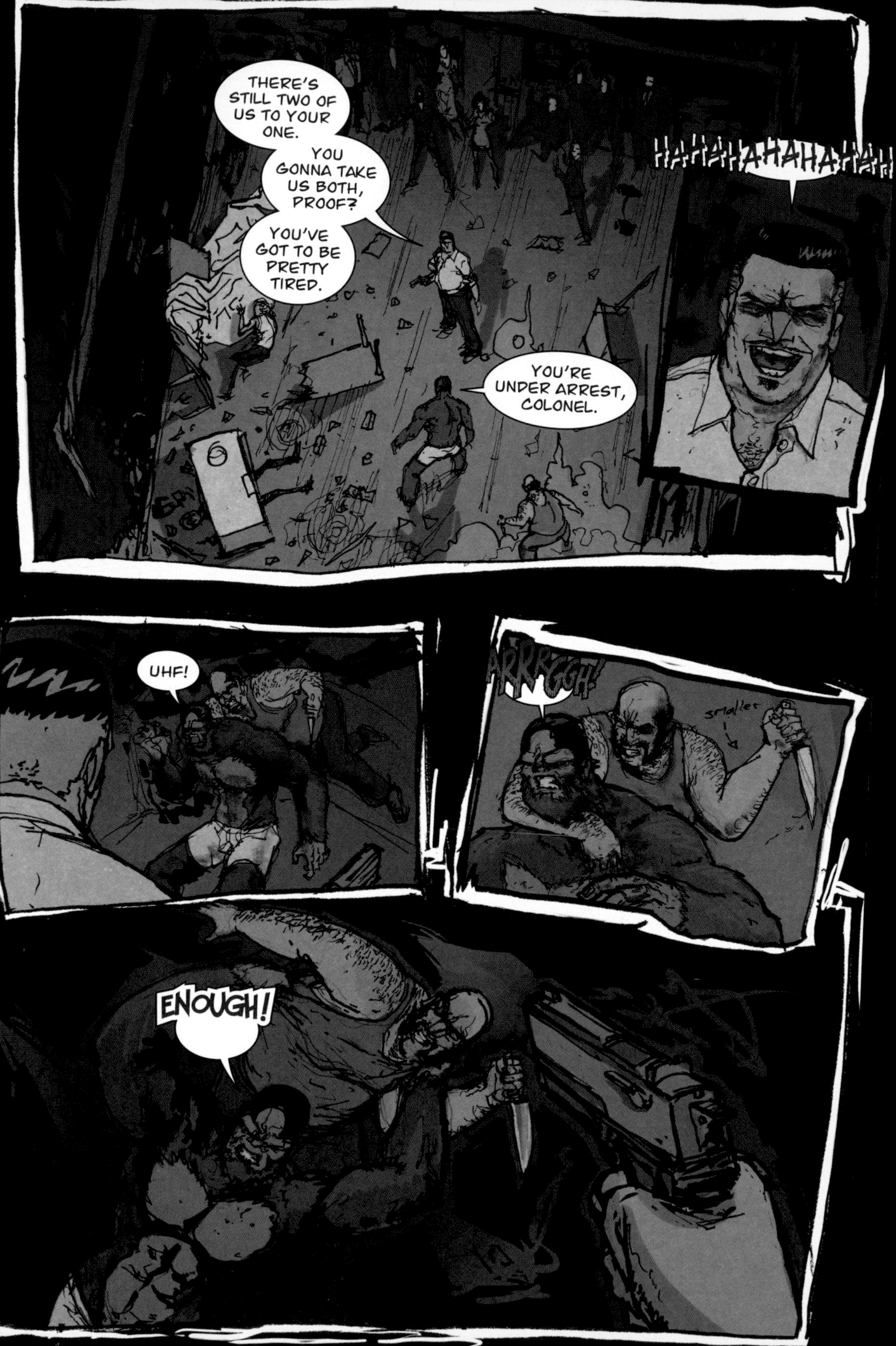
THERE'S STILL TWO OF US TO YOUR ONE.
YOU GONNA TAKE US BOTH, PROOF?
YOU'VE GOT TO BE PRETTY TIRED.
YOU'RE UNDER ARREST, COLONEL.
HAHAHAHAHAHAH
UHF!
ARRRGGH!
ENOUGH!

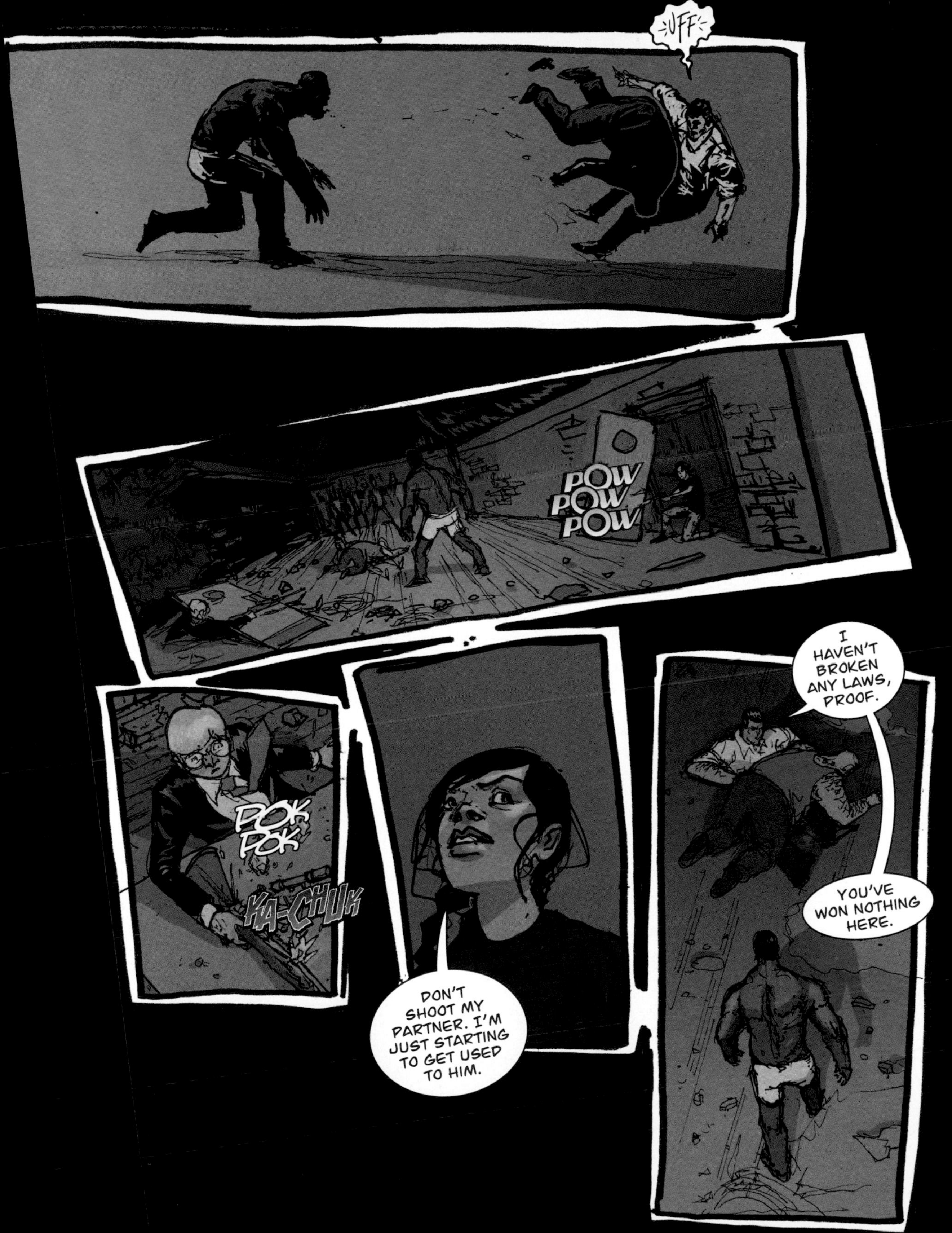
UFF
POW
POW
POW
POK
POK
KA-CHUK
DON'T SHOOT MY PARTNER. I'M JUST STARTING TO GET USED TO HIM.
I HAVEN'T BROKEN ANY LAWS, PROOF.
YOU'VE WON NOTHING HERE.

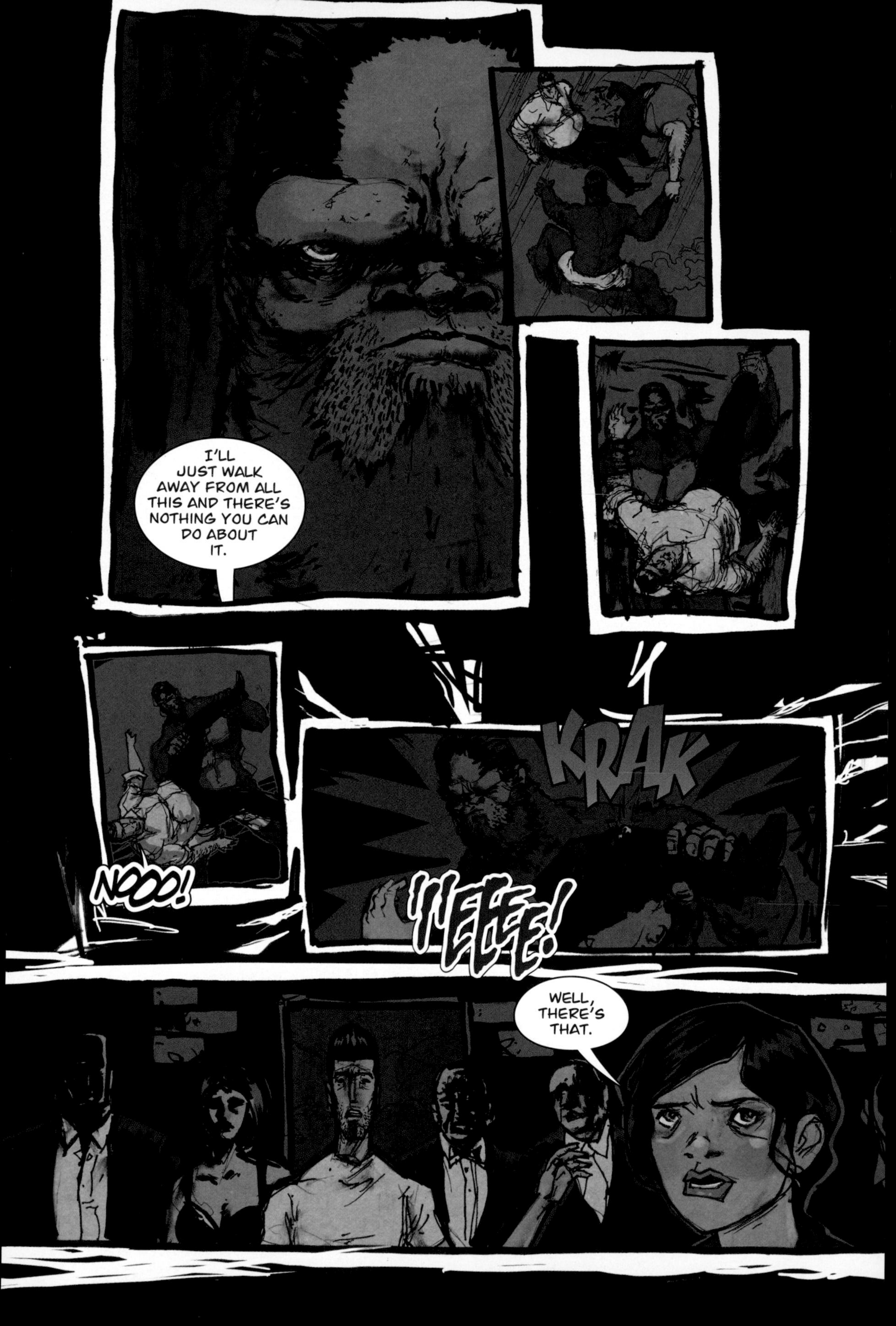
I'LL JUST WALK AWAY FROM ALL THIS AND THERE'S NOTHING YOU CAN DO ABOUT IT.
NOOO!
KRAK
WELL, THERE'S THAT.

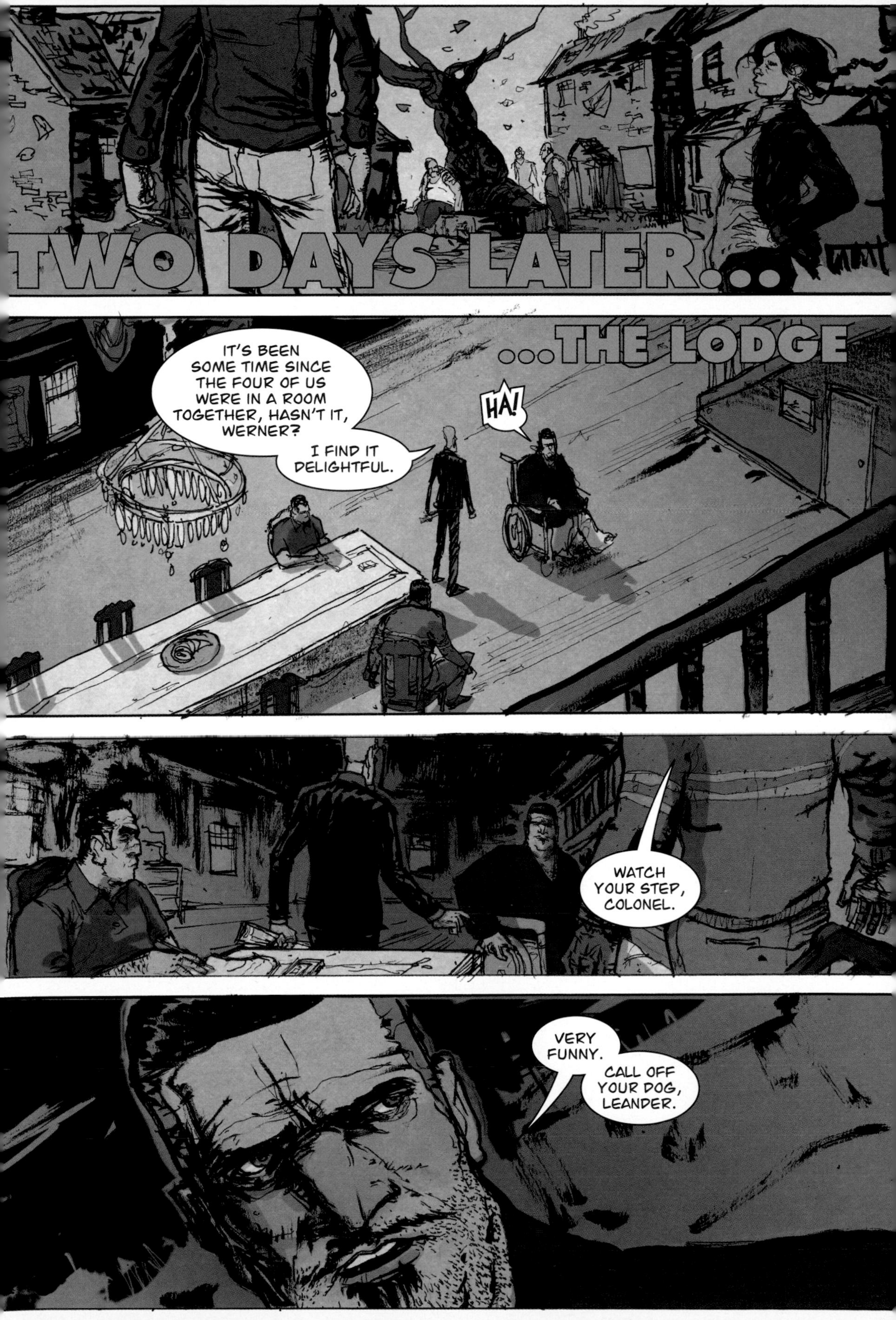
TWO DAYS LATER...
...THE LODGE
IT'S BEEN SOME TIME SINCE THE FOUR OF US WERE IN A ROOM TOGETHER, HASN'T IT, WERNER?
I FIND IT DELIGHTFUL.
HA!
WATCH YOUR STEP, COLONEL.
VERY FUNNY.
CALL OFF YOUR DOG, LEANDER.

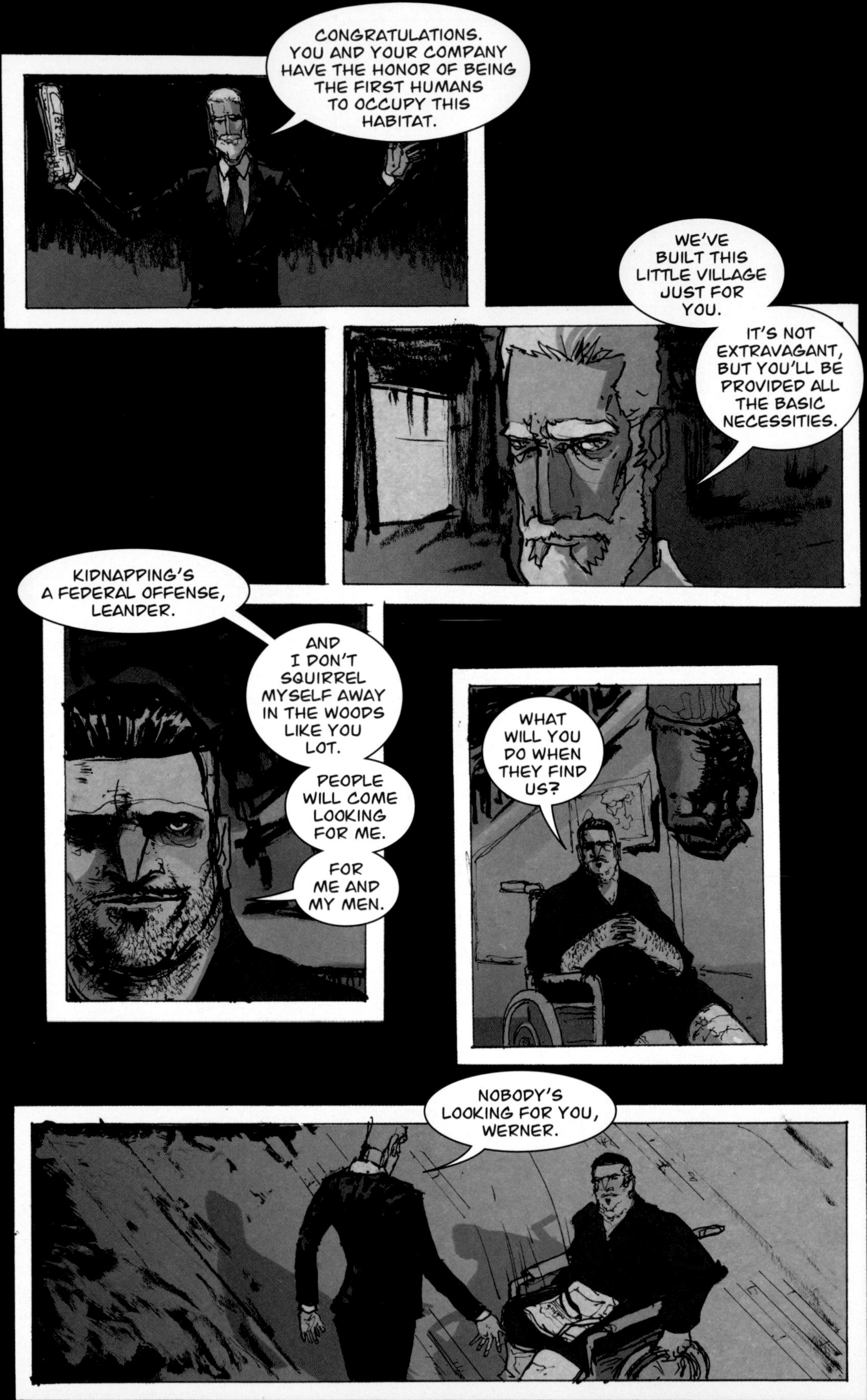
CONGRATULATIONS. YOU AND YOUR COMPANY HAVE THE HONOR OF BEING THE FIRST HUMANS TO OCCUPY THIS HABITAT.
WE'VE BUILT THIS LITTLE VILLAGE JUST FOR YOU.
IT'S NOT EXTRAVAGANT, BUT YOU'LL BE PROVIDED ALL THE BASIC NECESSITIES.
KIDNAPPING'S A FEDERAL OFFENSE, LEANDER.
AND I DON'T SQUIRREL MYSELF AWAY IN THE WOODS LIKE YOU LOT.
PEOPLE WILL COME LOOKING FOR ME.
FOR ME AND MY MEN.
WHAT WILL YOU DO WHEN THEY FIND US?
NOBODY'S LOOKING FOR YOU, WERNER.

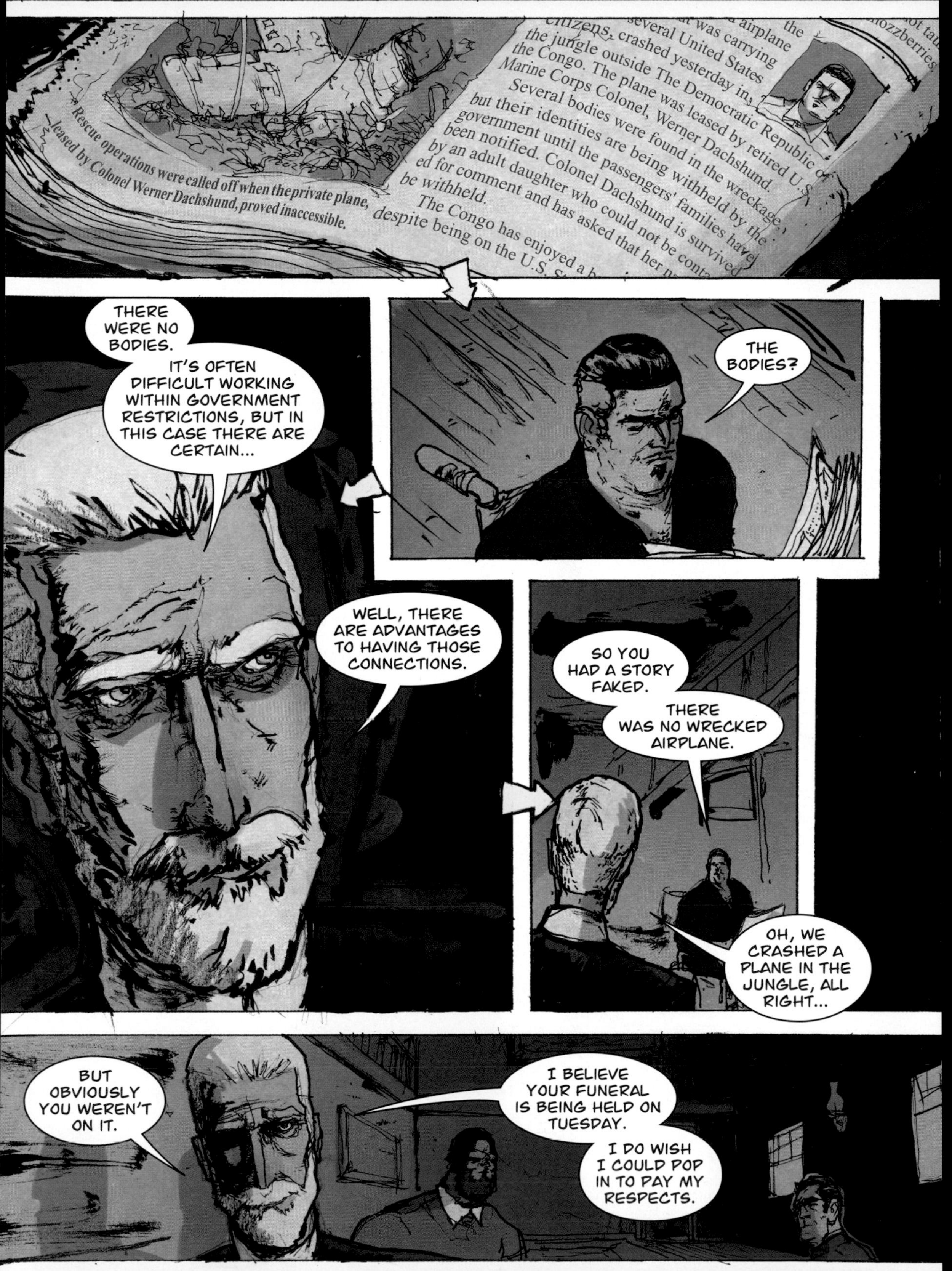

several United States
citizens, crashed yesterday in
the jungle outside The Democratic Republic of
the Congo. The plane was leased by retired U.S.
Marine Corps Colonel, Werner Dachshund.
Several bodies were found in the wreckage,
but their identities are being withheld by the
government until the passengers' families have
been notified. Colonel Dachshund is survived
by an adult daughter who could not be
ed for comment and has asked that her
be withheld.
The Congo has enjoyed a
despite being on the U.S.
Rescue operations were called off when the private plane, leased by Colonel Werner Dachshund, proved inaccessible.
THE BODIES?
THERE WERE NO BODIES.
IT'S OFTEN DIFFICULT WORKING WITHIN GOVERNMENT RESTRICTIONS, BUT IN THIS CASE THERE ARE CERTAIN...
WELL, THERE ARE ADVANTAGES TO HAVING THOSE CONNECTIONS.
SO YOU HAD A STORY FAKED.
THERE WAS NO WRECKED AIRPLANE.
OH, WE CRASHED A PLANE IN THE JUNGLE, ALL RIGHT...
BUT OBVIOUSLY YOU WEREN'T ON IT.
I BELIEVE YOUR FUNERAL IS BEING HELD ON TUESDAY.
I DO WISH I COULD POP IN TO PAY MY RESPECTS.

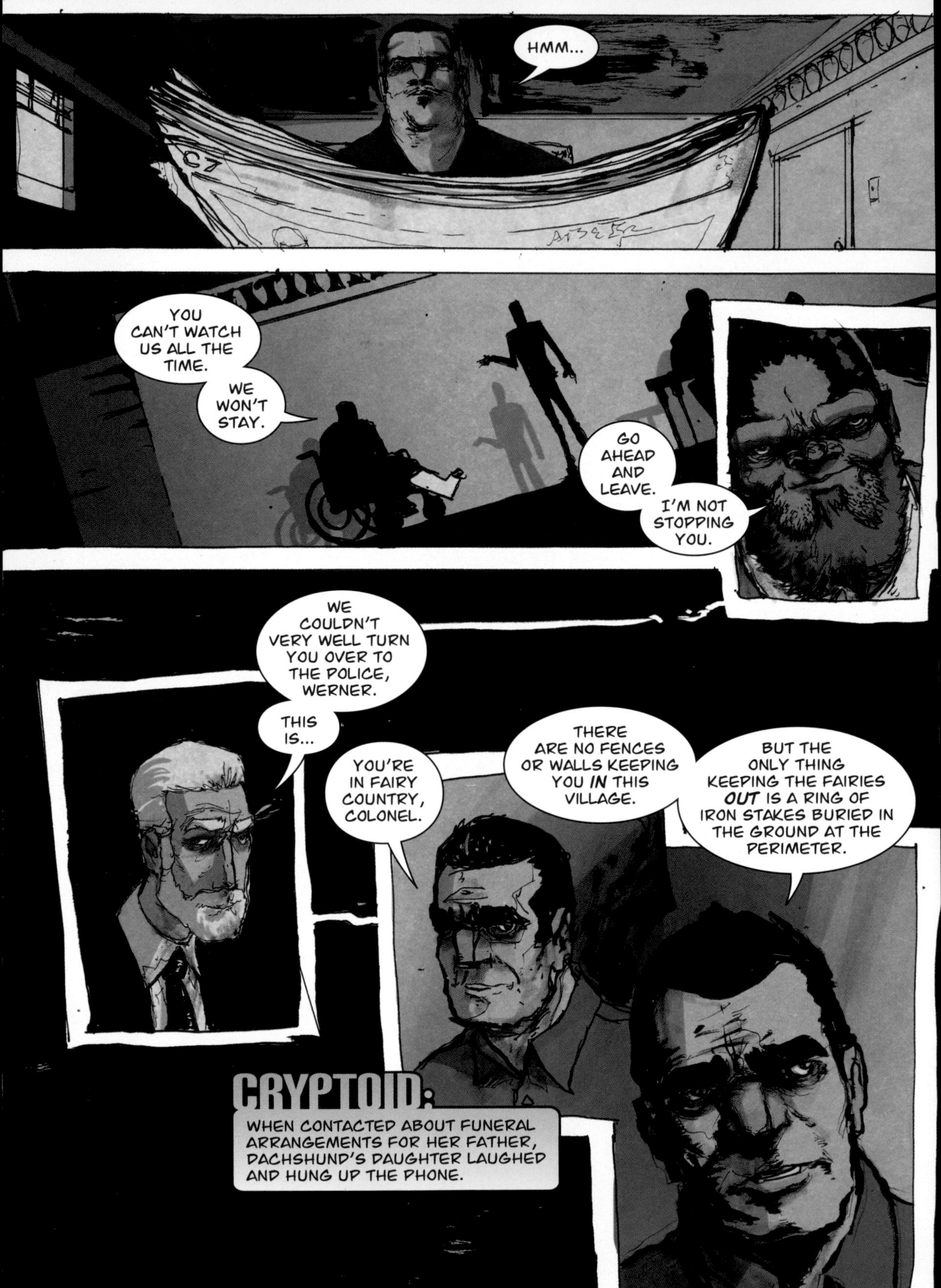
HMM...
YOU CAN'T WATCH US ALL THE TIME.
WE WON'T STAY.
GO AHEAD AND LEAVE.
I'M NOT STOPPING YOU.
WE COULDN'T VERY WELL TURN YOU OVER TO THE POLICE, WERNER.
THIS IS...
YOU'RE IN FAIRY COUNTRY, COLONEL.
THERE ARE NO FENCES OR WALLS KEEPING YOU *IN* THIS VILLAGE.
BUT THE ONLY THING KEEPING THE FAIRIES *OUT* IS A RING OF IRON STAKES BURIED IN THE GROUND AT THE PERIMETER.
CRYPTOID:
WHEN CONTACTED ABOUT FUNERAL ARRANGEMENTS FOR HER FATHER, DACHSHUND'S DAUGHTER LAUGHED AND HUNG UP THE PHONE.

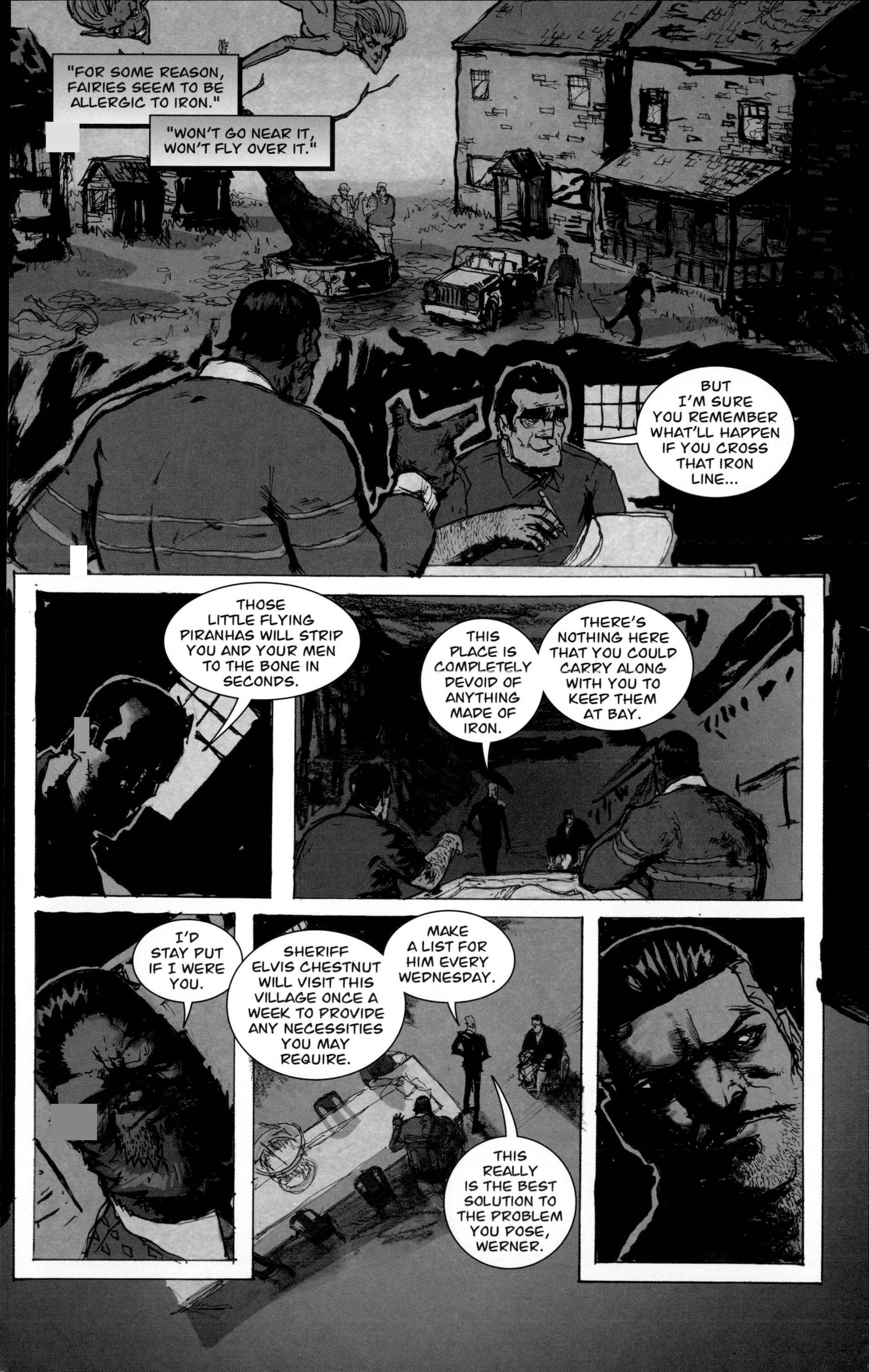
"FOR SOME REASON, FAIRIES SEEM TO BE ALLERGIC TO IRON."
"WON'T GO NEAR IT, WON'T FLY OVER IT."
BUT I'M SURE YOU REMEMBER WHAT'LL HAPPEN IF YOU CROSS THAT IRON LINE...
THOSE LITTLE FLYING PIRANHAS WILL STRIP YOU AND YOUR MEN TO THE BONE IN SECONDS.
THIS PLACE IS COMPLETELY DEVOID OF ANYTHING MADE OF IRON.
THERE'S NOTHING HERE THAT YOU COULD CARRY ALONG WITH YOU TO KEEP THEM AT BAY.
I'D STAY PUT IF I WERE YOU.
SHERIFF ELVIS CHESTNUT WILL VISIT THIS VILLAGE ONCE A WEEK TO PROVIDE ANY NECESSITIES YOU MAY REQUIRE.
MAKE A LIST FOR HIM EVERY WEDNESDAY.
THIS REALLY IS THE BEST SOLUTION TO THE PROBLEM YOU POSE, WERNER.

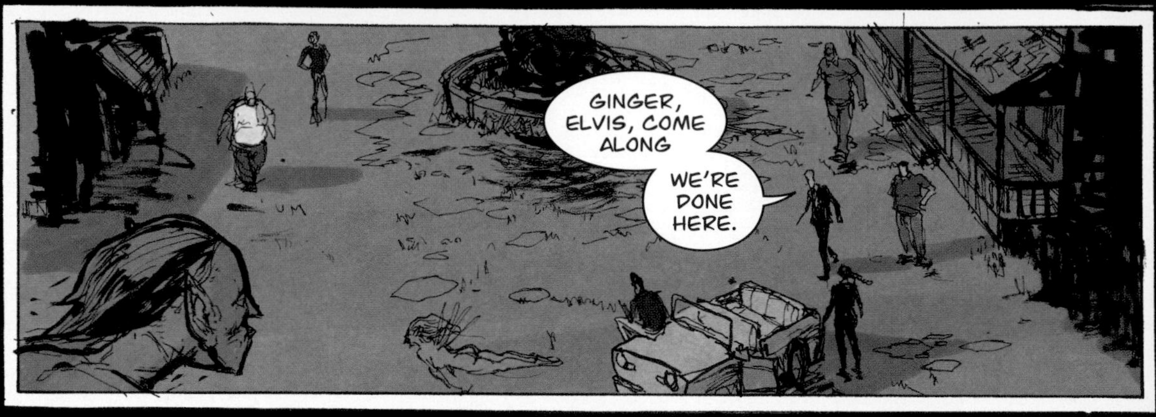
GINGER, ELVIS, COME ALONG
WE'RE DONE HERE.

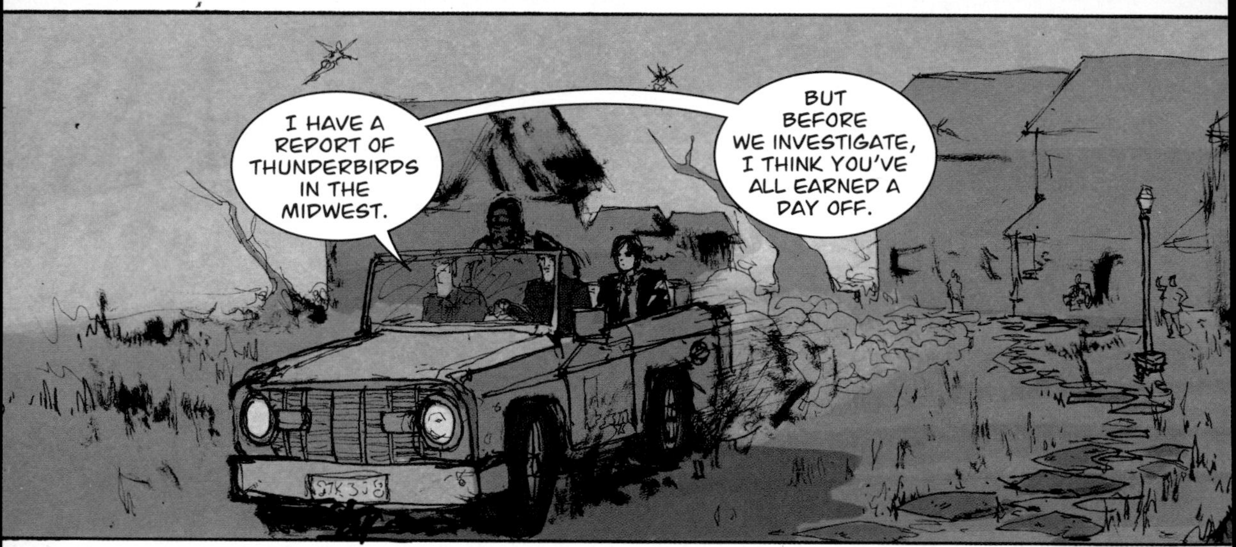
I HAVE A REPORT OF THUNDERBIRDS IN THE MIDWEST.
BUT BEFORE WE INVESTIGATE, I THINK YOU'VE ALL EARNED A DAY OFF.

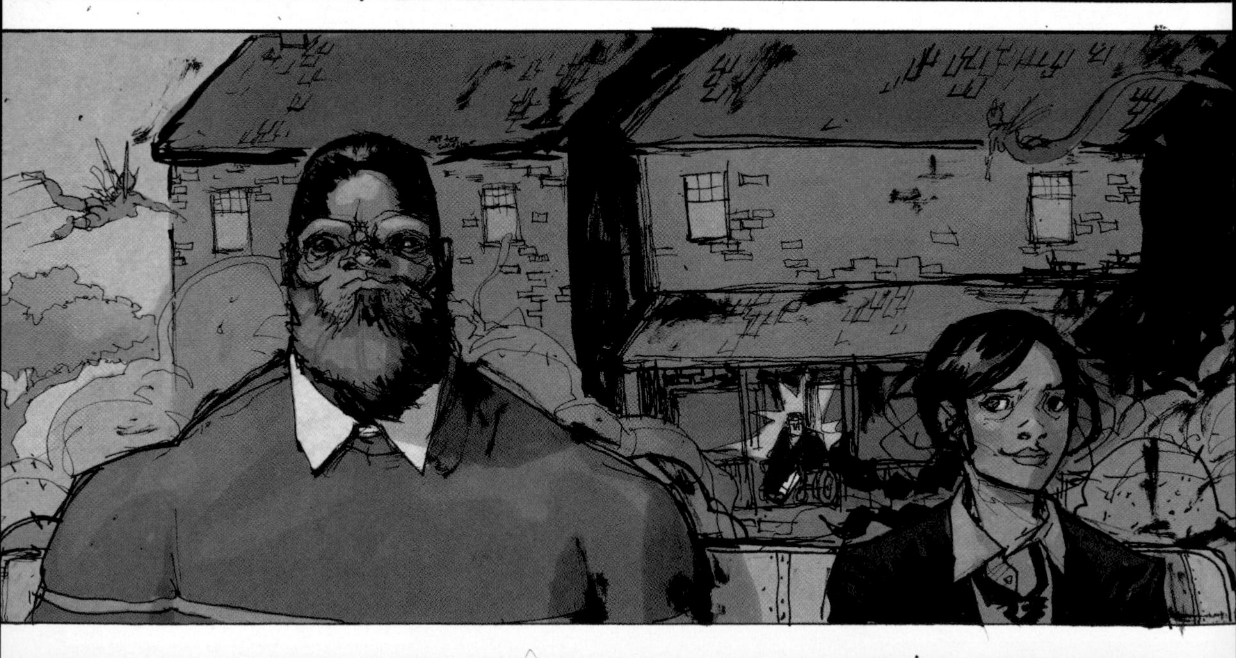

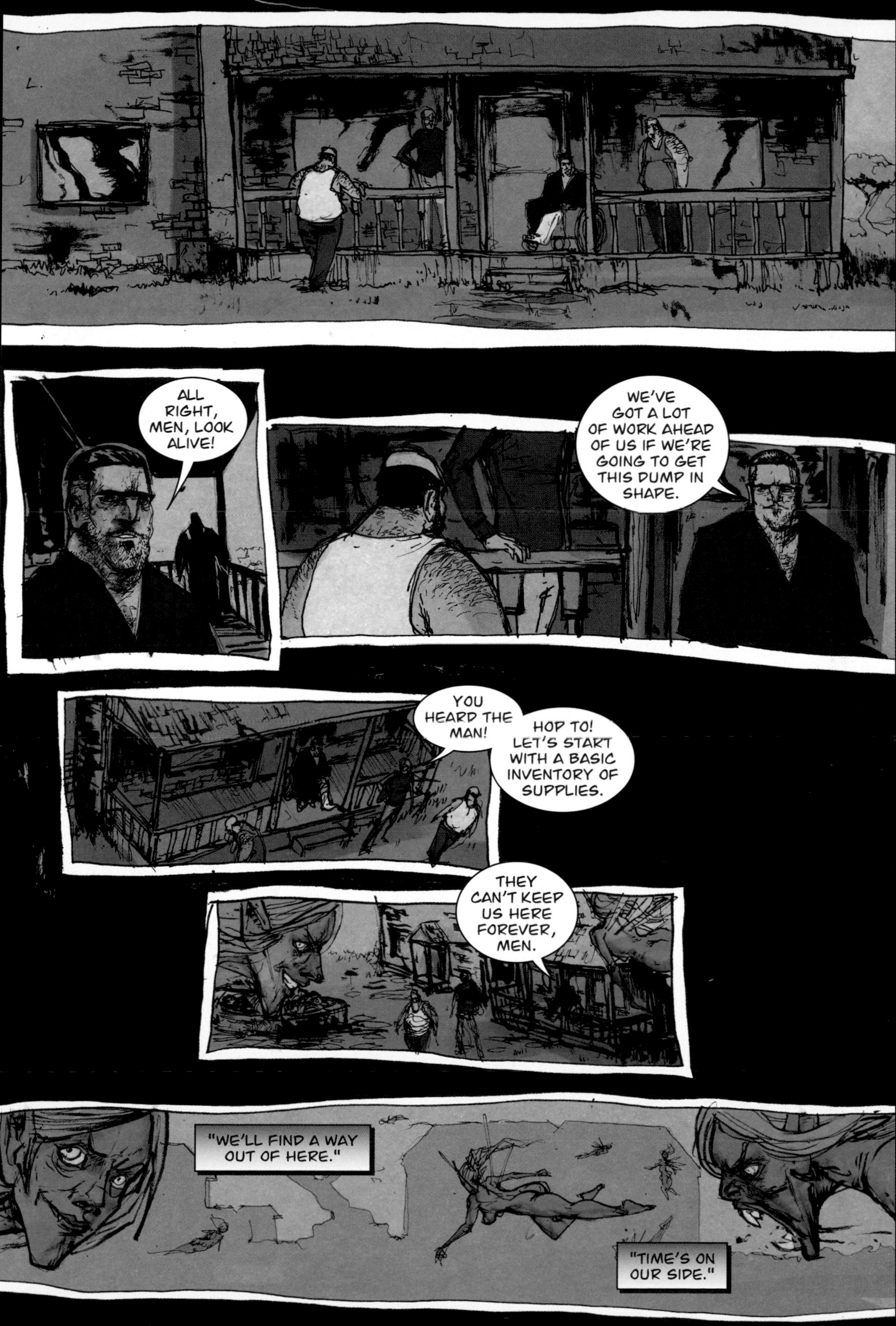
ALL RIGHT, MEN, LOOK ALIVE!
WE'VE GOT A LOT OF WORK AHEAD OF US IF WE'RE GOING TO GET THIS DUMP IN SHAPE.
YOU HEARD THE MAN!
HOP TO! LET'S START WITH A BASIC INVENTORY OF SUPPLIES.
THEY CAN'T KEEP US HERE FOREVER, MEN.
"WE'LL FIND A WAY OUT OF HERE."
"TIME'S ON OUR SIDE."

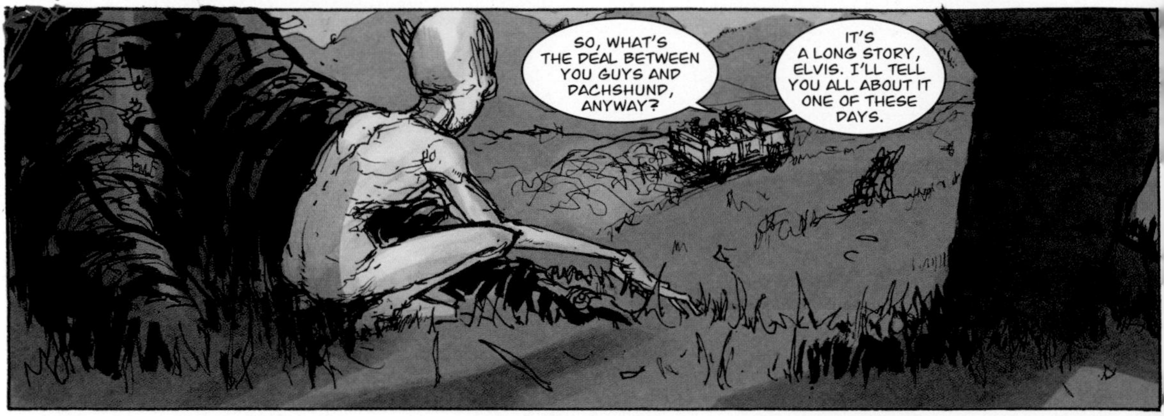
SO, WHAT'S THE DEAL BETWEEN YOU GUYS AND DACHSHUND, ANYWAY?
IT'S A LONG STORY, ELVIS. I'LL TELL YOU ALL ABOUT IT ONE OF THESE DAYS.

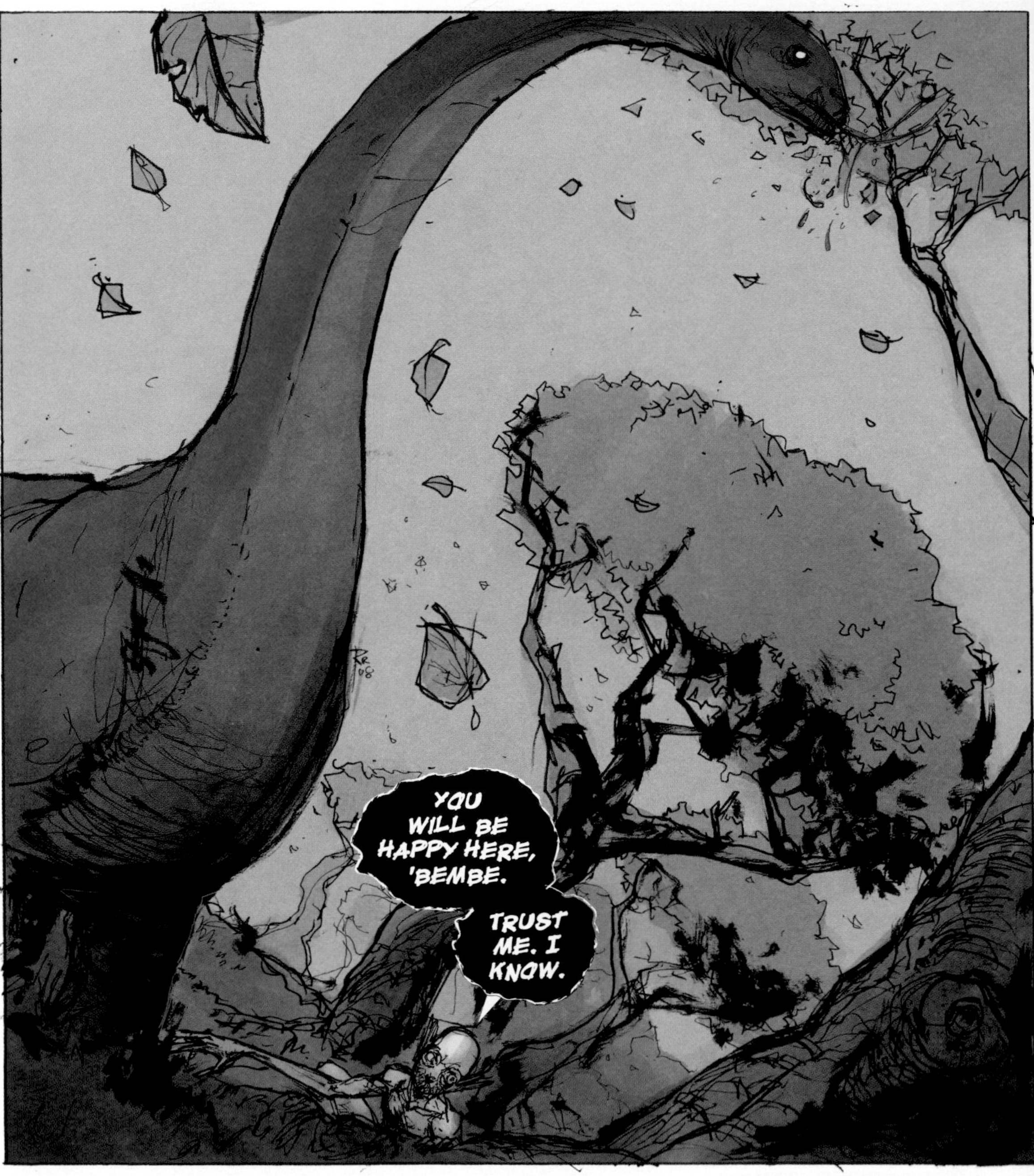
YOU WILL BE HAPPY HERE, 'BEMBE.
TRUST ME. I KNOW.

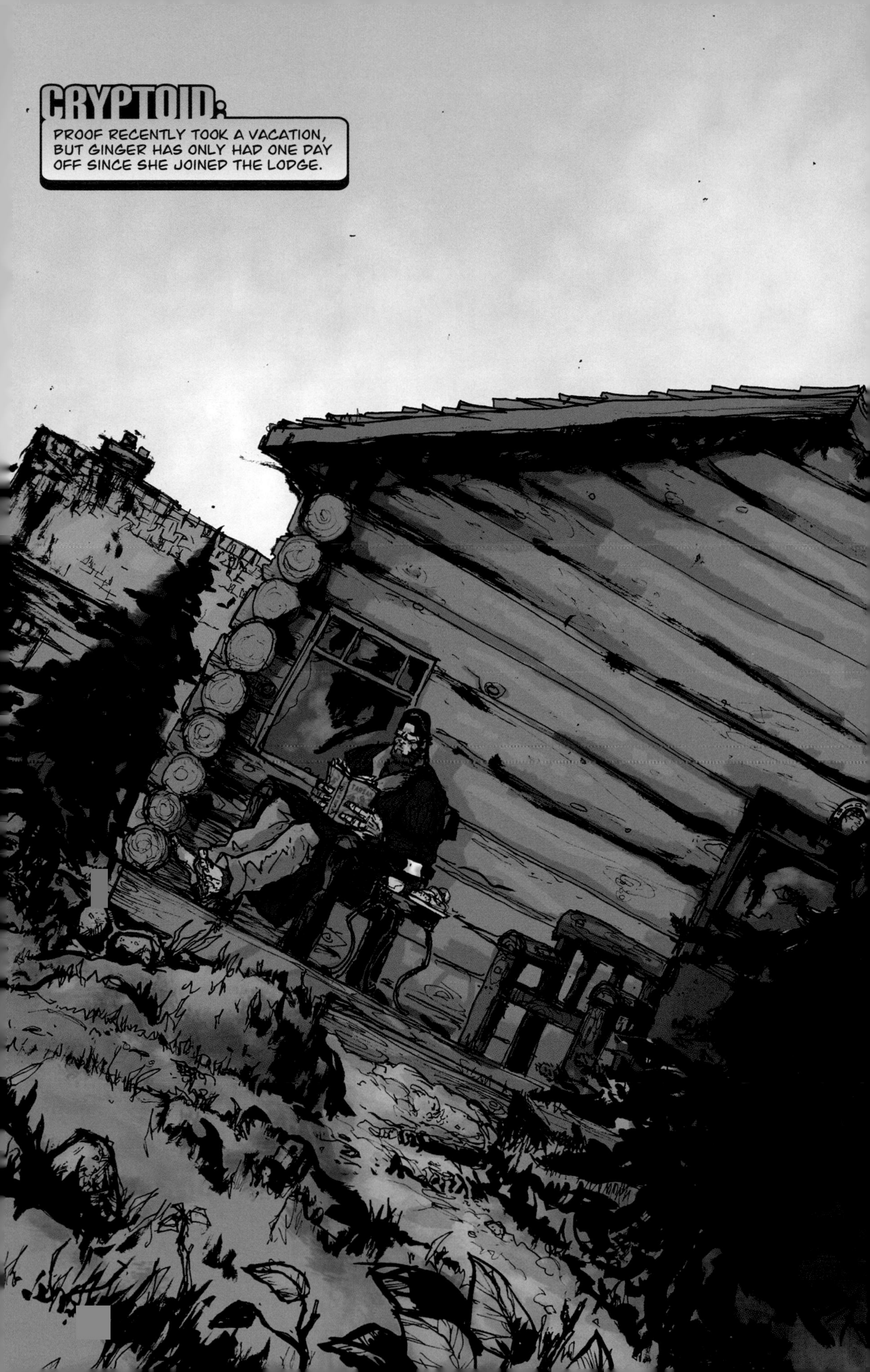
CRYPTOID:
PROOF RECENTLY TOOK A VACATION, BUT GINGER HAS ONLY HAD ONE DAY OFF SINCE SHE JOINED THE LODGE.

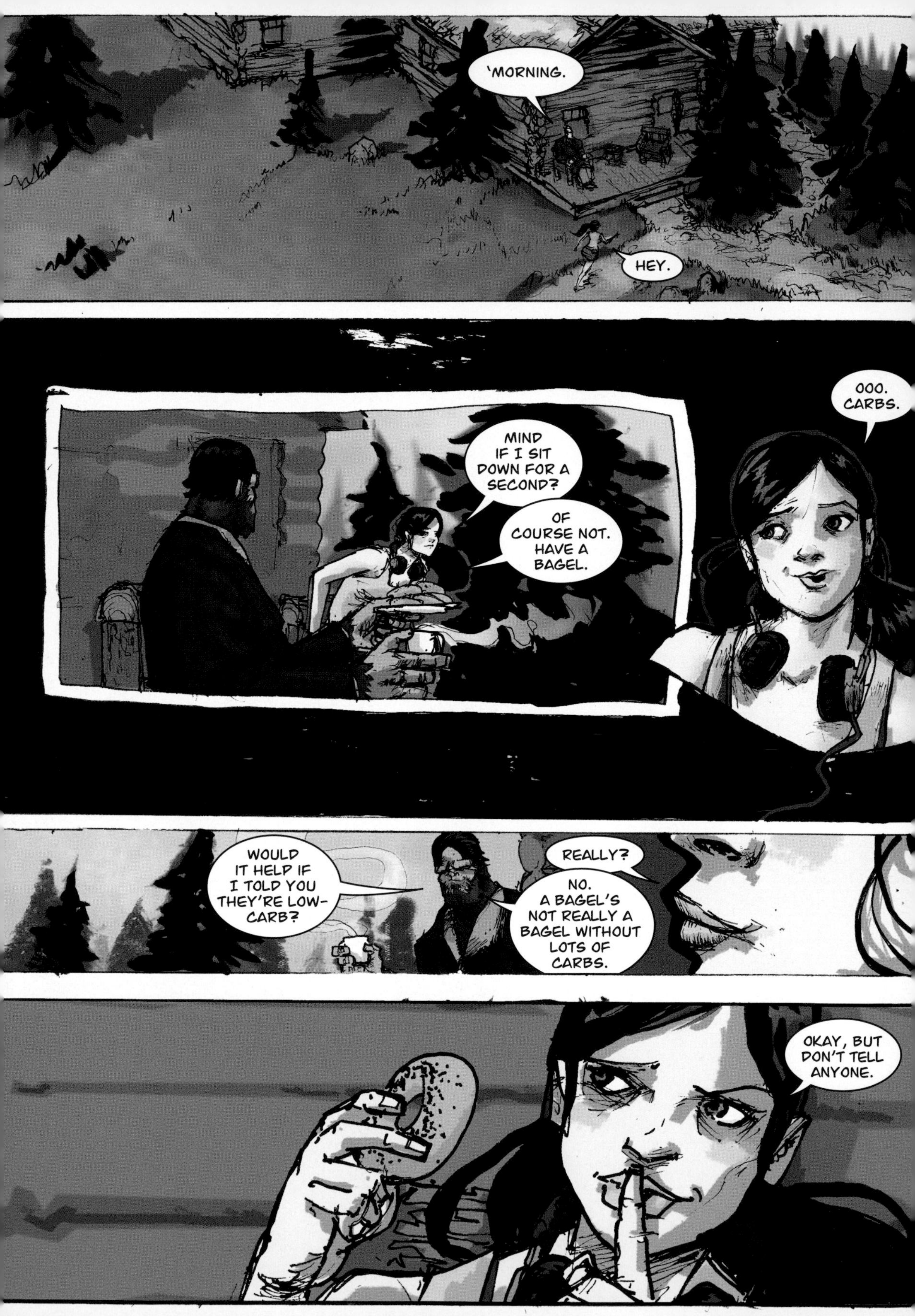
'MORNING.
HEY.
MIND IF I SIT DOWN FOR A SECOND?
OF COURSE NOT. HAVE A BAGEL.
OOO. CARBS.
WOULD IT HELP IF I TOLD YOU THEY'RE LOW-CARB?
REALLY?
NO. A BAGEL'S NOT REALLY A BAGEL WITHOUT LOTS OF CARBS.
OKAY, BUT DON'T TELL ANYONE.

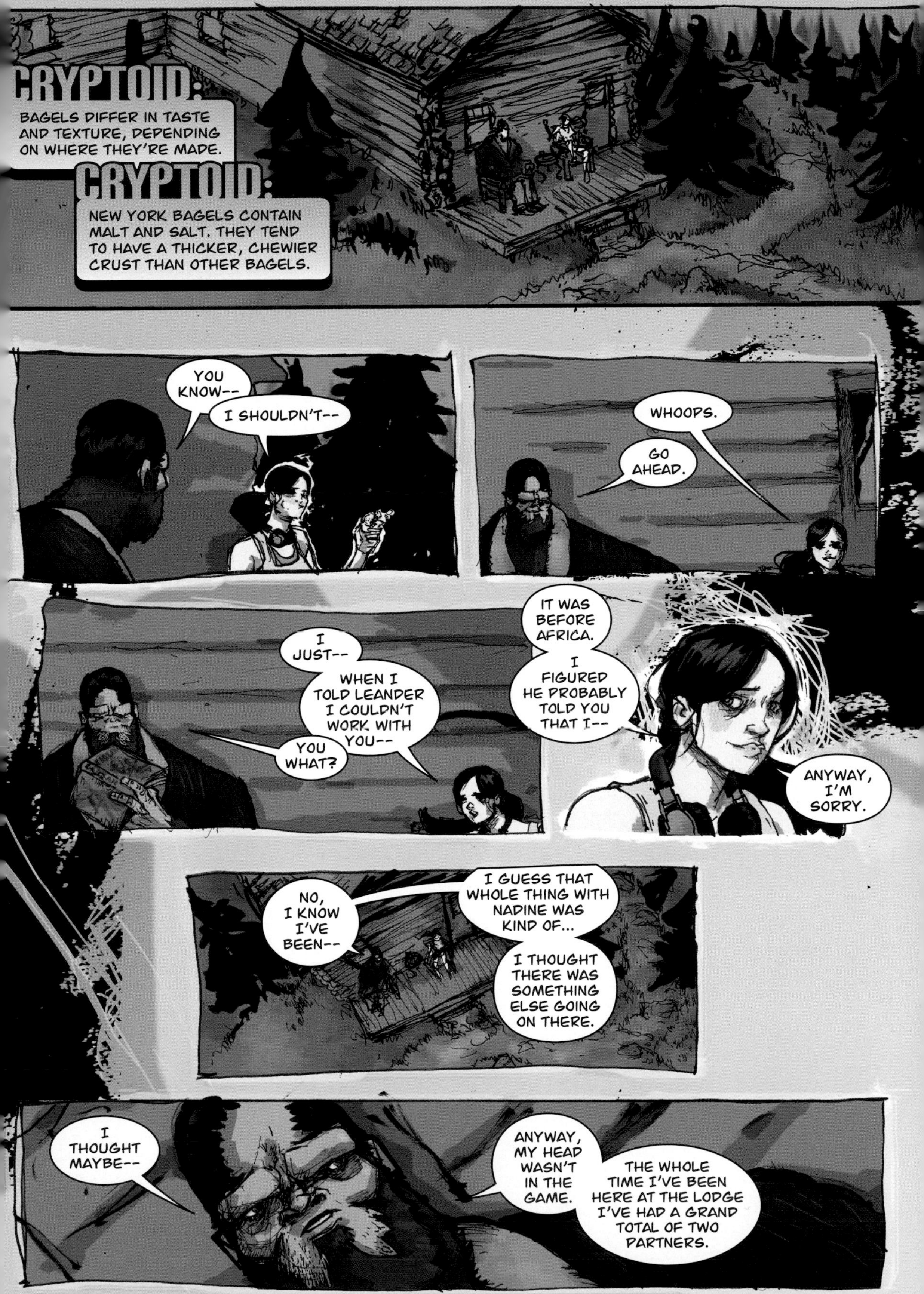
CRYPTOID:
BAGELS DIFFER IN TASTE AND TEXTURE, DEPENDING ON WHERE THEY'RE MADE.
CRYPTOID:
NEW YORK BAGELS CONTAIN MALT AND SALT. THEY TEND TO HAVE A THICKER, CHEWIER CRUST THAN OTHER BAGELS.
YOU KNOW--
I SHOULDN'T--
WHOOPS.
GO AHEAD.
I JUST--
WHEN I TOLD LEANDER I COULDN'T WORK WITH YOU--
YOU WHAT?
IT WAS BEFORE AFRICA.
I FIGURED HE PROBABLY TOLD YOU THAT I--
ANYWAY, I'M SORRY.
NO, I KNOW I'VE BEEN--
I GUESS THAT WHOLE THING WITH NADINE WAS KIND OF...
I THOUGHT THERE WAS SOMETHING ELSE GOING ON THERE.
I THOUGHT MAYBE--
ANYWAY, MY HEAD WASN'T IN THE GAME.
THE WHOLE TIME I'VE BEEN HERE AT THE LODGE I'VE HAD A GRAND TOTAL OF TWO PARTNERS.

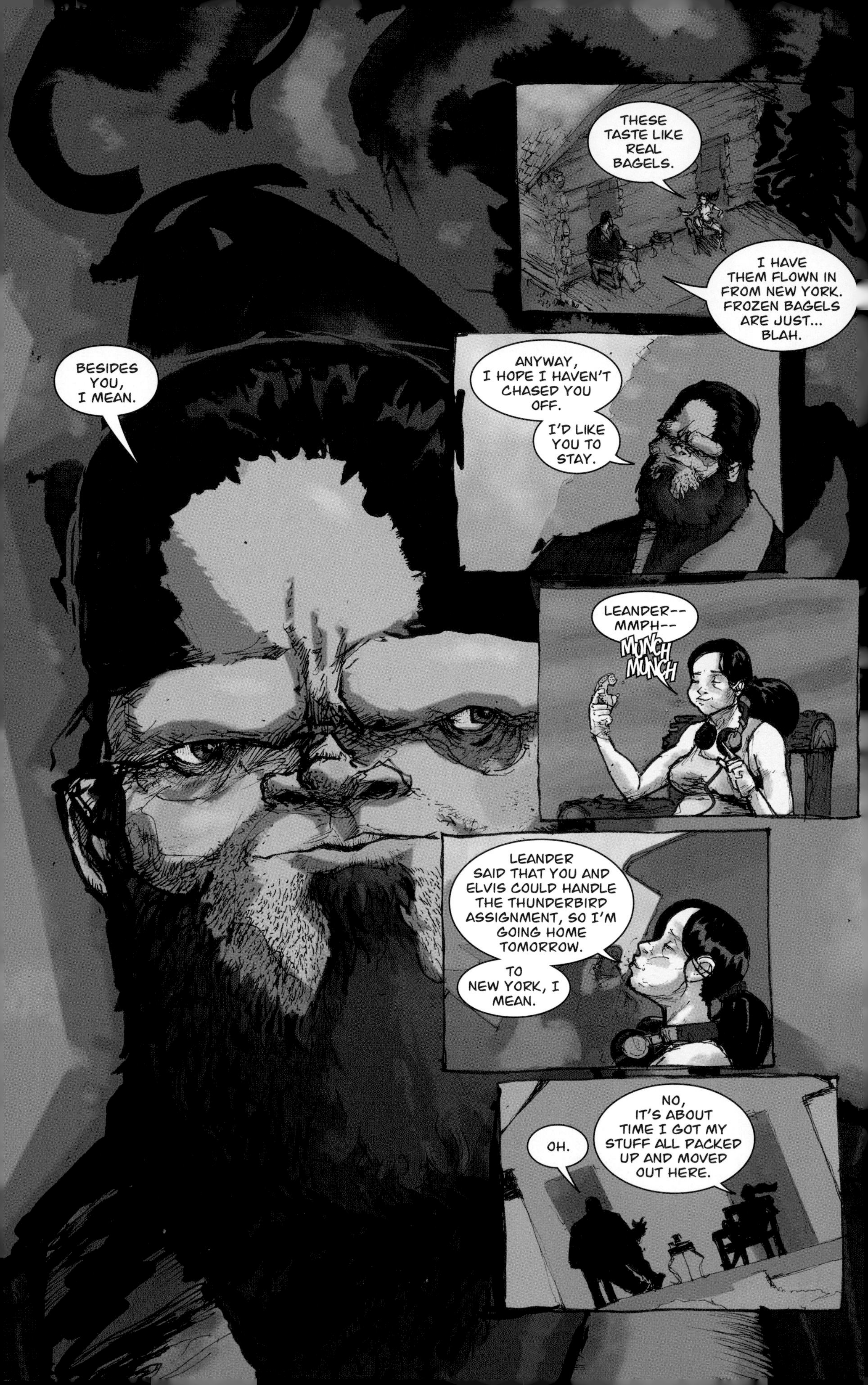
THESE TASTE LIKE REAL BAGELS.
I HAVE THEM FLOWN IN FROM NEW YORK. FROZEN BAGELS ARE JUST... BLAH.
ANYWAY, I HOPE I HAVEN'T CHASED YOU OFF.
I'D LIKE YOU TO STAY.
BESIDES YOU, I MEAN.
LEANDER-- MMPH--
MUNCH MUNCH
LEANDER SAID THAT YOU AND ELVIS COULD HANDLE THE THUNDERBIRD ASSIGNMENT, SO I'M GOING HOME TOMORROW.
TO NEW YORK, I MEAN.
OH.
NO, IT'S ABOUT TIME I GOT MY STUFF ALL PACKED UP AND MOVED OUT HERE.

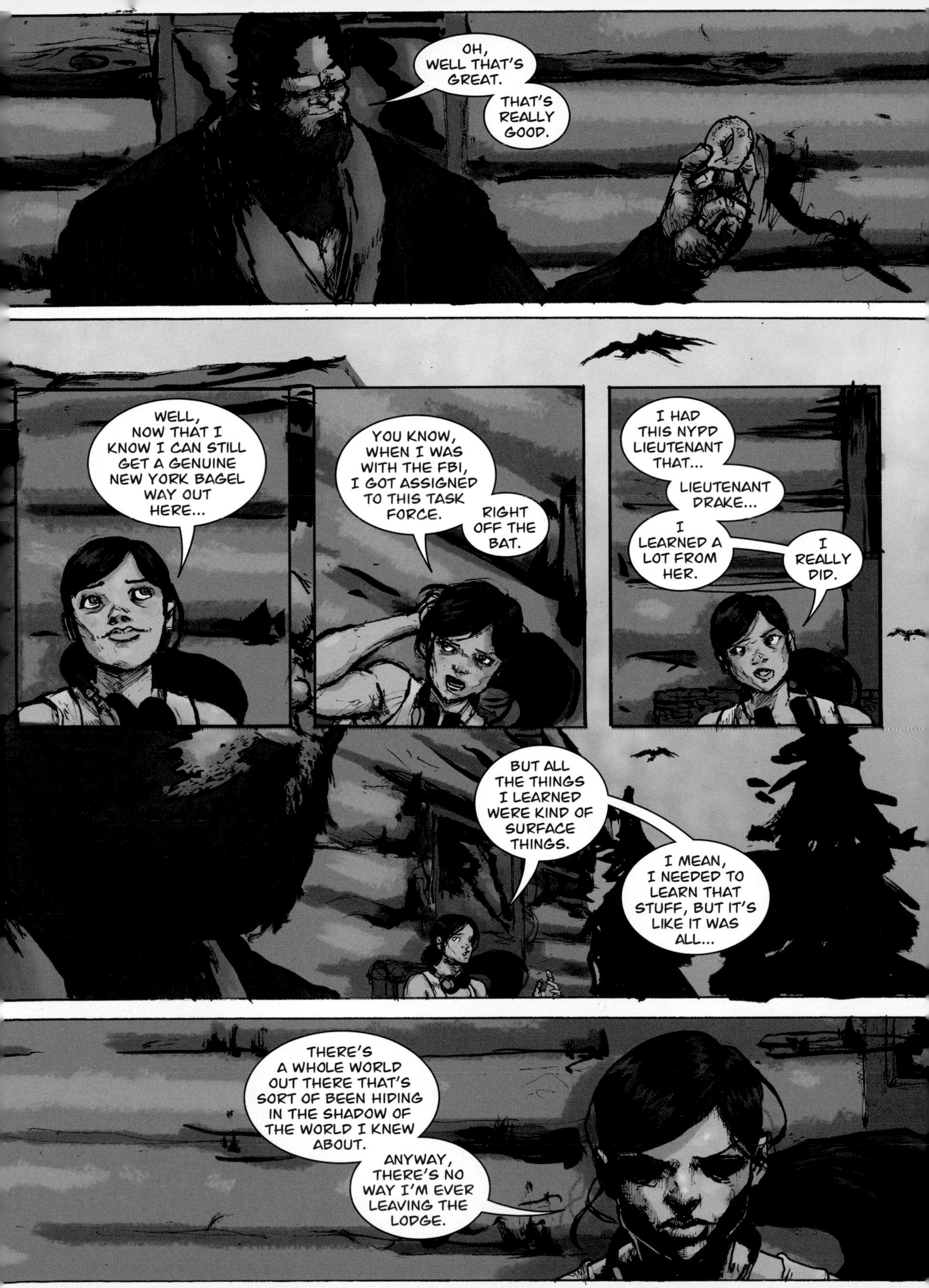
OH, WELL THAT'S GREAT.
THAT'S REALLY GOOD.
WELL, NOW THAT I KNOW I CAN STILL GET A GENUINE NEW YORK BAGEL WAY OUT HERE...
YOU KNOW, WHEN I WAS WITH THE FBI, I GOT ASSIGNED TO THIS TASK FORCE.
RIGHT OFF THE BAT.
I HAD THIS NYPD LIEUTENANT THAT...
LIEUTENANT DRAKE...
I LEARNED A LOT FROM HER.
I REALLY DID.
BUT ALL THE THINGS I LEARNED WERE KIND OF SURFACE THINGS.
I MEAN, I NEEDED TO LEARN THAT STUFF, BUT IT'S LIKE IT WAS ALL...
THERE'S A WHOLE WORLD OUT THERE THAT'S SORT OF BEEN HIDING IN THE SHADOW OF THE WORLD I KNEW ABOUT.
ANYWAY, THERE'S NO WAY I'M EVER LEAVING THE LODGE.

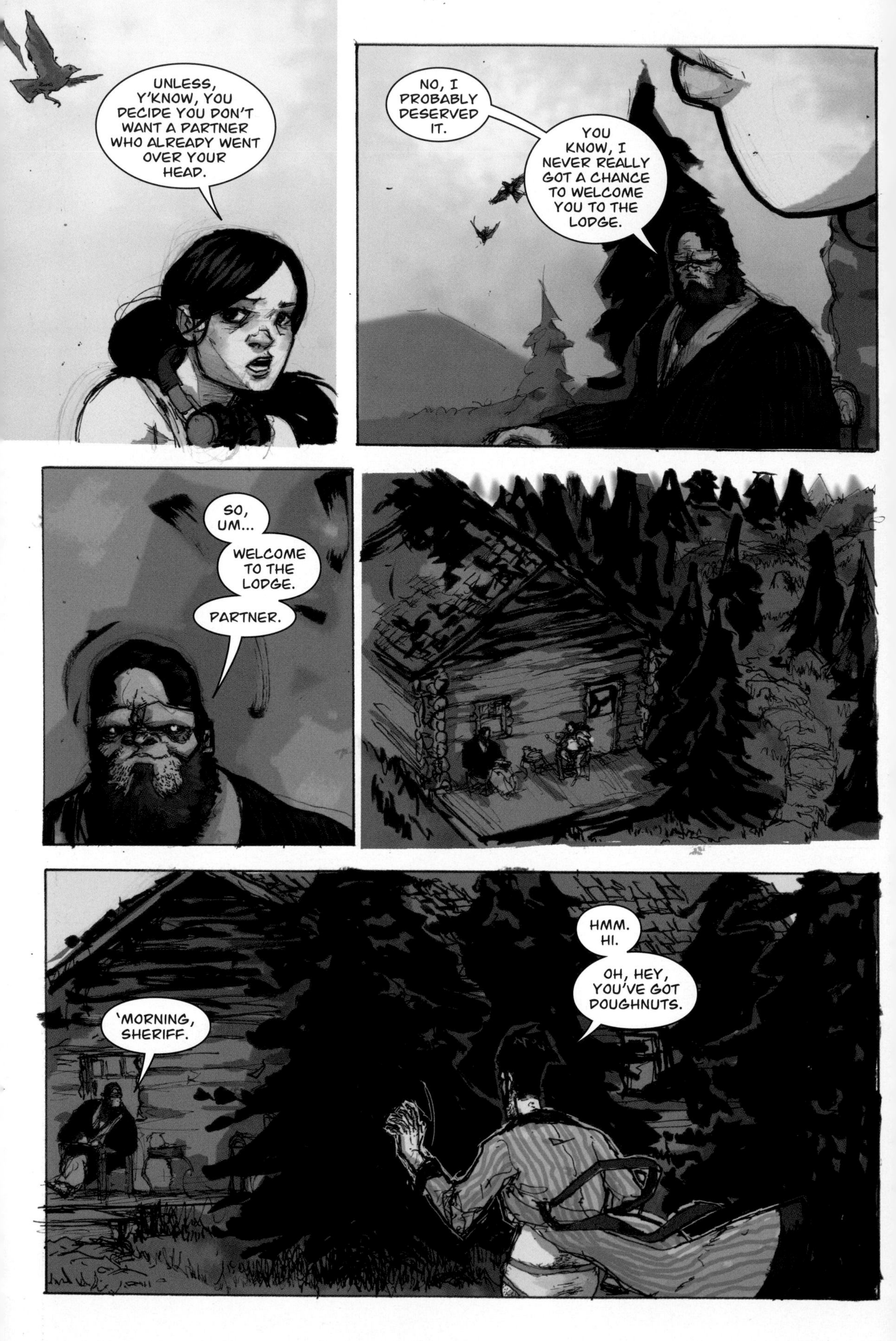
UNLESS, Y'KNOW, YOU DECIDE YOU DON'T WANT A PARTNER WHO ALREADY WENT OVER YOUR HEAD.
NO, I PROBABLY DESERVED IT.
YOU KNOW, I NEVER REALLY GOT A CHANCE TO WELCOME YOU TO THE LODGE.
SO, UM...
WELCOME TO THE LODGE.
PARTNER.
'MORNING, SHERIFF.
HMM. HI.
OH, HEY, YOU'VE GOT DOUGHNUTS.

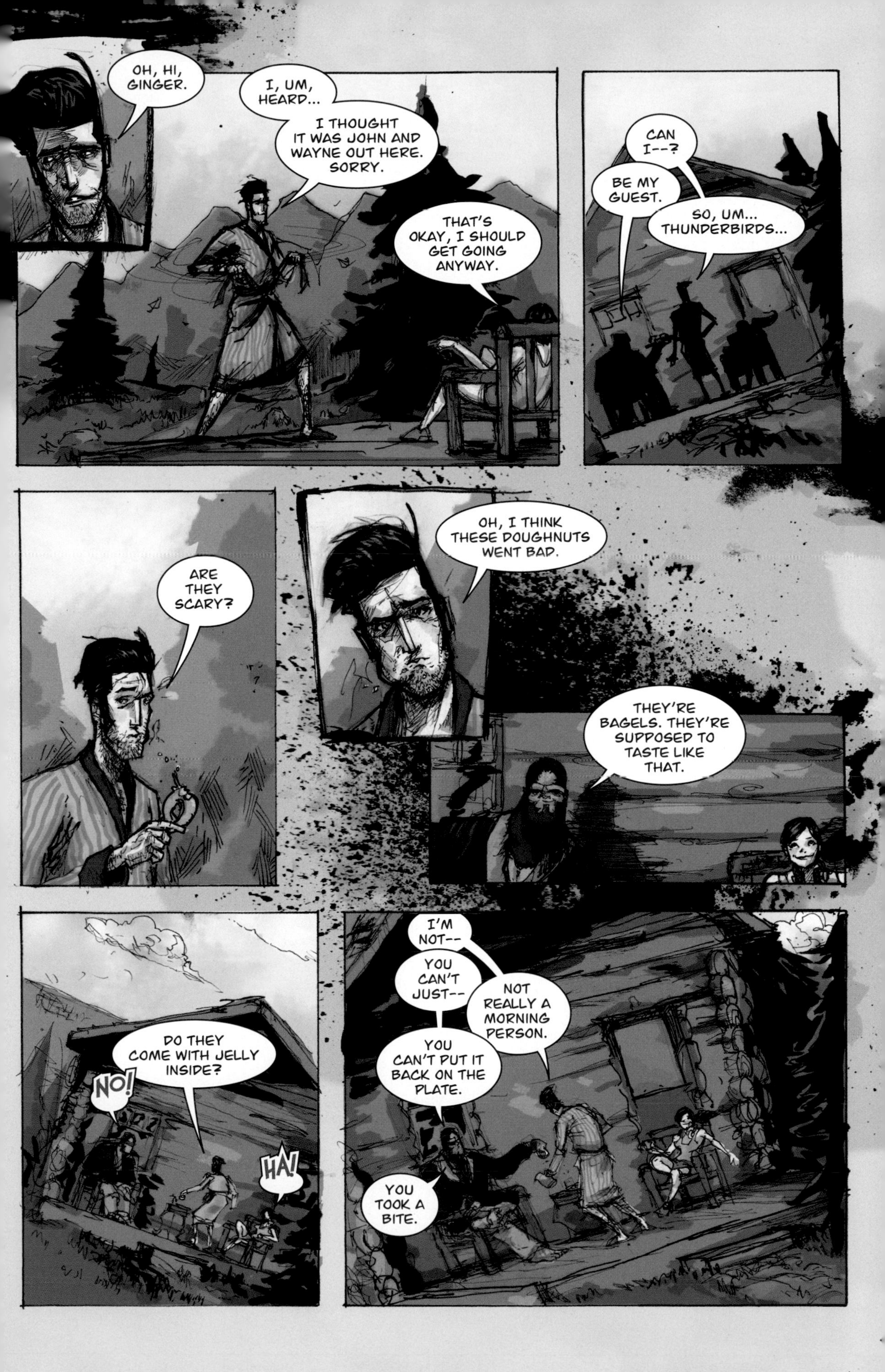
OH, HI, GINGER.
I, UM, HEARD...
I THOUGHT IT WAS JOHN AND WAYNE OUT HERE. SORRY.
THAT'S OKAY, I SHOULD GET GOING ANYWAY.
CAN I--?
BE MY GUEST.
SO, UM... THUNDERBIRDS...
ARE THEY SCARY?
OH, I THINK THESE DOUGHNUTS WENT BAD.
THEY'RE BAGELS. THEY'RE SUPPOSED TO TASTE LIKE THAT.
DO THEY COME WITH JELLY INSIDE?
NO!
HA!
I'M NOT--
YOU CAN'T JUST--
NOT REALLY A MORNING PERSON.
YOU CAN'T PUT IT BACK ON THE PLATE.
YOU TOOK A BITE.

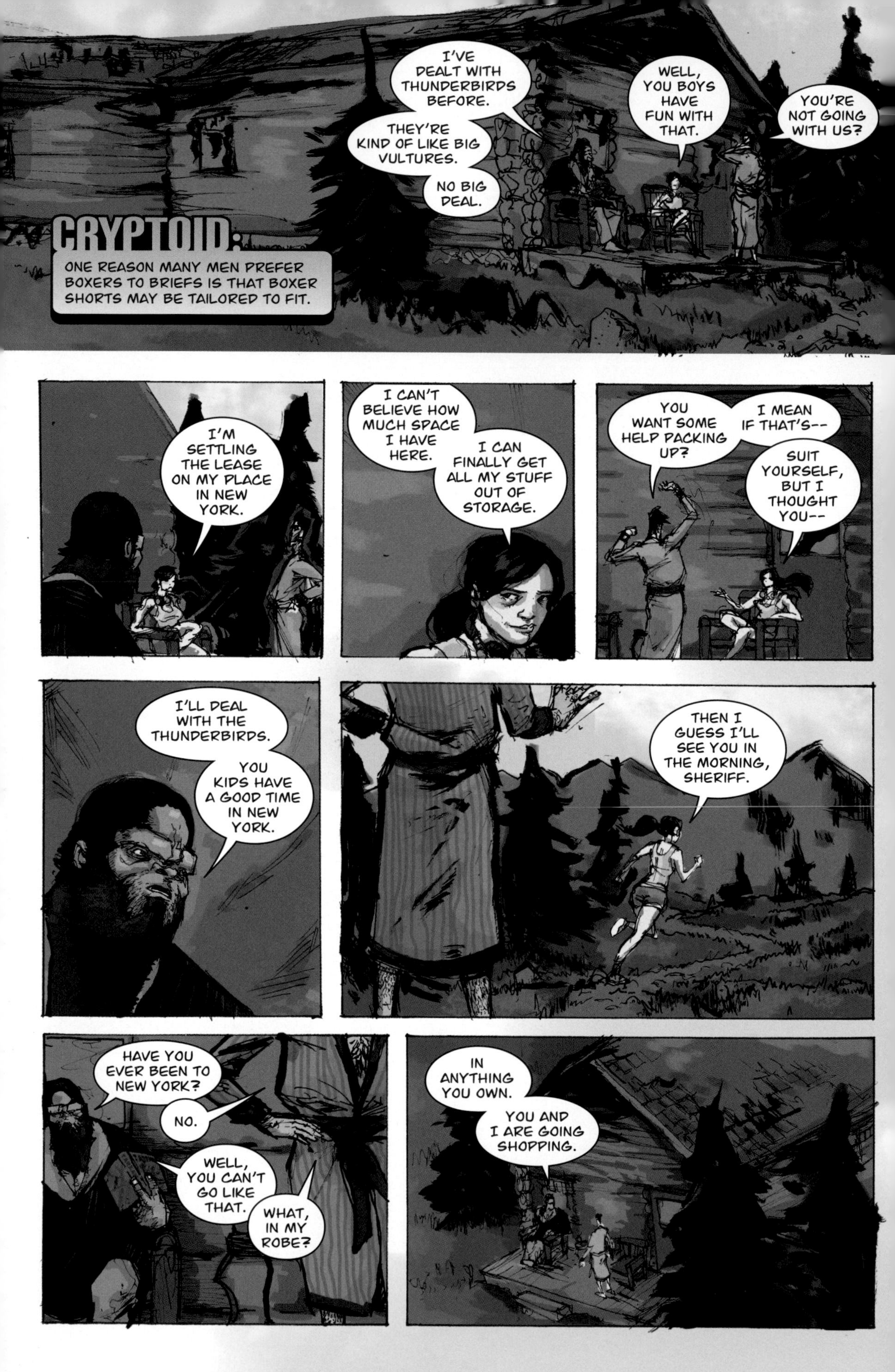
I'VE DEALT WITH THUNDERBIRDS BEFORE.
THEY'RE KIND OF LIKE BIG VULTURES.
NO BIG DEAL.
WELL, YOU BOYS HAVE FUN WITH THAT.
YOU'RE NOT GOING WITH US?
CRYPTOID:
ONE REASON MANY MEN PREFER BOXERS TO BRIEFS IS THAT BOXER SHORTS MAY BE TAILORED TO FIT.
I'M SETTLING THE LEASE ON MY PLACE IN NEW YORK.
I CAN'T BELIEVE HOW MUCH SPACE I HAVE HERE.
I CAN FINALLY GET ALL MY STUFF OUT OF STORAGE.
YOU WANT SOME HELP PACKING UP?
I MEAN IF THAT'S--
SUIT YOURSELF, BUT I THOUGHT YOU--
I'LL DEAL WITH THE THUNDERBIRDS.
YOU KIDS HAVE A GOOD TIME IN NEW YORK.
THEN I GUESS I'LL SEE YOU IN THE MORNING, SHERIFF.
HAVE YOU EVER BEEN TO NEW YORK?
NO.
WELL, YOU CAN'T GO LIKE THAT.
WHAT, IN MY ROBE?
IN ANYTHING YOU OWN.
YOU AND I ARE GOING SHOPPING.

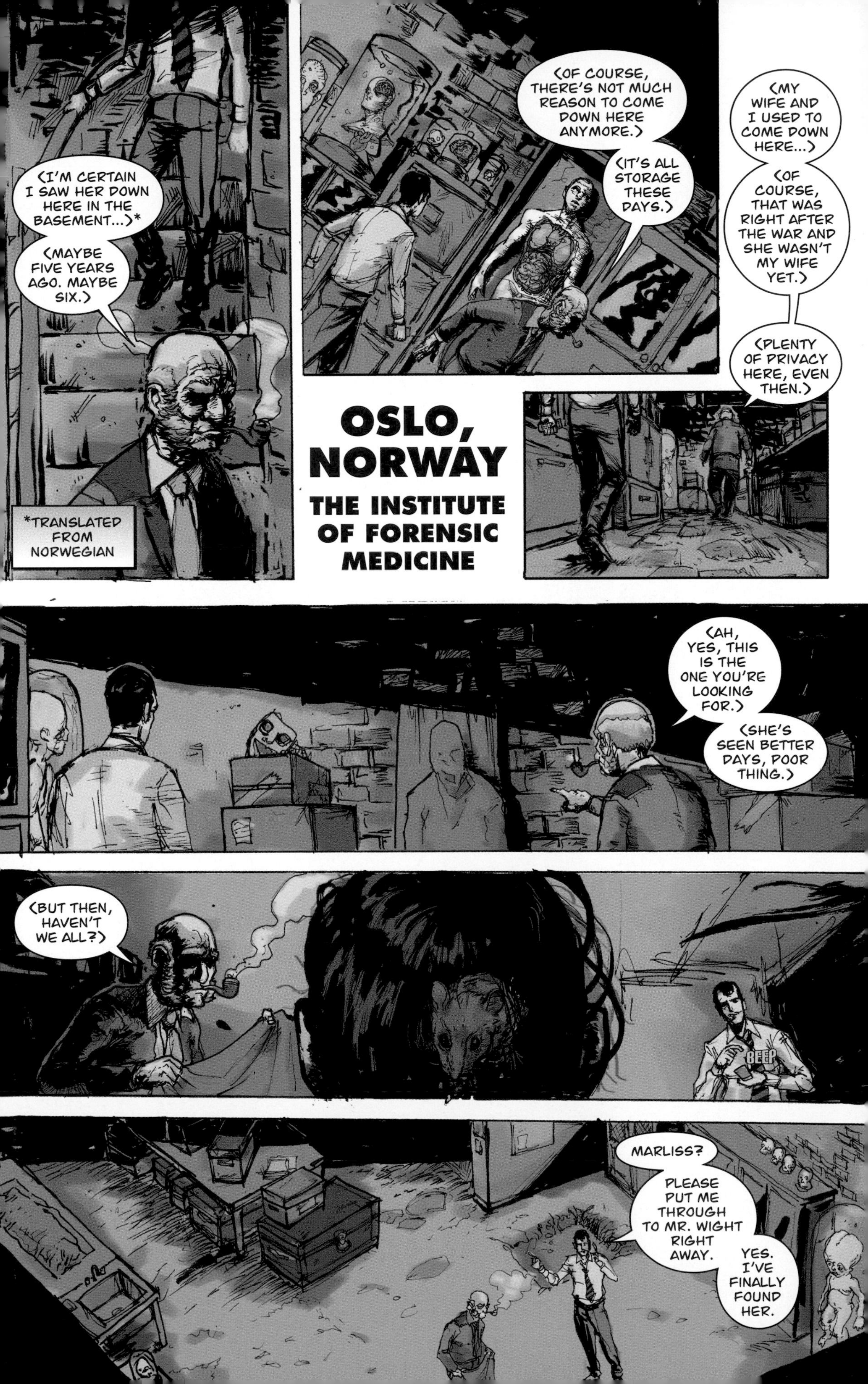

OSLO, NORWAY
THE INSTITUTE OF FORENSIC MEDICINE
(I'M CERTAIN I SAW HER DOWN HERE IN THE BASEMENT...)*
(MAYBE FIVE YEARS AGO. MAYBE SIX.)
*TRANSLATED FROM NORWEGIAN
(OF COURSE, THERE'S NOT MUCH REASON TO COME DOWN HERE ANYMORE.)
(IT'S ALL STORAGE THESE DAYS.)
(MY WIFE AND I USED TO COME DOWN HERE...)
(OF COURSE, THAT WAS RIGHT AFTER THE WAR AND SHE WASN'T MY WIFE YET.)
(PLENTY OF PRIVACY HERE, EVEN THEN.)
(AH, YES, THIS IS THE ONE YOU'RE LOOKING FOR.)
(SHE'S SEEN BETTER DAYS, POOR THING.)
(BUT THEN, HAVEN'T WE ALL?)
BEEP
MARLISS?
PLEASE PUT ME THROUGH TO MR. WIGHT RIGHT AWAY.
YES. I'VE FINALLY FOUND HER.

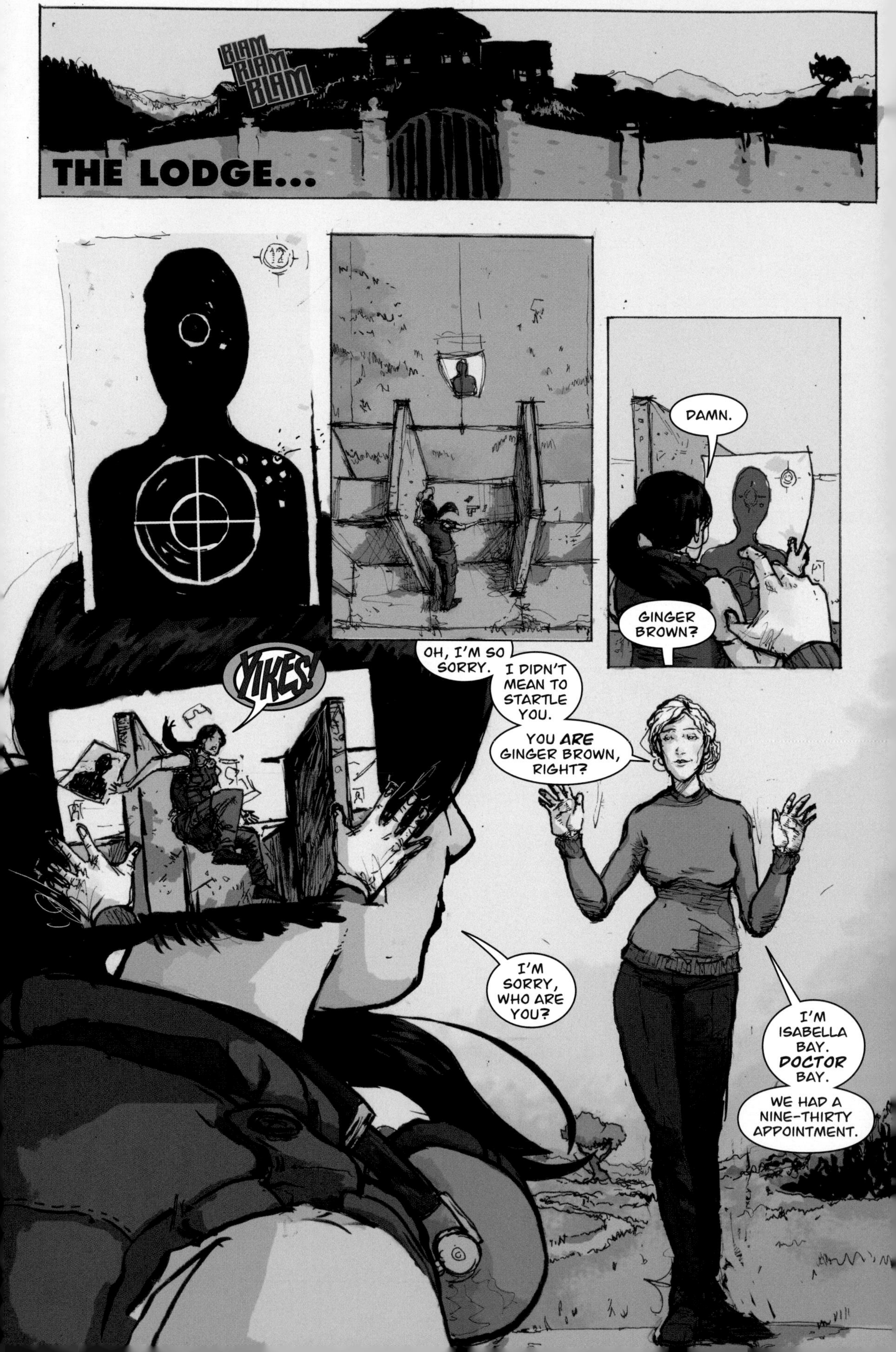
BLAM BLAM BLAM
THE LODGE...
DAMN.
GINGER BROWN?
YIKES!
OH, I'M SO SORRY.
I DIDN'T MEAN TO STARTLE YOU.
YOU ARE GINGER BROWN, RIGHT?
I'M SORRY, WHO ARE YOU?
I'M ISABELLA BAY. DOCTOR BAY.
WE HAD A NINE-THIRTY APPOINTMENT.

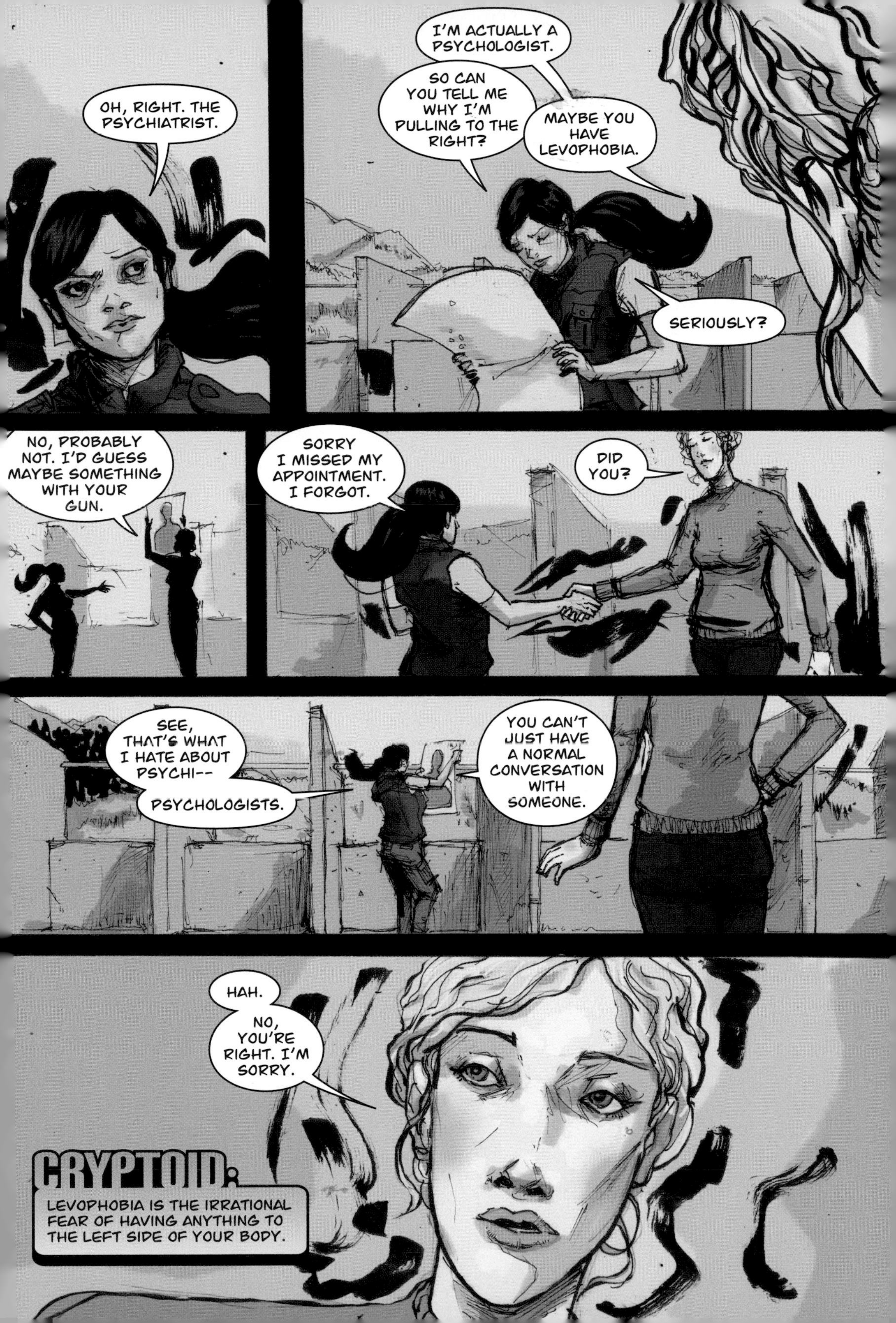
OH, RIGHT. THE PSYCHIATRIST.
I'M ACTUALLY A PSYCHOLOGIST.
SO CAN YOU TELL ME WHY I'M PULLING TO THE RIGHT?
MAYBE YOU HAVE LEVOPHOBIA.
SERIOUSLY?
NO, PROBABLY NOT. I'D GUESS MAYBE SOMETHING WITH YOUR GUN.
SORRY I MISSED MY APPOINTMENT. I FORGOT.
DID YOU?
SEE, THAT'S WHAT I HATE ABOUT PSYCHI--
PSYCHOLOGISTS.
YOU CAN'T JUST HAVE A NORMAL CONVERSATION WITH SOMEONE.
HAH.
NO, YOU'RE RIGHT. I'M SORRY.
CRYPTOID:
LEVOPHOBIA IS THE IRRATIONAL FEAR OF HAVING ANYTHING TO THE LEFT SIDE OF YOUR BODY.

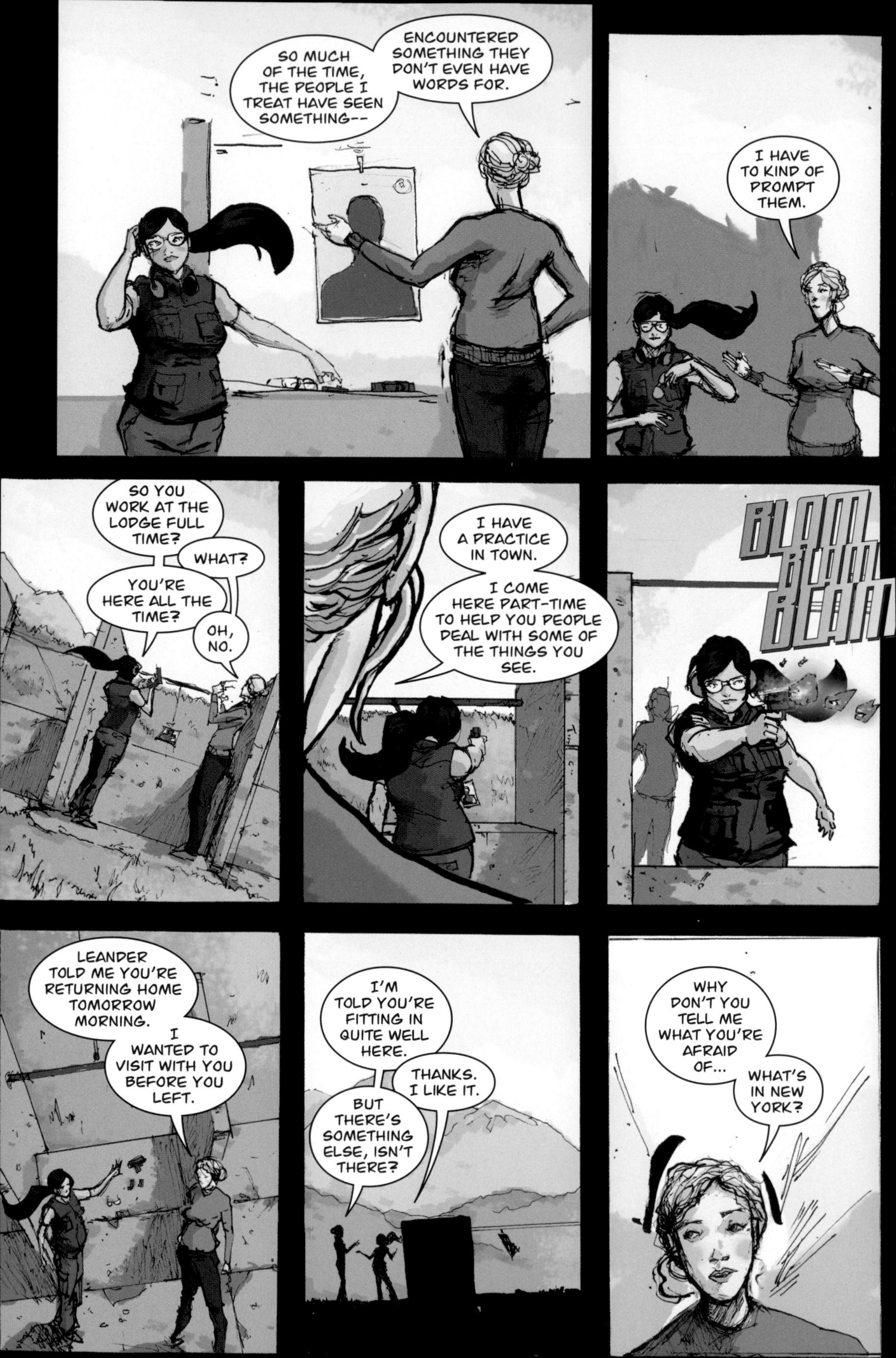
SO MUCH OF THE TIME, THE PEOPLE I TREAT HAVE SEEN SOMETHING--
ENCOUNTERED SOMETHING THEY DON'T EVEN HAVE WORDS FOR.
I HAVE TO KIND OF PROMPT THEM.
SO YOU WORK AT THE LODGE FULL TIME?
WHAT?
YOU'RE HERE ALL THE TIME?
OH, NO.
I HAVE A PRACTICE IN TOWN.
I COME HERE PART-TIME TO HELP YOU PEOPLE DEAL WITH SOME OF THE THINGS YOU SEE.
BLAM BLAM BLAM
LEANDER TOLD ME YOU'RE RETURNING HOME TOMORROW MORNING.
I WANTED TO VISIT WITH YOU BEFORE YOU LEFT.
I'M TOLD YOU'RE FITTING IN QUITE WELL HERE.
THANKS. I LIKE IT.
BUT THERE'S SOMETHING ELSE, ISN'T THERE?
WHY DON'T YOU TELL ME WHAT YOU'RE AFRAID OF...
WHAT'S IN NEW YORK?

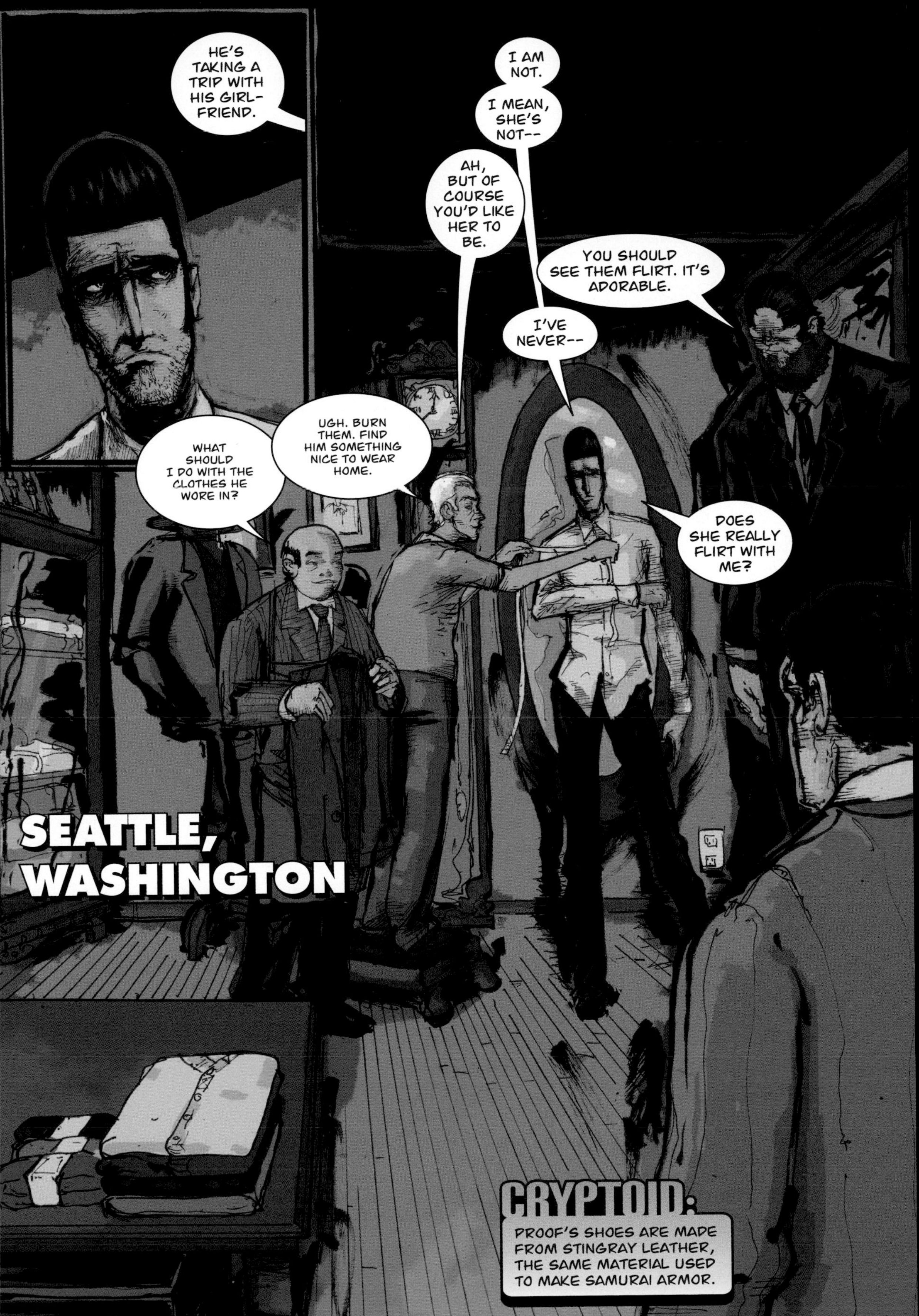
HE'S TAKING A TRIP WITH HIS GIRL-FRIEND.
I AM NOT.
I MEAN, SHE'S NOT--
AH, BUT OF COURSE YOU'D LIKE HER TO BE.
YOU SHOULD SEE THEM FLIRT. IT'S ADORABLE.
I'VE NEVER--
WHAT SHOULD I DO WITH THE CLOTHES HE WORE IN?
UGH. BURN THEM. FIND HIM SOMETHING NICE TO WEAR HOME.
DOES SHE REALLY FLIRT WITH ME?
SEATTLE, WASHINGTON
CRYPTOID:
PROOF'S SHOES ARE MADE FROM STINGRAY LEATHER, THE SAME MATERIAL USED TO MAKE SAMURAI ARMOR.

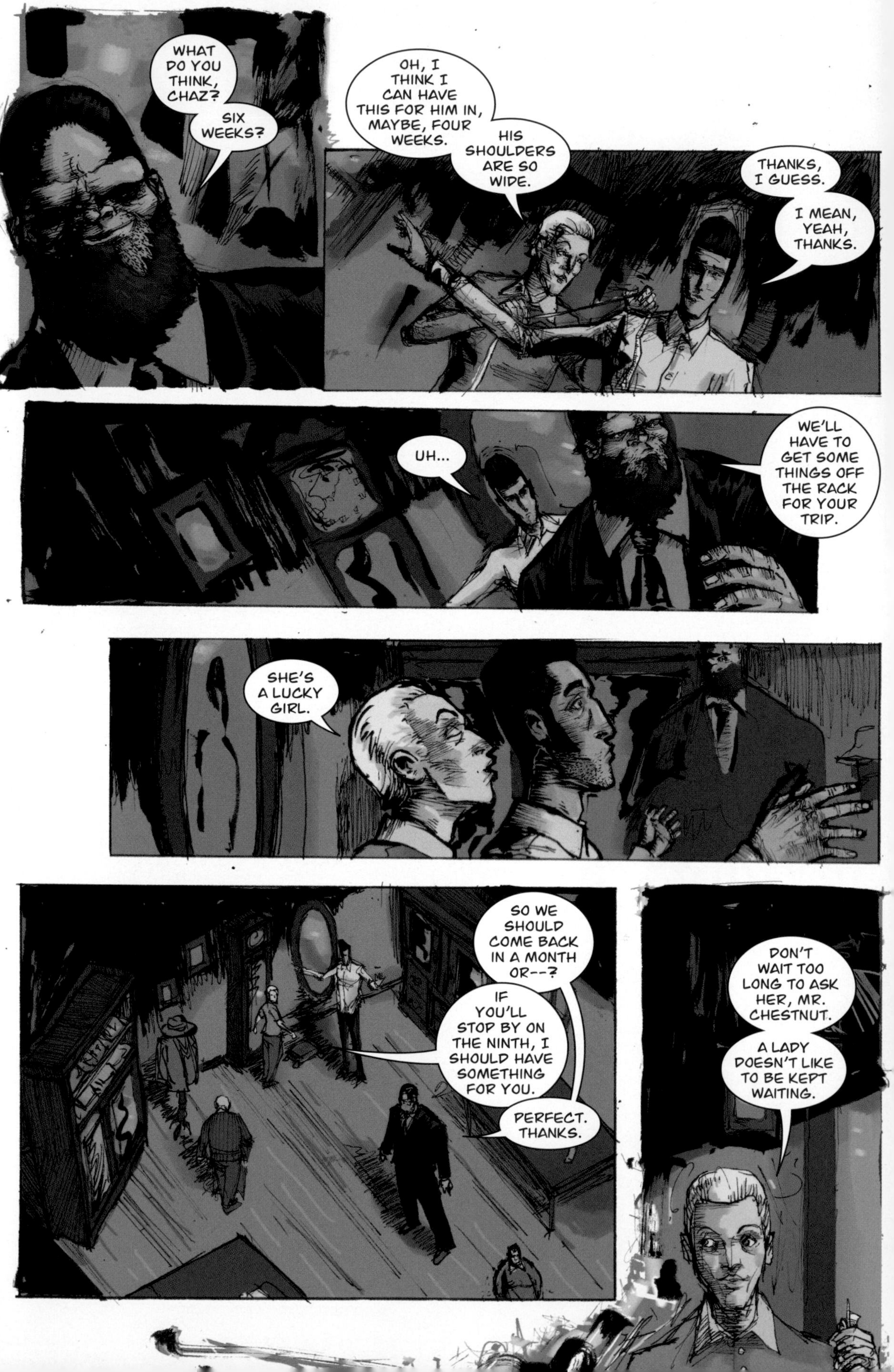
WHAT DO YOU THINK, CHAZ?
SIX WEEKS?
OH, I THINK I CAN HAVE THIS FOR HIM IN, MAYBE, FOUR WEEKS.
HIS SHOULDERS ARE SO WIDE.
THANKS, I GUESS.
I MEAN, YEAH, THANKS.
UH...
WE'LL HAVE TO GET SOME THINGS OFF THE RACK FOR YOUR TRIP.
SHE'S A LUCKY GIRL.
SO WE SHOULD COME BACK IN A MONTH OR--?
IF YOU'LL STOP BY ON THE NINTH, I SHOULD HAVE SOMETHING FOR YOU.
PERFECT. THANKS.
DON'T WAIT TOO LONG TO ASK HER, MR. CHESTNUT.
A LADY DOESN'T LIKE TO BE KEPT WAITING.

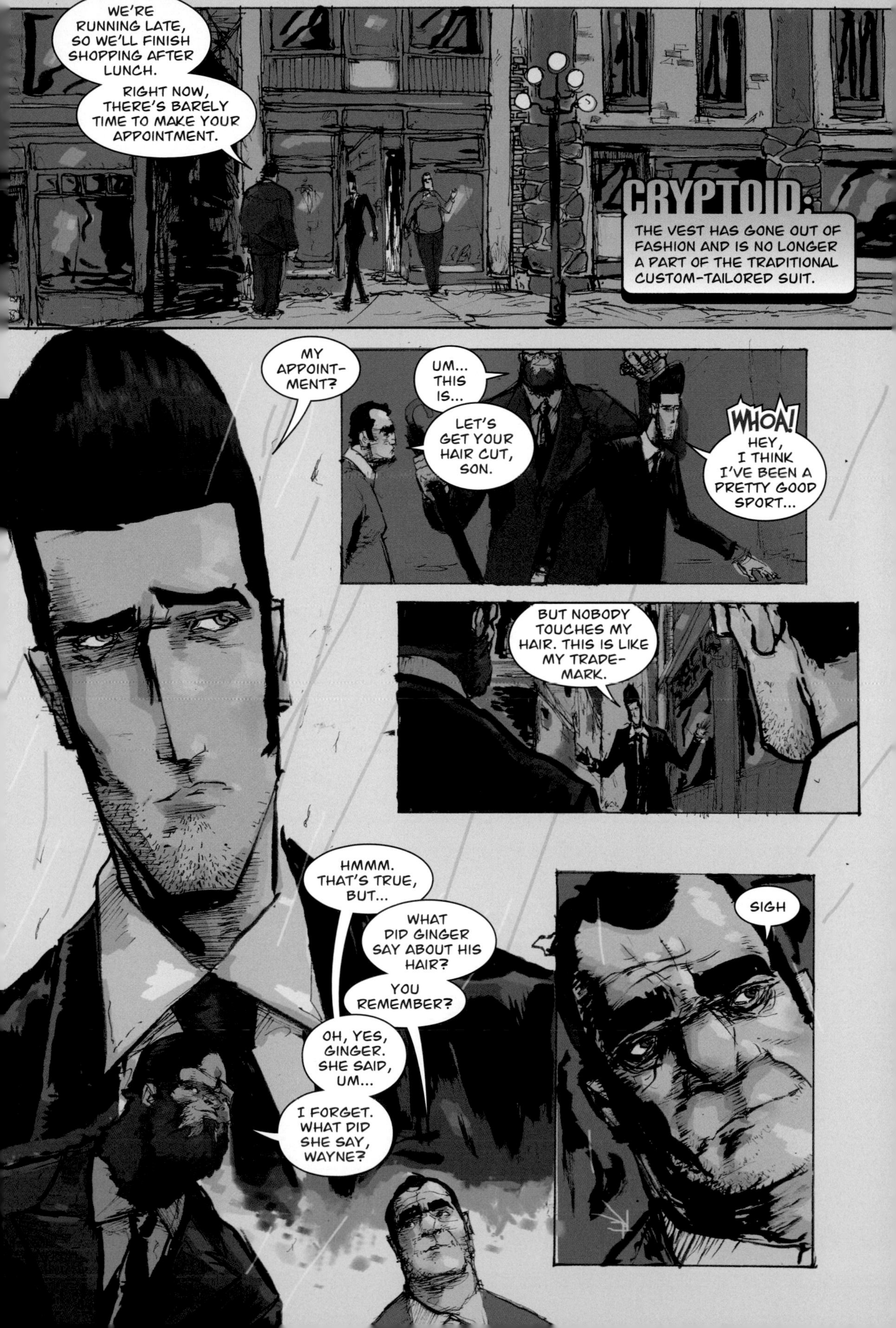
WE'RE RUNNING LATE, SO WE'LL FINISH SHOPPING AFTER LUNCH.
RIGHT NOW, THERE'S BARELY TIME TO MAKE YOUR APPOINTMENT.
CRYPTOID:
THE VEST HAS GONE OUT OF FASHION AND IS NO LONGER A PART OF THE TRADITIONAL CUSTOM-TAILORED SUIT.
MY APPOINTMENT?
UM... THIS IS...
LET'S GET YOUR HAIR CUT, SON.
WHOA!
HEY, I THINK I'VE BEEN A PRETTY GOOD SPORT...
BUT NOBODY TOUCHES MY HAIR. THIS IS LIKE MY TRADEMARK.
HMMM. THAT'S TRUE, BUT...
WHAT DID GINGER SAY ABOUT HIS HAIR?
YOU REMEMBER?
OH, YES, GINGER. SHE SAID, UM...
I FORGET. WHAT DID SHE SAY, WAYNE?
SIGH

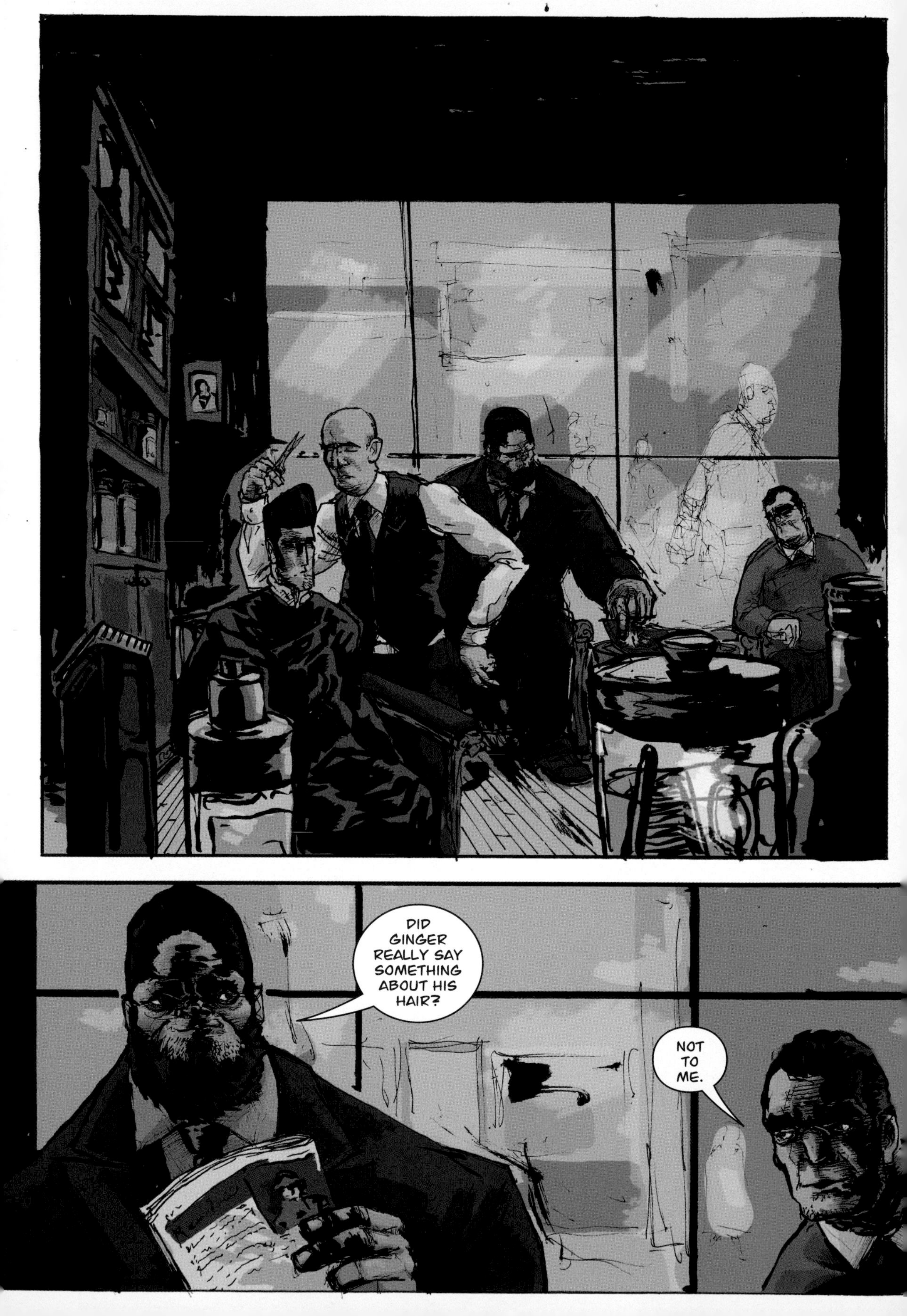
DID GINGER REALLY SAY SOMETHING ABOUT HIS HAIR?
NOT TO ME.

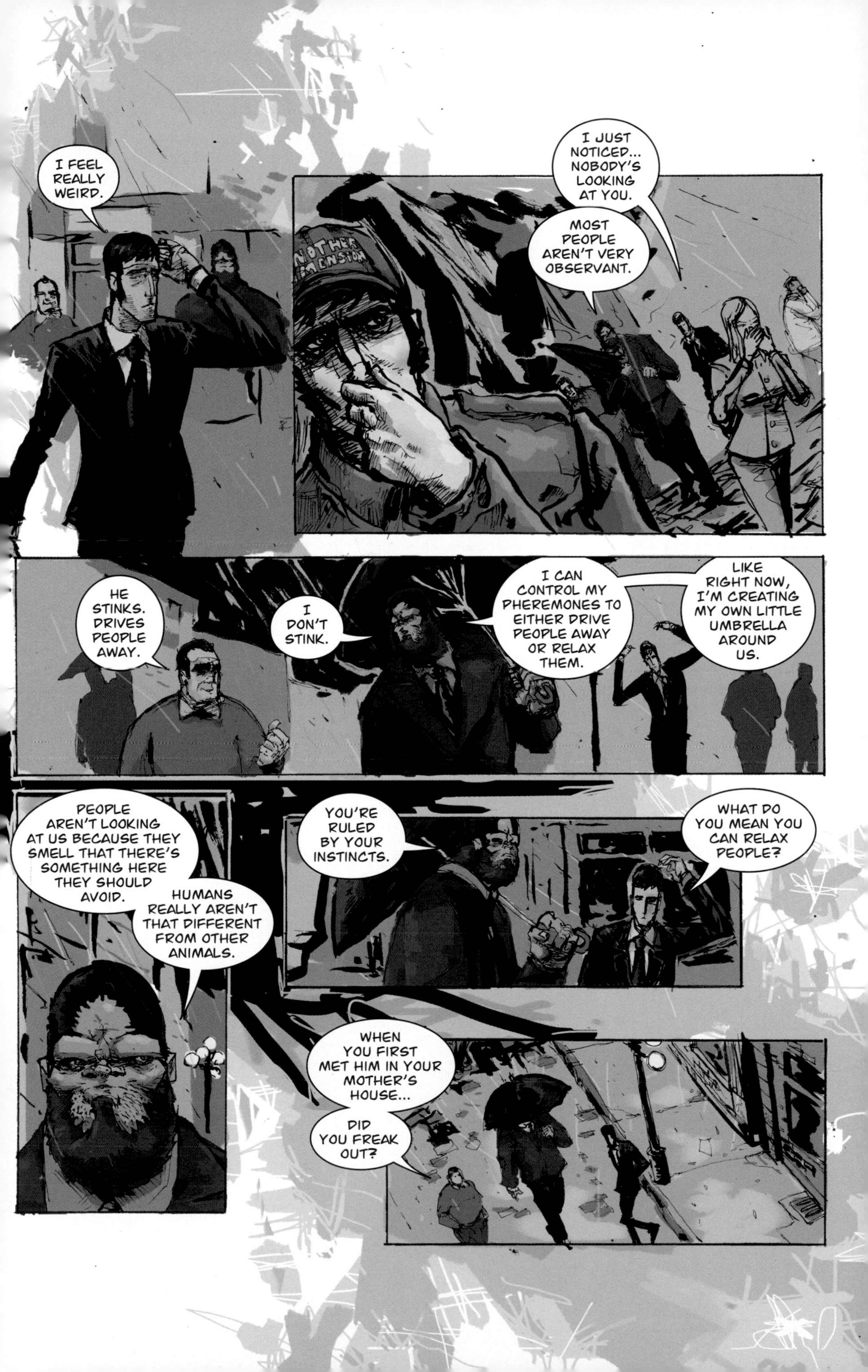

I FEEL REALLY WEIRD.
I JUST NOTICED... NOBODY'S LOOKING AT YOU.
MOST PEOPLE AREN'T VERY OBSERVANT.
NOTHER IMENSION
HE STINKS. DRIVES PEOPLE AWAY.
I DON'T STINK.
I CAN CONTROL MY PHEREMONES TO EITHER DRIVE PEOPLE AWAY OR RELAX THEM.
LIKE RIGHT NOW, I'M CREATING MY OWN LITTLE UMBRELLA AROUND US.
PEOPLE AREN'T LOOKING AT US BECAUSE THEY SMELL THAT THERE'S SOMETHING HERE THEY SHOULD AVOID.
HUMANS REALLY AREN'T THAT DIFFERENT FROM OTHER ANIMALS.
YOU'RE RULED BY YOUR INSTINCTS.
WHAT DO YOU MEAN YOU CAN RELAX PEOPLE?
WHEN YOU FIRST MET HIM IN YOUR MOTHER'S HOUSE...
DID YOU FREAK OUT?

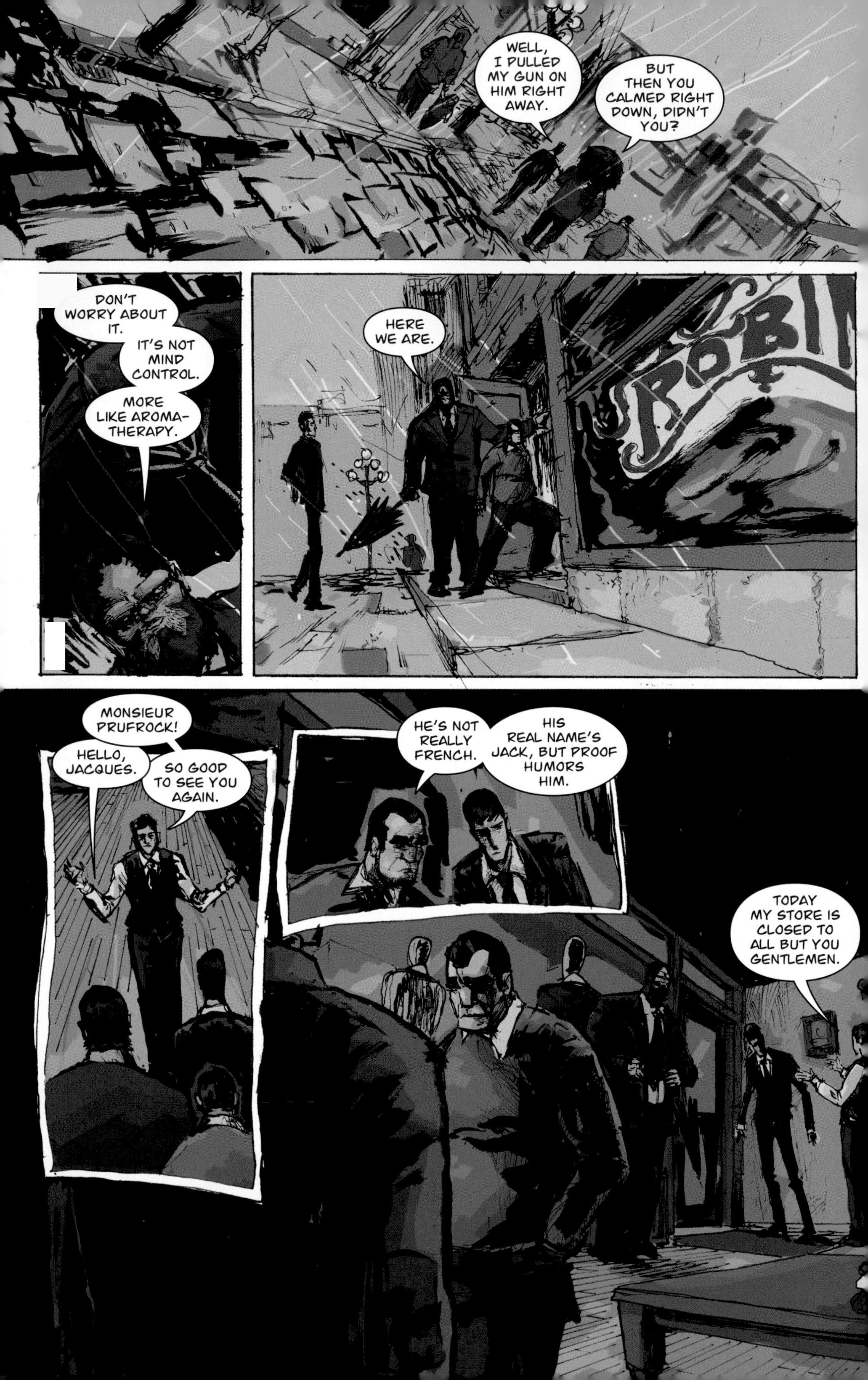
WELL, I PULLED MY GUN ON HIM RIGHT AWAY.
BUT THEN YOU CALMED RIGHT DOWN, DIDN'T YOU?
DON'T WORRY ABOUT IT.
IT'S NOT MIND CONTROL.
MORE LIKE AROMA-THERAPY.
HERE WE ARE.
MONSIEUR PRUFROCK!
HELLO, JACQUES.
SO GOOD TO SEE YOU AGAIN.
HE'S NOT REALLY FRENCH.
HIS REAL NAME'S JACK, BUT PROOF HUMORS HIM.
TODAY MY STORE IS CLOSED TO ALL BUT YOU GENTLEMEN.

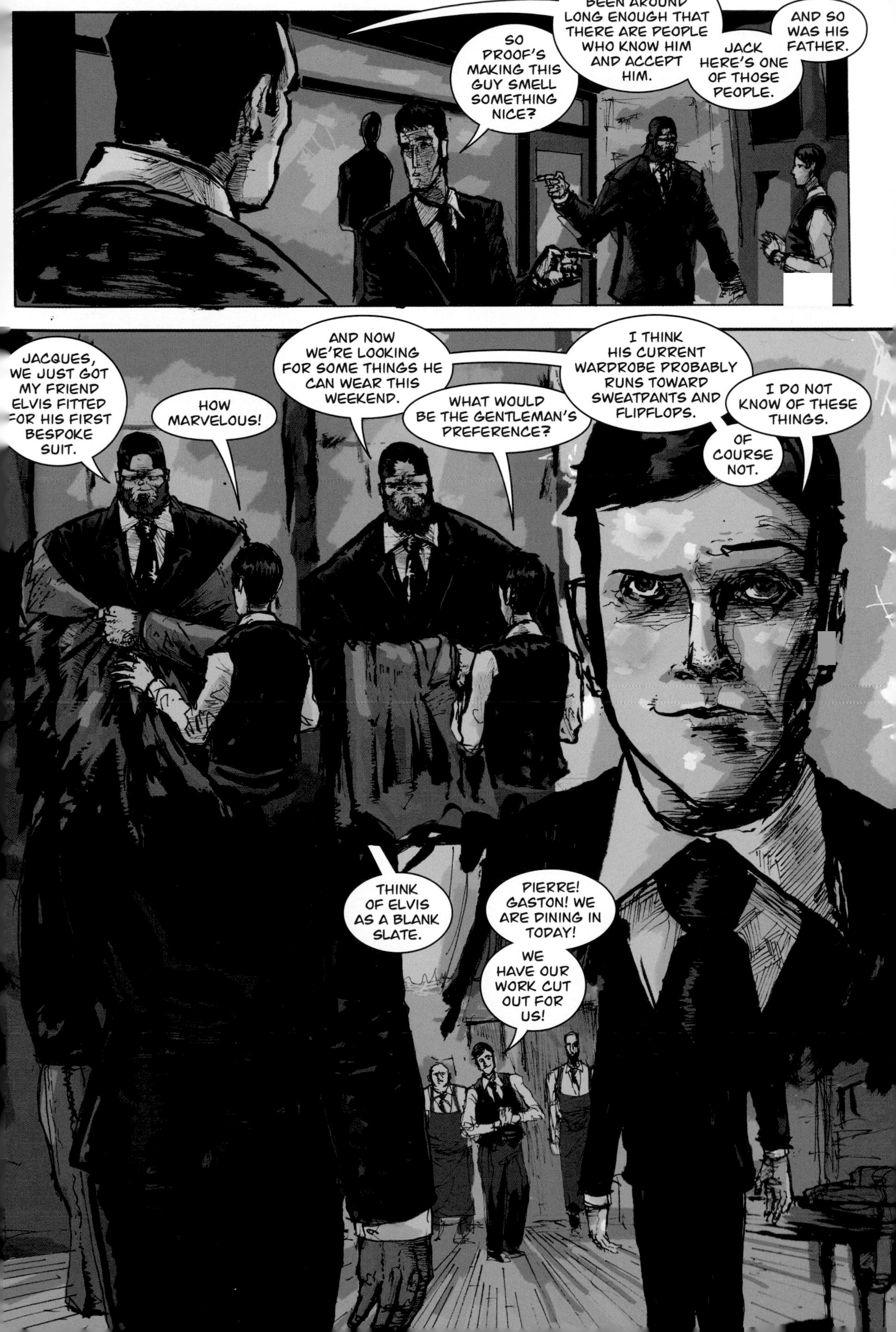
SO PROOF'S MAKING THIS GUY SMELL SOMETHING NICE?
NO, PROOF'S BEEN AROUND LONG ENOUGH THAT THERE ARE PEOPLE WHO KNOW HIM AND ACCEPT HIM.
JACK HERE'S ONE OF THOSE PEOPLE.
AND SO WAS HIS FATHER.
JACQUES, WE JUST GOT MY FRIEND ELVIS FITTED FOR HIS FIRST BESPOKE SUIT.
HOW MARVELOUS!
AND NOW WE'RE LOOKING FOR SOME THINGS HE CAN WEAR THIS WEEKEND.
WHAT WOULD BE THE GENTLEMAN'S PREFERENCE?
I THINK HIS CURRENT WARDROBE PROBABLY RUNS TOWARD SWEATPANTS AND FLIPFLOPS.
OF COURSE NOT.
I DO NOT KNOW OF THESE THINGS.
THINK OF ELVIS AS A BLANK SLATE.
PIERRE! GASTON! WE ARE DINING IN TODAY!
WE HAVE OUR WORK CUT OUT FOR US!

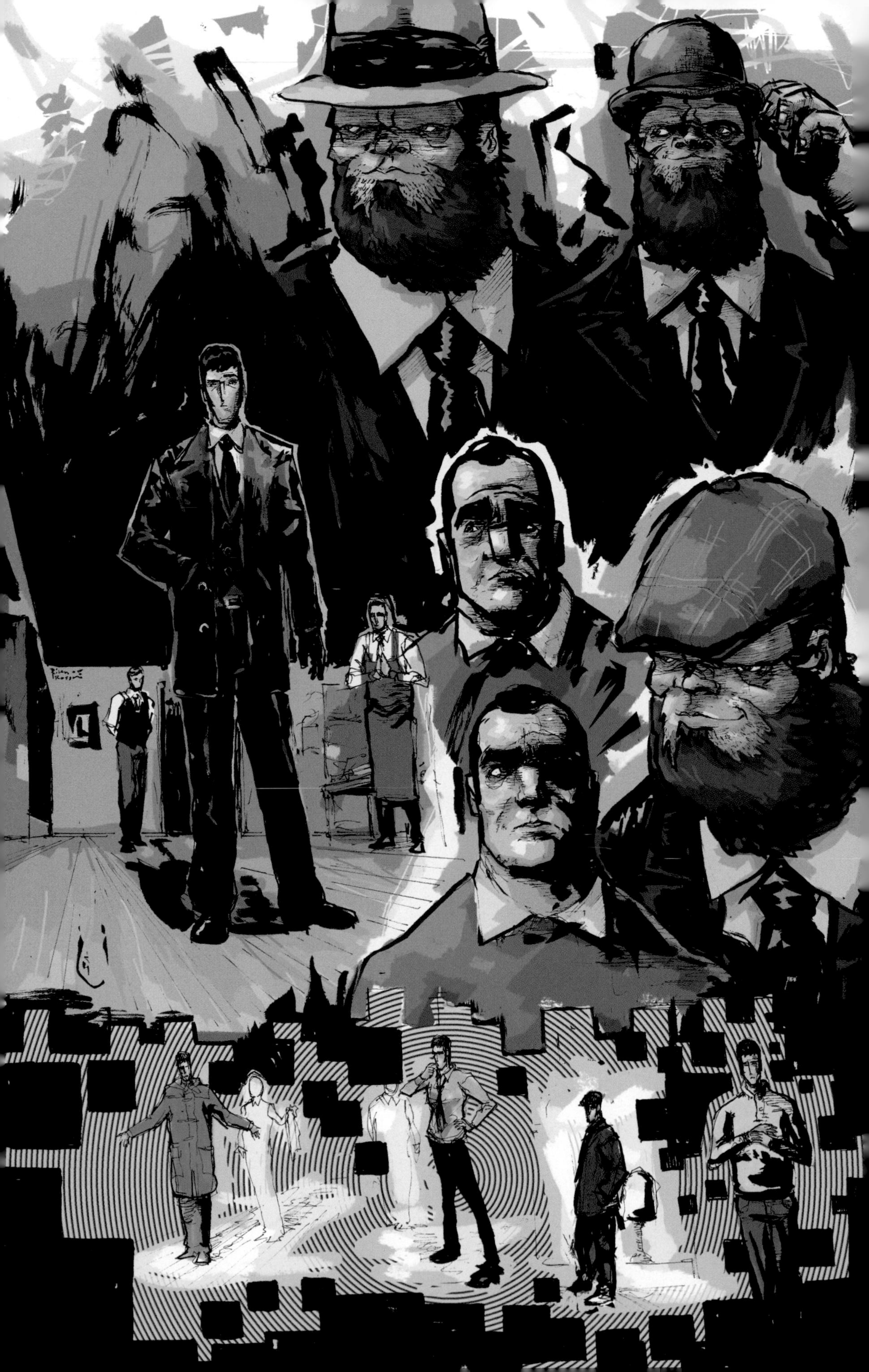

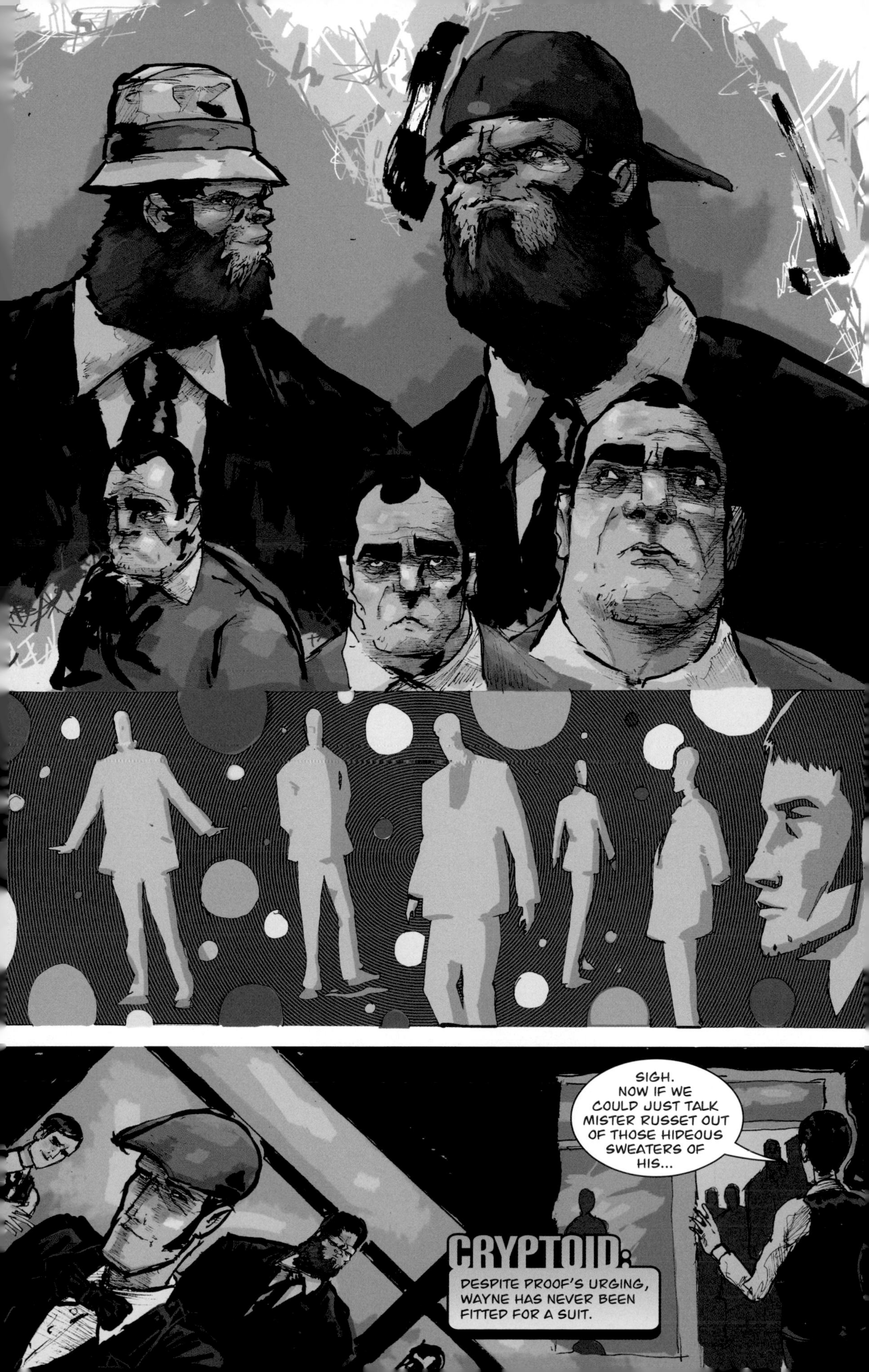
SIGH. NOW IF WE COULD JUST TALK MISTER RUSSET OUT OF THOSE HIDEOUS SWEATERS OF HIS...
CRYPTOID:
DESPITE PROOF'S URGING, WAYNE HAS NEVER BEEN FITTED FOR A SUIT.

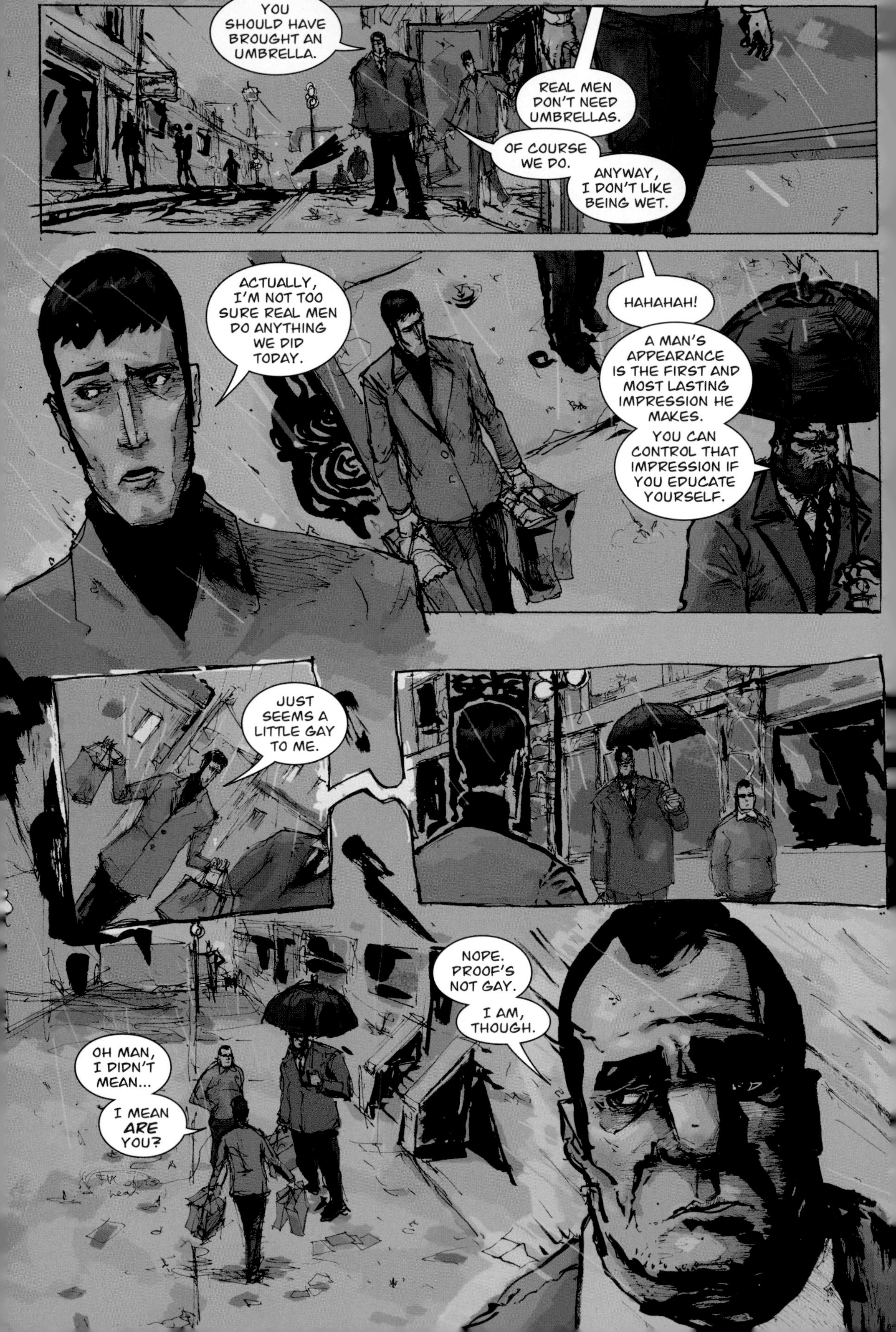
YOU SHOULD HAVE BROUGHT AN UMBRELLA.
REAL MEN DON'T NEED UMBRELLAS.
OF COURSE WE DO.
ANYWAY, I DON'T LIKE BEING WET.
ACTUALLY, I'M NOT TOO SURE REAL MEN DO ANYTHING WE DID TODAY.
HAHAHAH!
A MAN'S APPEARANCE IS THE FIRST AND MOST LASTING IMPRESSION HE MAKES.
YOU CAN CONTROL THAT IMPRESSION IF YOU EDUCATE YOURSELF.
JUST SEEMS A LITTLE GAY TO ME.
NOPE. PROOF'S NOT GAY.
I AM, THOUGH.
OH MAN, I DIDN'T MEAN...
I MEAN ARE YOU?

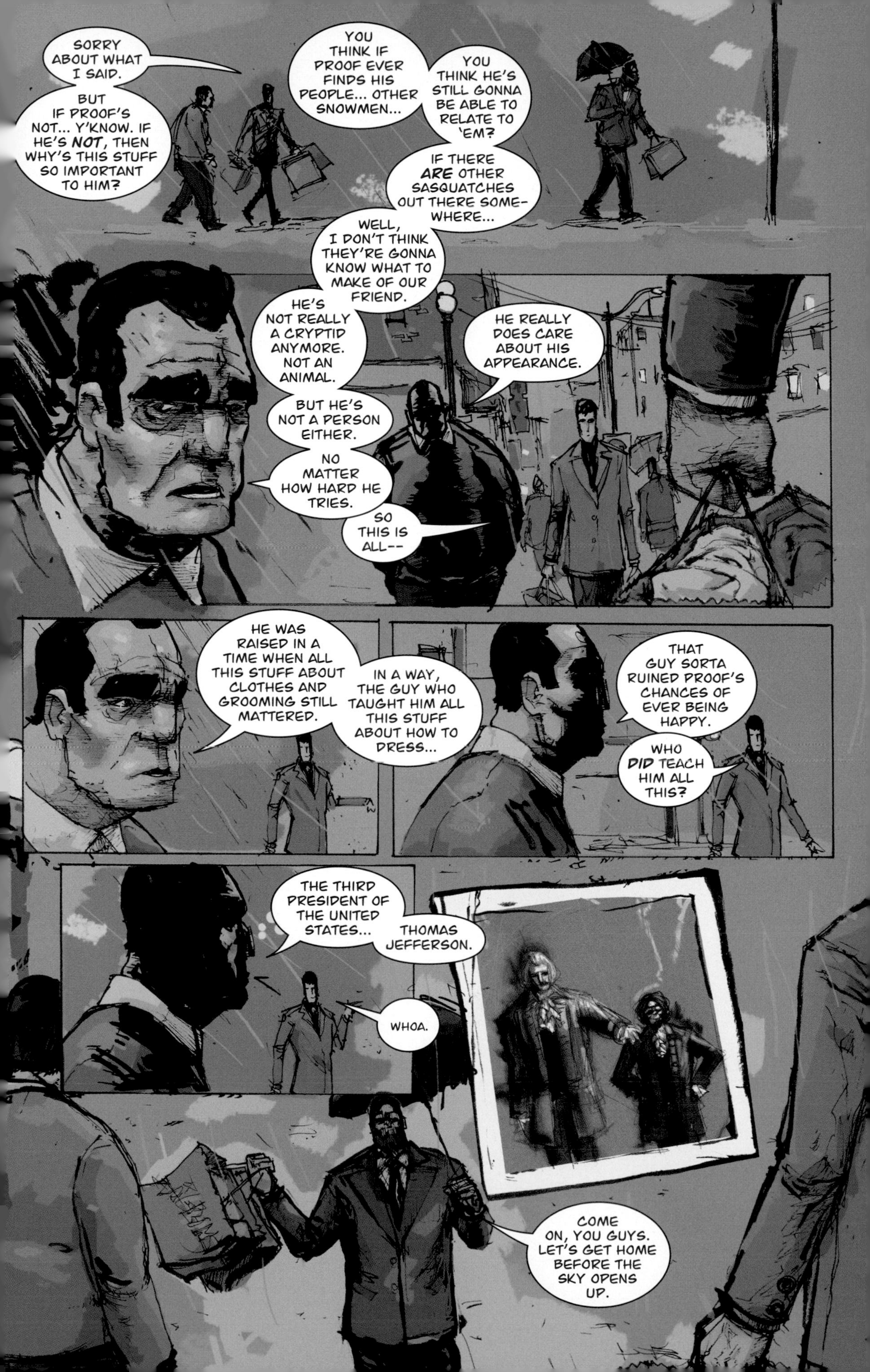
SORRY ABOUT WHAT I SAID.
BUT IF PROOF'S NOT... Y'KNOW. IF HE'S NOT, THEN WHY'S THIS STUFF SO IMPORTANT TO HIM?
YOU THINK IF PROOF EVER FINDS HIS PEOPLE... OTHER SNOWMEN...
YOU THINK HE'S STILL GONNA BE ABLE TO RELATE TO 'EM?
IF THERE ARE OTHER SASQUATCHES OUT THERE SOMEWHERE...
WELL, I DON'T THINK THEY'RE GONNA KNOW WHAT TO MAKE OF OUR FRIEND.
HE'S NOT REALLY A CRYPTID ANYMORE. NOT AN ANIMAL.
BUT HE'S NOT A PERSON EITHER.
NO MATTER HOW HARD HE TRIES.
HE REALLY DOES CARE ABOUT HIS APPEARANCE.
SO THIS IS ALL--
HE WAS RAISED IN A TIME WHEN ALL THIS STUFF ABOUT CLOTHES AND GROOMING STILL MATTERED.
IN A WAY, THE GUY WHO TAUGHT HIM ALL THIS STUFF ABOUT HOW TO DRESS...
THAT GUY SORTA RUINED PROOF'S CHANCES OF EVER BEING HAPPY.
WHO DID TEACH HIM ALL THIS?
THE THIRD PRESIDENT OF THE UNITED STATES...
THOMAS JEFFERSON.
WHOA.
COME ON, YOU GUYS. LET'S GET HOME BEFORE THE SKY OPENS UP.

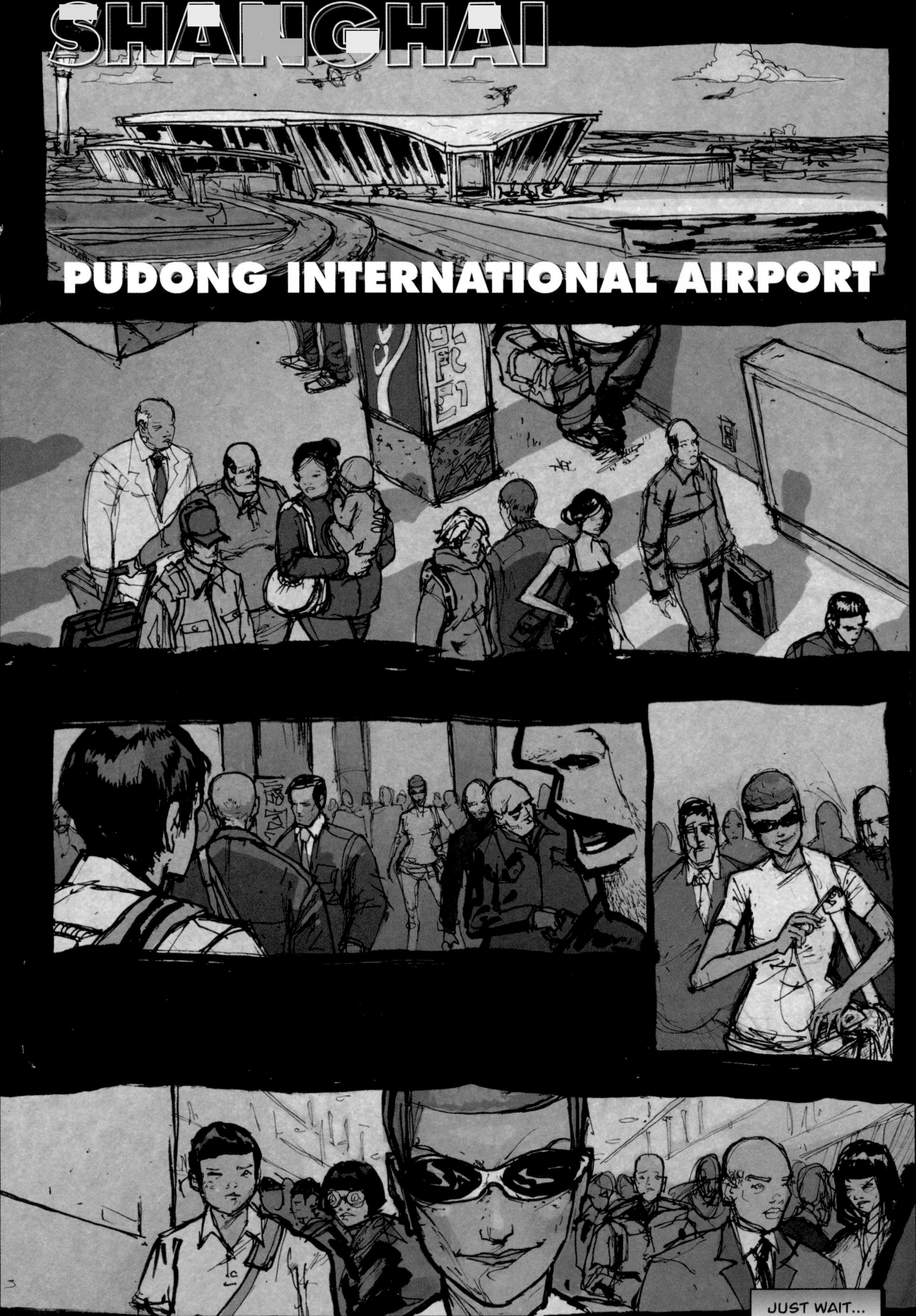
SHANGHAI
PUDONG INTERNATIONAL AIRPORT
JUST WAIT...

HEY KIDS! BIG-GAME CAN BE BIG FUN!

Cut along the dotted lines and tie each end of a string to the Colonel's earholes.

Then tuck a napkin into your shirt collar and let the world know "I want my meat rare!"

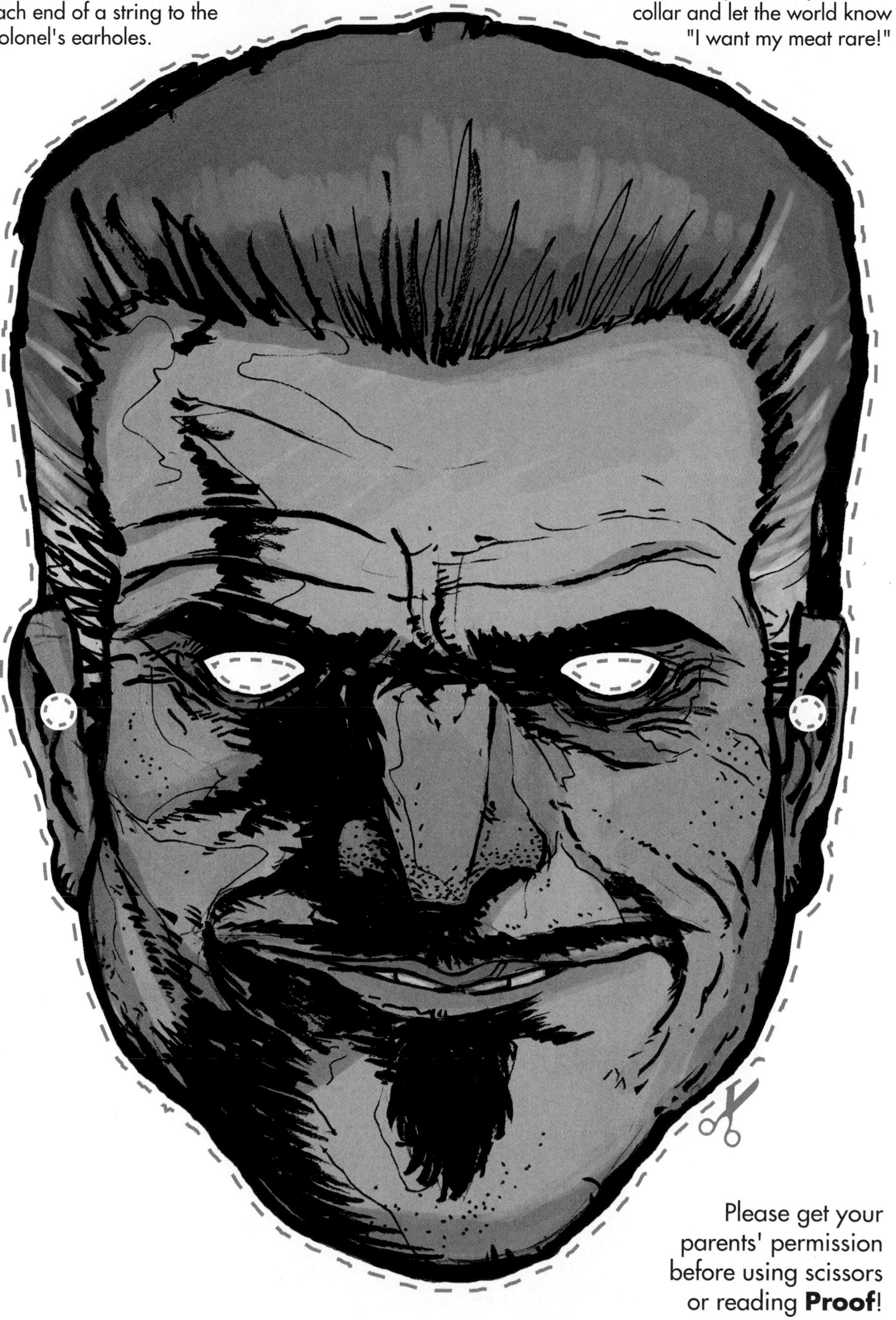

Please get your parents' permission before using scissors or reading **Proof**!

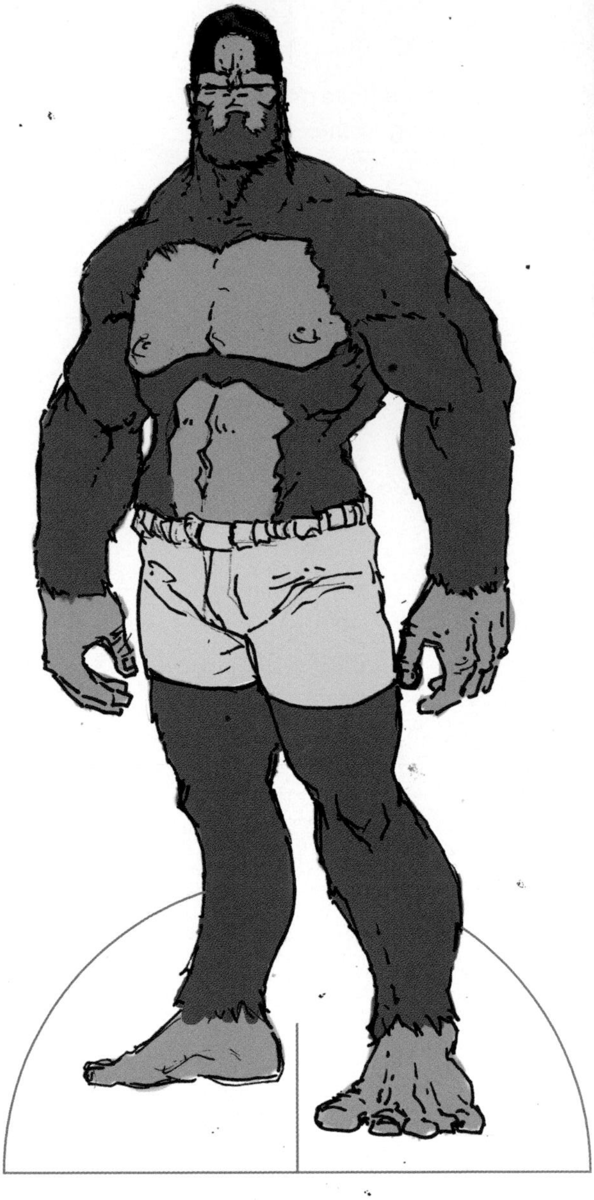

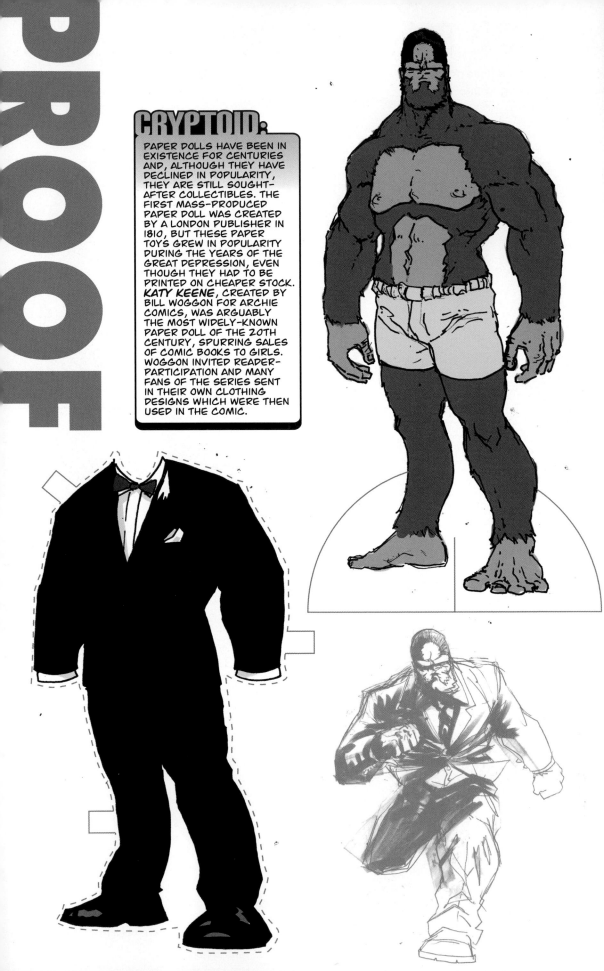

CRYPTOID:

PAPER DOLLS HAVE BEEN IN EXISTENCE FOR CENTURIES AND, ALTHOUGH THEY HAVE DECLINED IN POPULARITY, THEY ARE STILL SOUGHT-AFTER COLLECTIBLES. THE FIRST MASS-PRODUCED PAPER DOLL WAS CREATED BY A LONDON PUBLISHER IN 1810, BUT THESE PAPER TOYS GREW IN POPULARITY DURING THE YEARS OF THE GREAT DEPRESSION, EVEN THOUGH THEY HAD TO BE PRINTED ON CHEAPER STOCK. ***KATY KEENE***, CREATED BY BILL WOGGON FOR ARCHIE COMICS, WAS ARGUABLY THE MOST WIDELY-KNOWN PAPER DOLL OF THE 20TH CENTURY, SPURRING SALES OF COMIC BOOKS TO GIRLS. WOGGON INVITED READER-PARTICIPATION AND MANY FANS OF THE SERIES SENT IN THEIR OWN CLOTHING DESIGNS WHICH WERE THEN USED IN THE COMIC.

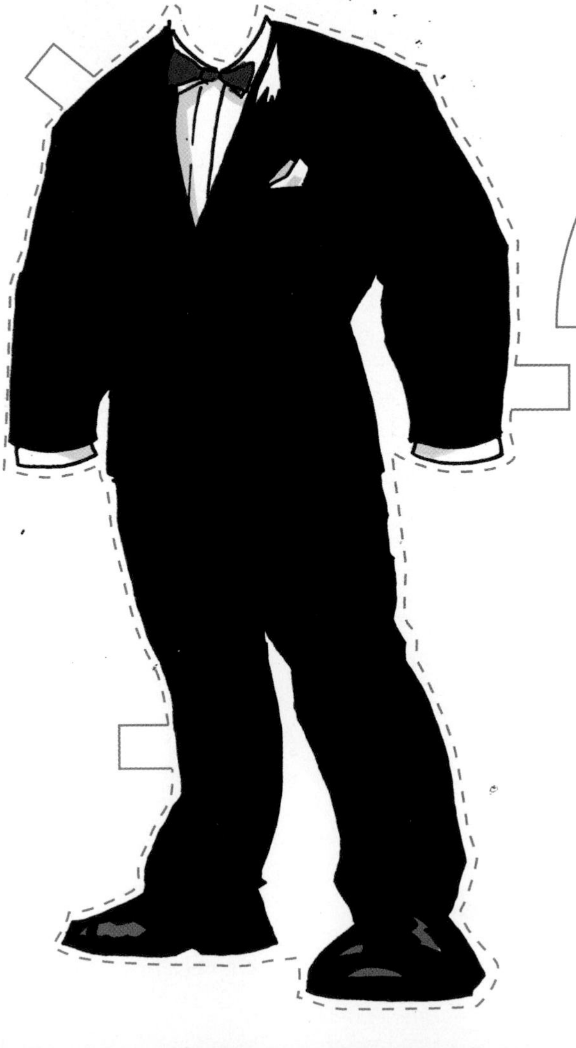

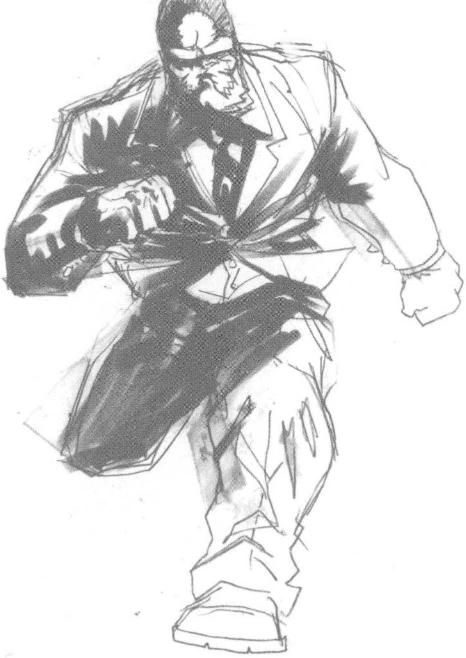

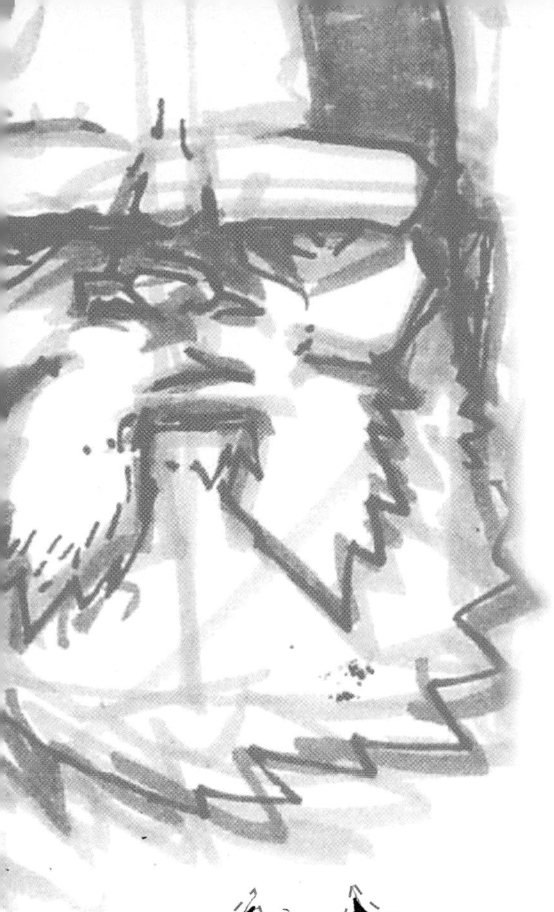
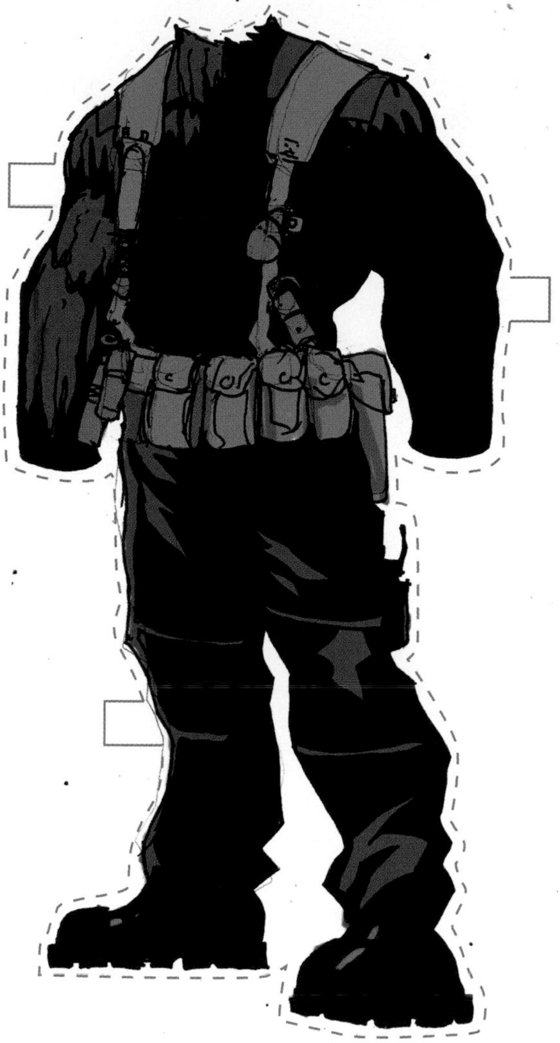
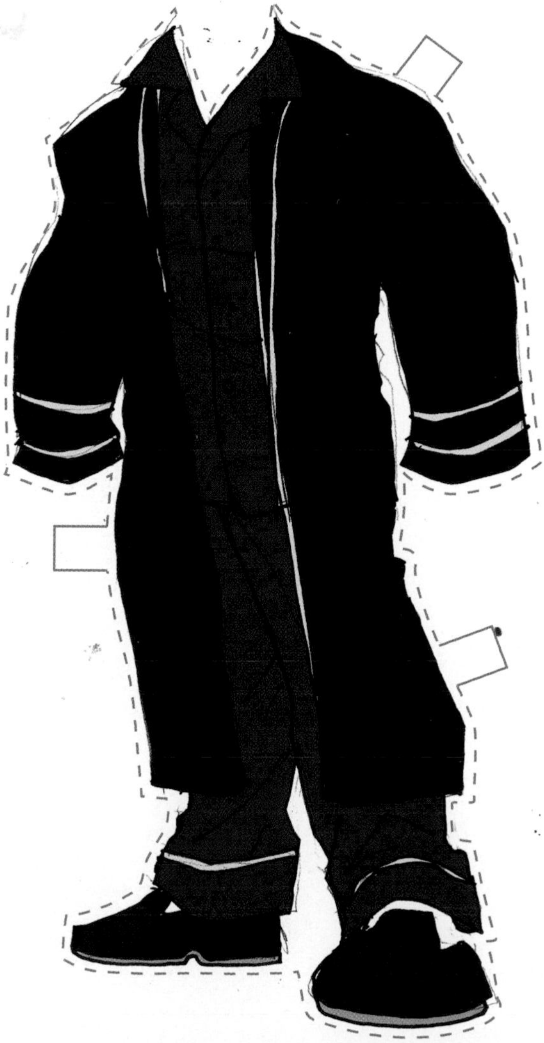
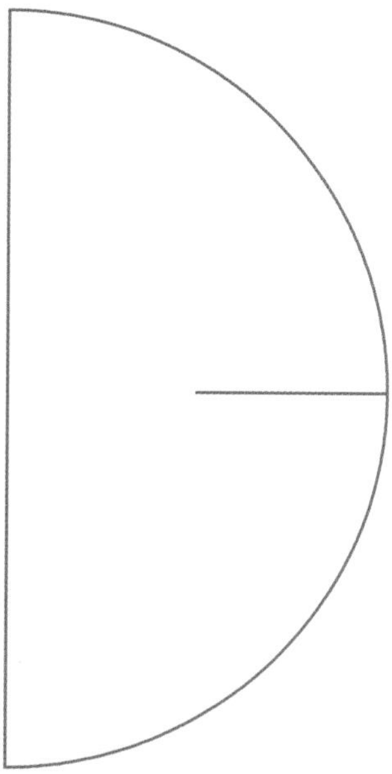

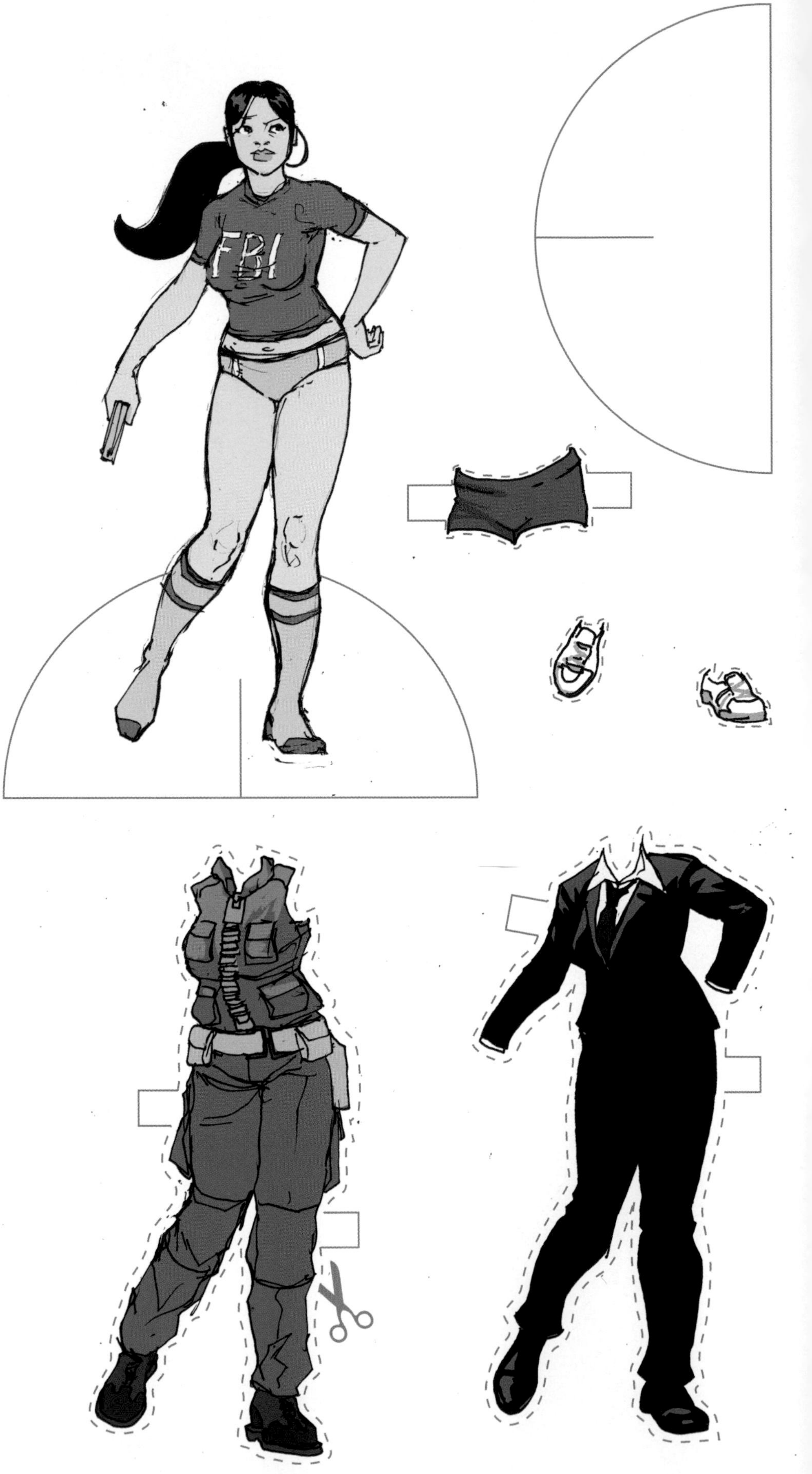
FBI

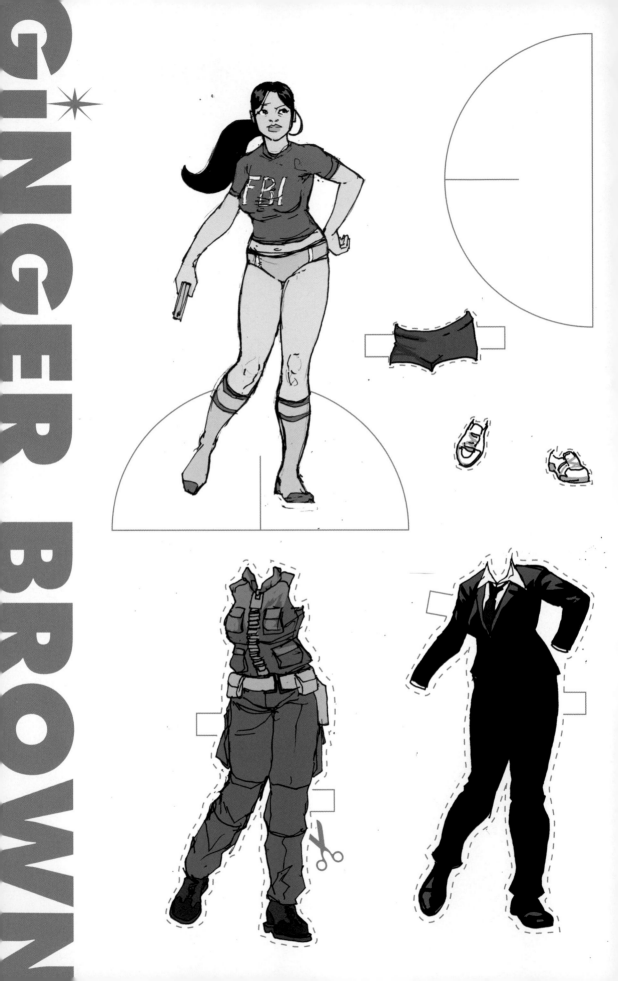

ELVIS CHESTNUT

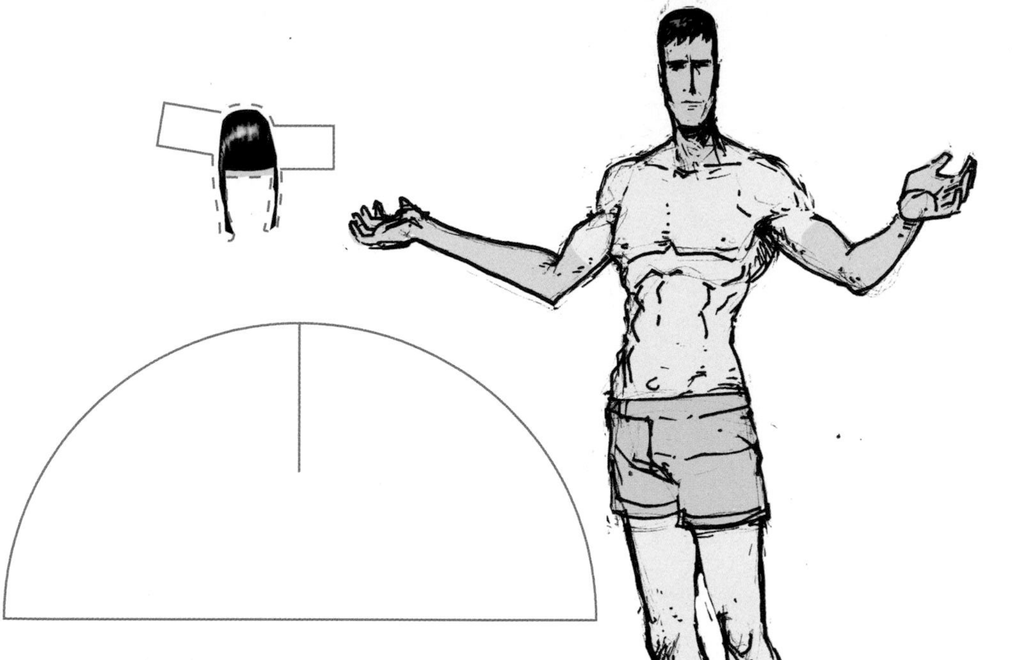

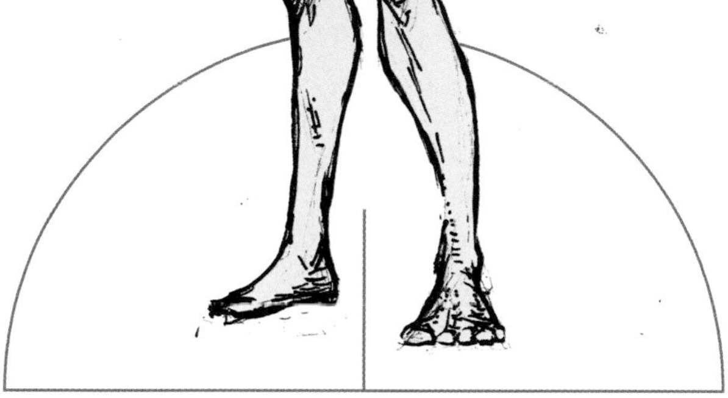

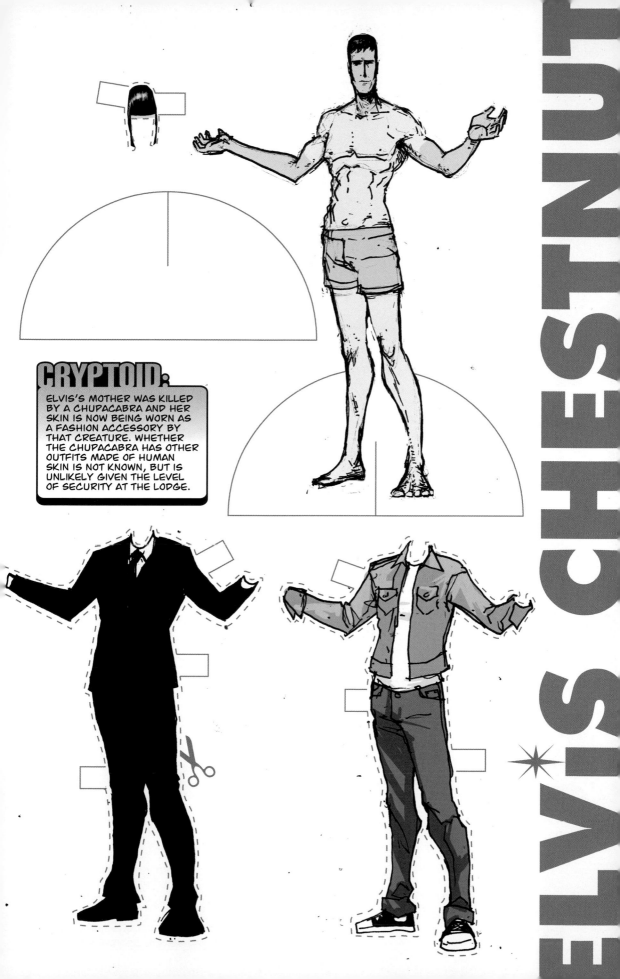

CRYPTOID:

ELVIS'S MOTHER WAS KILLED BY A CHUPACABRA AND HER SKIN IS NOW BEING WORN AS A FASHION ACCESSORY BY THAT CREATURE. WHETHER THE CHUPACABRA HAS OTHER OUTFITS MADE OF HUMAN SKIN IS NOT KNOWN, BUT IS UNLIKELY GIVEN THE LEVEL OF SECURITY AT THE LODGE.

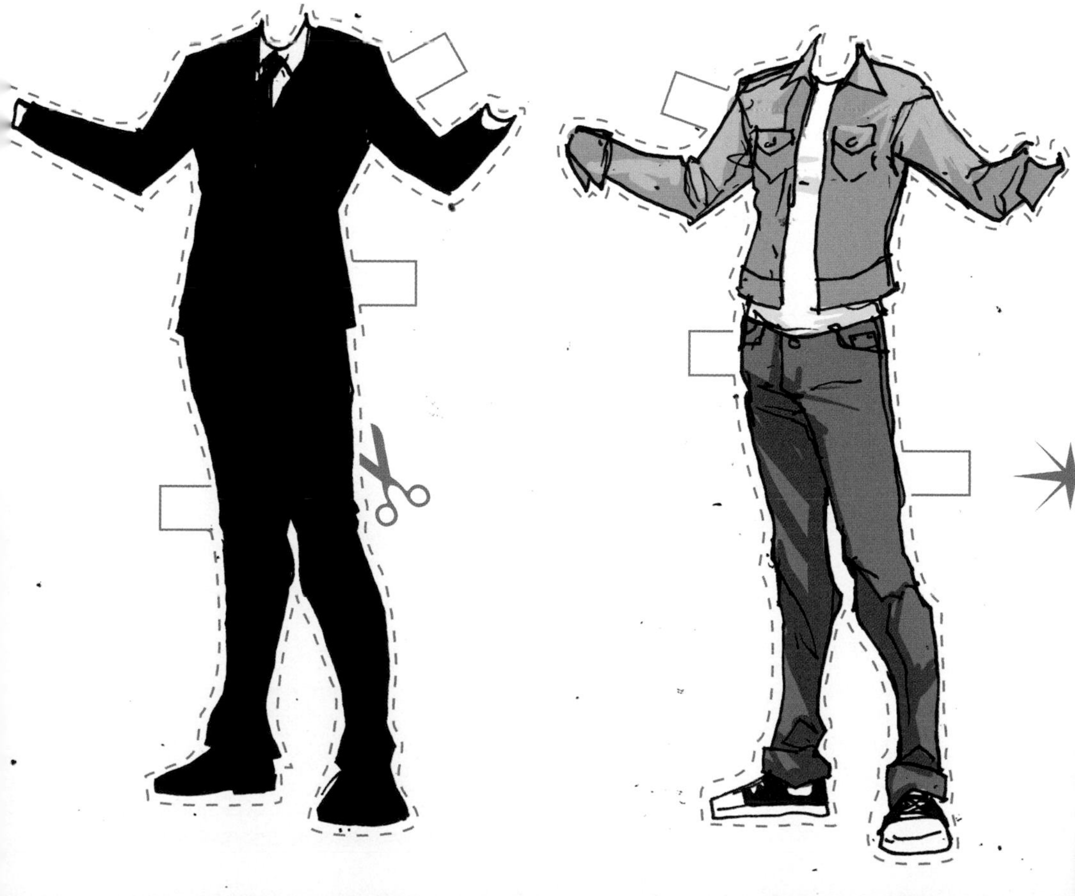

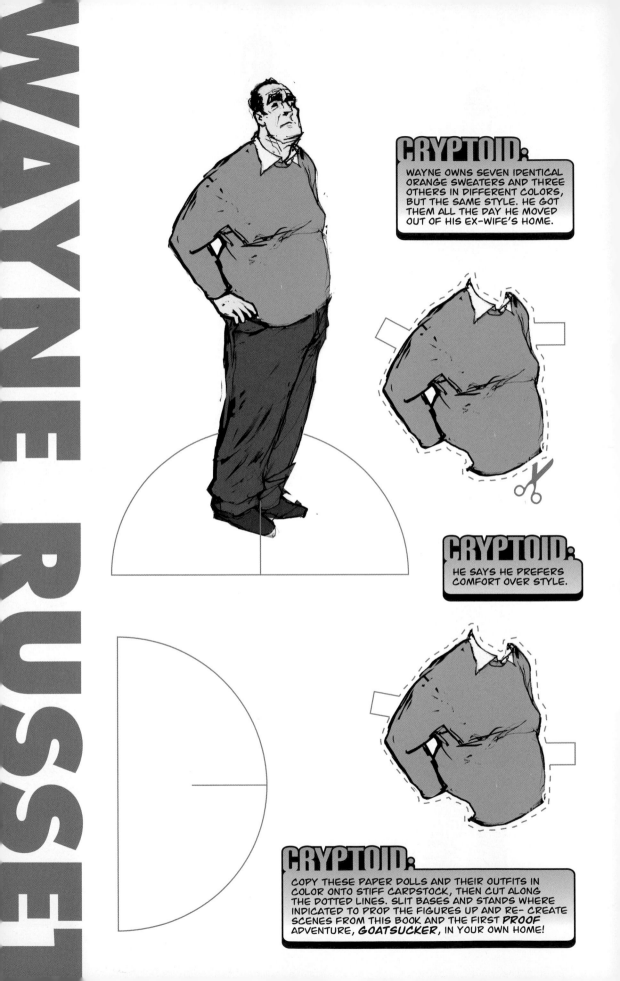

WAYNE RUSSE

CRYPTOID:

WAYNE OWNS SEVEN IDENTICAL ORANGE SWEATERS AND THREE OTHERS IN DIFFERENT COLORS, BUT THE SAME STYLE. HE GOT THEM ALL THE DAY HE MOVED OUT OF HIS EX-WIFE'S HOME.

CRYPTOID:

HE SAYS HE PREFERS COMFORT OVER STYLE.

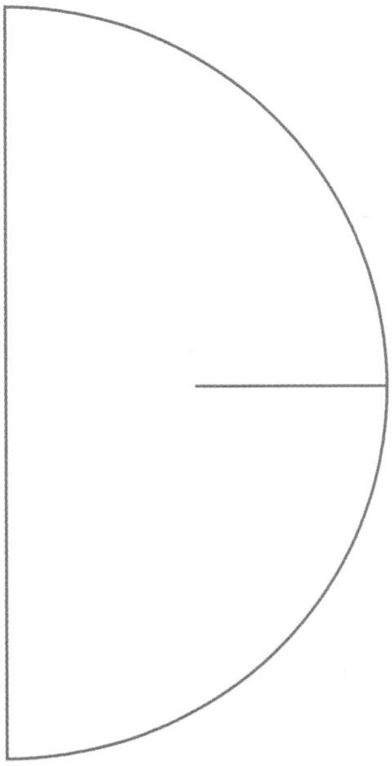

CRYPTOID:

COPY THESE PAPER DOLLS AND THEIR OUTFITS IN COLOR ONTO STIFF CARDSTOCK, THEN CUT ALONG THE DOTTED LINES. SLIT BASES AND STANDS WHERE INDICATED TO PROP THE FIGURES UP AND RE- CREATE SCENES FROM THIS BOOK AND THE FIRST *PROOF* ADVENTURE, *GOATSUCKER*, IN YOUR OWN HOME!

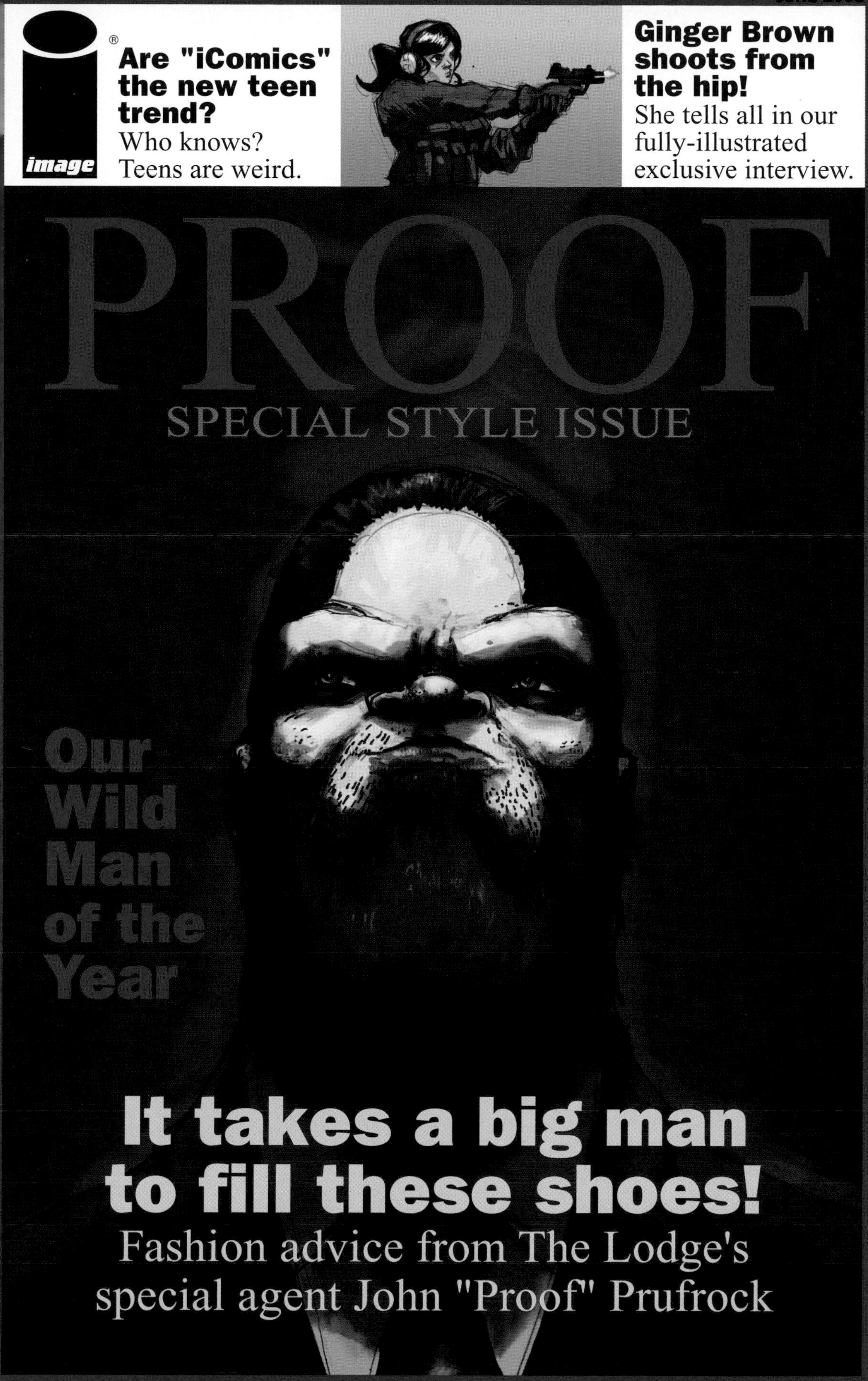
JUNE 2008
image
Are "iComics" the new teen trend?
Who knows? Teens are weird.
Ginger Brown shoots from the hip!
She tells all in our fully-illustrated exclusive interview.
PROOF
SPECIAL STYLE ISSUE
Our Wild Man of the Year
It takes a big man to fill these shoes!
Fashion advice from The Lodge's special agent John "Proof" Prufrock

A Perfect Gentleman (Proof number nine)
The Script
Written by Alex Grecian for Riley Rossmo

A note to the reader: *As a general rule, nobody sees these scripts except Riley and our colorist. So this wasn't really meant to stand alone as a satisfying story. As usual, this script is chock-ful of parenthetical asides to Riley and to our colorist, Adam, who was just starting the book with this issue. I make repeated reference here to a book called* The Gentleman's Guide to Grooming and Style, *a wonderful big red book, full of fashion and grooming tips. More important, it's full of large glossy photographs that depict guys dressed in the kind of clothing that neither Riley nor I have ever owned or even seen up-close. We weren't necessarily prepared to create a "style" issue of a comic, but this book helped us enormously. Oh, one more thing...* Proof *is famous for its "Cryptoids," but there aren't many to be seen here. I generally write tham after seeing the art, so I'll have an idea of where they'll fit best and how they'll enhance the story.*
-Alex

Page 1 --

1 -- Full page. Tight on Proof. He's sitting in a deck chair on a cobblestone patio outside at The Lodge. Behind him are some scrawny trees. It's a bright sunny morning and he's wearing pin-striped pajamas under a silk robe with slippers. He has his little reading glasses on and is reading an issue of *GQ*. He's got a steaming cup of coffee and a thermal pot with more coffee on the round wrought-iron table next to him, as well as a little plate with a bagel on it. The bagel has lox and cream cheese on it and there's a single huge bite taken out of it. There's another, bigger plate, in the middle of the table with a few more bagels on it. Bagels, not doughnuts. I imagine he's dressed something like the guy on page 335 of the *Gentleman's Guide to Grooming and Style*, but not as slovenly and his posture's somewhat better (he should look relaxed though). I don't like the red robe. He should be wearing something darker, like maybe the black robe with white piping at the top of the facing page of that book (or the outfit on the far right of the cover). Dust that book off, incidentally. We'll be using it a lot in this issue 'cause I sure don't know this stuff off the top of my head (it'll make the Cryptoids easy to research though). Felix is curled up at Proof's feet. Just a calm ideal morning here. I'm not writing any business for Felix because there may not be any room for it in this scene. The first nine pages are really dialogue heavy and I'm worried about having the space in each panel for lettering.

  TITLE
  A Perfect Gentleman
  CREDITS
  Words: Alex Grecian
  Pictures: Riley Rossmo
  Colors: Adam Guzowski

Page 2 --

1 -- Biggish panel. Pull back and the patio is in a little glade behind The Lodge. We can see the main building where the apartments are, maybe 20 yards away, so it's not like he's had to trek out here, but there's still the illusion of semi-privacy. Proof's looking up and taking a sip of coffee as Ginger approaches along a path. She's wearing jogging shorts and a tank-top shirt and is pulling her headphones out of her ears as she comes up

to Proof. Probably can't see it, 'cause it'd be too small, but she's been listening to her iPod as she takes a morning run. She's a little sweaty and has her hair back in a ponytail. I like that every time we see Ginger in an off-moment here at The Lodge, she's exercising.

PROOF

'Morning.

GINGER

Hey.

2 -- She's pulling out a chair next to Proof. Proof's pushing the big plate of bagels toward her.

GINGER

Mind if I sit down for a second?

PROOF

Of course not. Have a bagel.

3 -- Ginger curls her nose up, but she's smiling.

GINGER

Ooo. Carbs.

4 -- Proof's grinning at her. We're looking at him over Ginger's shoulder so she's in here.

PROOF

Would it help if I told you they're carb-free?

GINGER

Really?

PROOF (cont'd)

No. A bagel's not really a bagel without carbs.

5 -- She's picking one up. Putting a finger to her lips in a shushing gesture.

GINGER

Okay, but don't tell anyone.

Page 3 --

1 -- Knowing you, this is the panel for this page where you'll leave all the room for dialogue, but Proof and Ginger are just sitting quietly. Proof's reading his magazine and Ginger's munching her bagel, looking off into the trees. She's thinking about stuff.

2 -- Same. Proof's looked up from the magazine and Ginger's lowered the bagel. There's just one bite left. They're both trying to talk at the same time.

PROOF

You know--

GINGER

I shouldn't--

3 -- They're both smiling, slightly embarrassed.

GINGER

Whoops.

PROOF

Go ahead.

4 -- Same. Smiles are gone, though.

GINGER
I just--
GINGER (cont'd)
When I told Leander I couldn't work with you--
PROOF
You what?

5 -- Push in on Ginger.
GINGER
It was before Africa.
GINGER (cont'd)
I figured he probably told you that I--
GINGER (cont'd)
Anyway, I'm sorry.

6 -- Pull back and get Proof in here.
PROOF
No, I know I've been...
GINGER
That whole thing with Nadine was kind of...
PROOF (cont'd)
I thought there was something else going on there.

7 -- Push in on Proof now.
PROOF
I thought maybe--
PROOF (cont'd)
Anyway, I should've thought about how it was for you.
PROOF (cont'd)
The whole time I've been here at The Lodge I've had a grand total of two
partners.

Page 4 --
1 -- Tight on Proof. He's smiling.
PROOF
Besides you, I mean.

2 -- Ginger's reaching for another bagel.
GINGER
These taste like actual New York bagels.
PROOF
I have them flown in. Frozen bagels are just... Blah.

3 -- More talking. You should breeze through this stuff.
PROOF
Anyway, I hope I haven't chased you off.
PROOF (cont'd)
I'd like you to stay.

4 -- Ginger's taken a bite of bagel already and is chewing. Her eyes are half-closed and she's holding up a finger like "wait a second." She likes her bagels.

5 -- Same. This first word balloon is gonna be huge though.
>   GINGER
> Leander said that you and Elvis could handle the Thunderbird assignment, so
> I'm going home tomorrow.
>   GINGER (cont'd)
> To New York, I mean.

6 -- Both of 'em in this panel.
>   PROOF
> Oh.
>   GINGER
> No, it's about time I got my stuff all packed up and moved out here.

Page 5 --
1 -- Proof's smiling. He's reaching for a bagel now.
>   PROOF
> Oh, well that's great.
>   GINGER
> Well, now that I know I can still get a genuine New York bagel way out here...

2 -- Ginger's looking up at the trees, smiling.

3 -- Push in on Ginger and let's stay on her for a few panels. Some stuff she needs to get off her chest and out of the way.
>   GINGER.
> You know, when I was with the FBI, I got assigned to this task force.
>   GINGER (cont'd)
> Right off the bat.

4 -- Same.
>   GINGER
> I had this NYPD lieutenant that...
>   GINGER (cont'd)
> Lieutenant Drake...
>   GINGER (cont'd)
> That I learned a lot from
>   GINGER (cont'd)
> I really did.

5 -- Same.
>   GINGER
> But all the things I learned were just surface things.
>   GINGER (cont'd)
> I mean, I needed to learn that stuff, but it's like it was all sort of...

6 -- Same.

GINGER

There's a whole world out there that's sort of been hiding in the shadow of the world I knew about.

GINGER (cont'd)

Anyway, there's no way I'm ever leaving The Lodge.

Page 6 --

1 -- A little more Ginger here, then we'll bring in Elvis.

GINGER

Unless, y'know, you decide you don't want a partner who already went over your head.

2 -- Proof smiles at her.

PROOF

I kind of deserved it.

PROOF (cont'd)

I never got a chance to really welcome you to The Lodge.

3 -- Proof looks a little sheepish.

PROOF

So, um...

PROOF (cont'd)

Welcome to The Lodge.

PROOF (cont'd)

Partner.

4 -- Quiet panel while they both look at the trees and eat their bagels.

5 -- Bigger panel. Here comes Elvis down that little path through the trees. He's carrying a mug of coffee which is slopping over a bit as he walks. He's wearing a ratty bathrobe with wide purple, black and teal stripes (that's what my favorite bathrobe looked like before my wife made me get rid of it, soon after we started dating). The robe's open and Elvis is wearing baggy tighty-whities. He's running his free hand through his hair and looks groggy. This might be a bit tricky... He needs to be coming from a direction that allows us to see him, but he doesn't see Ginger because the trees are hiding her.

PROOF

'Morning, Sheriff.

ELVIS

Hmm. Hi.

ELVIS (cont'd)

Oh, hey, you've got doughnuts out here.

Page 7 --

1 -- Elvis sees Ginger. He's already set the coffee cup on the table and is pulling his robe shut, maybe tying the sash. He's smiling at her. Not a big over-the-top embarrassed kinda reaction, just a "happy to see her, hope she didn't see my junk" kinda thing going on here. Ginger's talking about going, but she's not getting up from her chair.

ELVIS

Oh, hi, Ginger.

ELVIS (cont'd)
I heard...
ELVIS (cont'd)
Thought John and Wayne were out here. Sorry.
GINGER
That's okay, I need to get going anyway.

2 -- Elvis slumps into another wrought-iron chair and reaches for a bagel. Proof's quietly amused. So is Ginger if we can see her here. They're both really fond of Elvis, but in different ways.
ELVIS
Can I--?
PROOF
Be my guest.
ELVIS (cont'd)
So, um... Thunderbirds...

3 -- Elvis bites into a bagel, but is looking sideways at Ginger.
ELVIS
Are they scary?

4 -- Elvis is staring at his bagel. Proof's mildly dismayed by Elvis's lack of experience. Ginger's hiding her smile behind her hand.
ELVIS
I think these doughnuts went bad.
PROOF
They're bagels. They're supposed to taste like that.

5 -- Elvis is putting the bagel, missing a bite, back on the big plate in the middle of the table with all the other bagels. Proof looks anguished.
ELVIS
Do they come with jelly inside?
GINGER
Ha!
PROOF
No.

6 -- Proof's grabbed the bagel that Elvis just put back, holding it with two fingers the way you might hold a bag of poop. Elvis is reaching for the thermal coffee decanter. He's embarrassed. (Adam, when you color this maybe add just a little extra pink to his cheeks.) He knows he's a rube, but doesn't quite get what's so funny.
ELVIS
I'm not--
PROOF
You can't just--
ELVIS (cont'd)
Not really a morning person.

1 -- Proof's tossing the bagel into the grass and Ginger's standing to go. Elvis is pouring coffee into his mug.

> PROOF
> I've dealt with Thunderbirds before.
> PROOF (cont'd)
> They're kind of like big vultures.
> PROOF (cont'd)
> No big deal.

2 -- Both guys are looking at Ginger, who's putting her iPod headphones back in her ears.

> GINGER
> Well, you boys have fun with that.
> ELVIS
> You're not going with us?
> GINGER (cont'd)
> I'm settling the lease on my place in New York.

3 -- Push in on Ginger.

> GINGER
> I can't believe how much space I have here.
> GINGER (cont'd)
> I can finally get all my stuff out of storage.

4 -- Elvis is trying to be extremely casual. He's looking at Ginger. Ginger's looking at Proof, who doesn't need to be in the panel.

> ELVIS
> You want some help packing up?
> ELVIS (cont'd)
> I mean if that's--
> GINGER
> Suit yourself, but I thought you--

5 -- Push in on Proof

> PROOF
> I'll deal with the Thunderbirds.
> PROOF (cont'd)
> Seriously.
> PROOF (cont'd)
> You kids have a good time in New York.

6 -- Ginger's walking away down the path to The Lodge.

> GINGER
> See you in the morning, Sheriff.

7 -- Elvis has never tried harder in his life to look cool. Proof's grinning at him. We may not be able to see Elvis's face in this panel and that's okay.

> PROOF
> Have you been to New York before?

                    ELVIS
No.
                    PROOF (cont'd)
Well, you're not going like that.

8 -- Elvis looks confused.
                    ELVIS
What, in my robe?
                    PROOF
In anything you own.
                    PROOF (cont'd)
You and I are going shopping today.

Page 9 --

1 -- Two men are walking down a dimly lit stone staircase. One's old and hunched and the other man is young and taller. We may come back to them in the Julia arc and we may not, so I haven't named them yet. I'll just call them Old Man and Young Man, 'cause I'm clever that way. The Old Man is wearing a tweed suit with elbow patches and smoking a pipe. Maybe he even has a cane. The young man is in a dress shirt and slacks, maybe a tie.
                    OLD MAN
<I'm certain I saw her down here in the basement...>*
                    OLD MAN (cont'd)
<Maybe five years ago. Maybe six.>
                    CAPTION
*Translated from Norwegian
                    CAPTION (cont'd)
The Institute of Forensic Medicine
                    CAPTION (cont'd)
Oslo

2 -- The men are walking past a lacquered cadaver with its skin stretched open and pinned back to show its internal organs. On a shelf behind them is an array of human heads, floating in big jars of formaldehyde.
                    OLD MAN
<Of course, there's not much reason to come down here anymore.>
                    OLD MAN (cont'd)
<It's all storage these days.>

3 -- We're behind them, looking at a dark corner of the basement. There's a vaguely human shape there, covered with a dusty blanket.
                    OLD MAN
<My wife and I used to come down here...>
                    OLD MAN (cont'd)
<Of course that was right after the war and she wasn't my wife yet.>
                    OLD MAN (cont'd)
<Plenty of privacy here, even then.>

4 -- Now we're looking at these two guys from the POV of the thing under the blanket. The Old Man's pulling the blanket off. No big display of showmanship here. The Young

Man's holding a cell phone, dialing a number.

                    OLD MAN
     <Ah, yes, she is still here.>
                    OLD MAN (cont'd)
     <She's seen better days, poor thing.>

5 -- The Young Man's talking on the phone now. The Old Man's staring sadly at the thing under the blanket.

                    OLD MAN
     <But then, haven't we all?>
                    YOUNG MAN
     Marliss?
                    YOUNG MAN (cont'd)
     Put me through to Mr. Wight right away.
                    YOUNG MAN (cont'd)
     I've finally found her.

Page 10 --

1 -- Establishing shot of The Lodge. We need to hint that some time has passed, so show the sun, high in the sky.

2 -- Tight on one of those paper targets that everybody uses at firing ranges. You've seen these on TV a zillion times. It's a crude black silhouette of a person's head and torso with concentric circles marked on it in white. There are five holes in it already and a sixth is being created. There's one hole already in the head, two in the left shoulder, one farther down in the area of the left arm and one in the gut, but Ginger's pulling to the right, so it's grouped close to the others. This final shot is hitting the target-perp square-ly in the chest.

                    SFX
     Blam

3 -- Pull back and we're at the Lodge's firing range. This can look like any generic firing range and there's lots of images out there on the Internet. I'll find a few to send your way. Ginger's taking off the headphone things. Her gun's on the counter in front of her. She's wearing safety glasses. If we can see the target, it's zooming up the line toward her.

4 -- We're looking over Ginger's shoulder. She's holding the target, looking at it. A woman's hand is reaching out from off-panel, from our POV, to tap her on the shoulder.

                    GINGER
     Damn.
                    ISABELLA (off-panel)
     Ginger Brown?

5 -- Ginger jumps a country mile. Pull back and get Isabella in here. This is our intro-duction to her, so let's make sure we like her character design. It occurred to me that we have an awful lot of dark-complected ethnic women in this series, especially since we're gonna reintroduce Belinda Drake. Should we have a blond white chick? Personally, I'm partial to brunettes anyway, but it might not be a bad idea to expand the makeup of The Lodge a bit. As always, it's up to you when it comes to this stuff.

GINGER

Aaah!

ISABELLA

Oh, I'm so sorry.

ISABELLA (cont'd)

I didn't mean to startle you.

6 -- Push in on Isabella and let's get a good look at her here. She needs to be attractive, but in an understated way. She's an intellectual type, someone you might like to snuggle up to in front of a fire and discuss Camus. And look at how many word balloons need to fit above her.

ISABELLA

You are Ginger Brown, right?

GINGER

I'm sorry, who are you?

ISABELLA (cont'd)

I'm Isabella Bay. Doctor Bay.

ISABELLA (cont'd)

We had a nine-thirty appointment.

Page 11 --

1 -- Push in on Ginger. She's taking off the safety glasses.

GINGER

Oh, right. The psychiatrist.

ISABELLA

I'm actually a psychologist.

2 -- Ginger's looking down at her target.

GINGER

So can you tell me why I'm pulling to the right?

ISABELLA

Maybe you have levophobia.

GINGER (cont'd)

Seriously?

Cryptoid here about levophobia being a common phobia. A fear of things to the left side of a person's body.

3 -- Isabella's taking a look at the target.

ISABELLA

No, probably not. I'd guess maybe something with your gun.

4 -- The two women are shaking hands.

GINGER

Sorry I missed my appointment. I forgot.

ISABELLA

Did you?

5 -- Ginger's turned her back and is clipping another target to the line above her.

> GINGER
> See, that's what I hate about psychi--
> GINGER (cont'd)
> Psychologists.
> GINGER (cont'd)
> You can't just have a normal conversation with someone.

6 -- Isabella's laughing. The designs I've seen for her since I wrote that last page make her seem a bit mousy and severe, but let's have her be one of those women who, if you can make them laugh, they're suddenly beautiful, you know what I mean? She's lovely in this panel, not menacing or rude. I think people spend a lot of time trying to make her laugh.

> ISABELLA
> Ha ha ha
> ISABELLA (cont'd)
> You're right. I'm sorry.

Page 12 --

1 -- Ginger's pushed the button that sends the target to the back of the range. I have no idea where that button usually is (I'm guessing it's under the counter), so I'll do some research before you have to draw this. Right now I just wanna finish this script.

> ISABELLA
> So much of the time, the people I treat have seen something--
> ISABELLA (cont'd)
> Encountered something they don't even have words for.

2 -- Ginger's handing Isabella a pair of safety glasses and headphones.

> ISABELLA
> I have to kind of prompt them.

3 -- Ginger's waiting for Isabella to finish putting on the safety equipment, which Isabella's doing. The headphones are already on her head, and she's pulling one of the ear pieces away so she can hear Ginger. She's still just holding the glasses.

> GINGER
> So you work at The Lodge full time?
> ISABELLA
> What?
> GINGER (cont'd)
> You're here all the time?

4 -- Isabella's suited up and Ginger's taking aim down the line.

> ISABELLA
> Oh, no.
> ISABELLA (cont'd)
> I have a practice in town.
> ISABELLA (cont'd)
> I come here part-time to help you people deal with some of the things you see.

5 -- Ginger's firing.

SFX
Blam Blam Blam Blam Blam Blam

6 -- Both women are taking off their headphones. Ginger's gun is laying on the counter.
                    ISABELLA
Leander told me you're returning home tomorrow morning.
                    ISABELLA (cont'd)
I wanted to visit with you before you left.

7 -- The target's moving up the line again, toward the two women.
                    ISABELLA
I'm told you're fitting in quite well here.
                    GINGER
Thanks. I like it.
                    ISABELLA (cont'd)
But there's something else, isn't there?

8 -- Push in on Isabella.
                    ISABELLA
Why don't you tell me what you're afraid of...
                    ISABELLA (cont'd)
What's in New York?

Page 13 --
1 -- I love to start a page with a long panel that runs across the top of a page. That's
how I see this one. We're tight on Elvis, who looks extremely worried. He's wearing a
white dress shirt with a collar. We can't see much more, just his head and shoulders.
                    PROOF (off-panel)
He's meeting his girlfriend's family tomorrow.

2 -- Big panel. Fills the rest of the page. Okay, we're in the tailor's shop. The tailor's
behind Elvis, measuring his shoulders. Proof and Wayne are off to one side, observing.
There's another guy, off to the other side, the tailor's assistant. The details are really
important in this panel, but of course I'll cover up a lot of your hard work with word
balloons. Let's name the tailor Chaz. His assistant's name is Eddie and I think he should
be Asian. Chaz is roughly 45 years old with blonde hair, lots of product, I picture him
as a more weasely-looking Gordon Ramsey. He's wearing a designer t-shirt and ironed
blue jeans, loafers (like the ones on page 184 of the *Gentleman's Guide*) without socks
and a belt (don't have the belt be too long; my wife tells me that's out of style now).
Eddie, the assistant, is wearing a pin-striped suit and looks impeccable, his hair cut very
short, almost as short as yours. Elvis is standing on a small platform as Chaz measures
him. He's wearing suit pants that are much too long for him, so he's stepping on the
hems. Eddie is holding a dummy suit jacket for Elvis to eventually try on (he's just holding it, not trying to get Elvis to wear it). Elvis's arms are down at his sides and Chaz is
peeking around him to talk to Proof. Proof's wearing a bespoke suit and looks as perfect as you've ever drawn him. Elvis is mortified. Wayne is wearing his comfy orange
sweater and slacks. For the inside of this shop, I can't find much in the *Gentleman's
Guide*, but there's a big picture on page 193 that might be a little helpful and there are
small photos on pages 157 and 307 that show more detail. Lots of rich woodwork and
bolts of cloth.

                    ELVIS
I am not.
                    ELVIS (cont'd)
I mean, she's not--
                    CHAZ
Ah, but of course you'd like her to be.
                    PROOF
You should see them flirt. It's adorable.
                    ELVIS (cont'd)
I've never--
                    ELVIS (cont'd)
Does she really flirt with me?
                    CAPTION
Seattle, Washington

Page 14 --
1 -- Proof is grinning big, but ignoring Elvis's question.
                    PROOF
What do you think, Chaz?
                    PROOF (cont'd)
Six weeks?

2 -- Pull back and get Elvis and Chaz in here. Chaz is measuring down the length of Elvis's arm.
                    CHAZ
Oh, I think I can have this for him in maybe four weeks.
                    CHAZ (cont'd)
His shoulders are so wide.

3 -- Proof's thinking, looking up. Elvis is trying to look at Chaz, but can't really see him because Chaz is behind him, measuring the other arm.
                    ELVIS
Thanks, I guess...
                    ELVIS (cont'd)
I mean, yeah, thanks.
                    PROOF
We'll have to get some things off the rack for your trip.

4 -- Push in and Chaz has leaned in from behind to murmur in Elvis's ear. Elvis is blushing.
                    CHAZ
She's a lucky girl.

5 -- Pull back again and Chaz is consulting with Eddie. Elvis is standing like a scarecrow.
                    PROOF
So you'll be back here in a month or--?
                    CHAZ
If you'll stop by on the ninth, we should have something for you.
                    PROOF (cont'd)
Perfect. Thanks.

6 -- Push in on Chaz. He's grinning.
                    CHAZ
          Don't wait too long to ask her, Mr. Chestnut.
                    CHAZ (cont'd)
          A lady doesn't like to be kept waiting.

Page 15 --
1 -- Big panel here, then a succession of fairly small panels. Proof, Wayne and Elvis are standing on the sidewalk outside the tailor's shop. There are lots and lots of photos in the *Gentleman's Guide* of how the outside of a place like this would look. A light rain is starting. Proof's got an umbrella hooked over his arm, not opened yet, and is now wearing an overcoat and hat. He's checking his pocket watch.
                    PROOF
          We're running late, so we'll finish shopping after lunch.
                    PROOF (cont'd)
          Right now there's barely time to make your appointment.

2 -- Tight on Elvis.
                    ELVIS
          My appointment?

3 -- Proof's kind of awkwardly touching Elvis's pompadore. Wayne's grimacing.
                    PROOF
          Um... This is...
                    WAYNE
          Let's get your hair cut, son.

4 -- Elvis looks aghast. He's pulling back a little.
                    ELVIS
          Nobody touches my hair. This is my trademark.

5 -- Proof and Wayne are looking at each other.
                    PROOF
          Hmmm. That's true, but...
                    WAYNE
          What did Ginger say about his hair?
                    PROOF (cont'd)
          Oh, yes, Ginger. She said, um...
                    PROOF (cont'd)
          I forget. What did she say, Wayne?

6 -- Tight on Wayne. You can't show his head shaking, but he's got a tight-lipped regretful look on his face.

Page 16 --
1 -- Big panel. Fill most of the page. Elvis is sitting in a barber's chair with one of those giant bibs on to catch falling hair. There are a couple of pictures of decent barbershops in the *Gentleman's Guide*, but don't make this a noisy Super Cuts type of place. Proof would never go to one of those. A middle-aged barber is standing behind the chair,

studying Elvis's hair. The barber should be old-school. I see him in a dress shirt and vest, but without the suit jacket, his tie tucked into the vest.

2 -- Proof and Wayne are sitting in chairs off to the side, waiting, each of them holding a magazine. I'll stick in covers later. I think Wayne's got *Outdoorsman* and Proof's got *GQ* again. They're talking without looking at each other, so they're not actually reading their magazines.

> PROOF
>
> Did Ginger really say something about his hair?
>
> WAYNE
>
> Not to me.

Page 17 --

1 -- The three of them are exiting the barbershop. Elvis is looking up, in the direction of his new hair style. Proof and Wayne are looking up, too, but at the pouring rain. I don't know what you've got in mind for his hair now, but it would have to be fairly conservative for Proof to approve of it. The nice thing is that you can change his hair at any future point to whatever you like and we don't have to write it into the series. Now that we've cut his hair once, all bets are off. On the following pages, if Elvis isn't doing anything else, you might want to have him tentatively touching the top of his head.

2 -- They're walking down the street. Passersby are paying no attention to them. One guy's holding his hand over his nose as he passes. Proof's opening his umbrella and Elvis is gawking at the people passing them.

> ELVIS
>
> Nobody's looking at you.
>
> PROOF
>
> Most people aren't very observant.

3 -- Proof's umbrella serves as a backdrop (and gives you less to draw) for Wayne and Elvis to talk. Wayne is avoiding being under the umbrella, so don't have it over him. Put Elvis closer to Proof.

> WAYNE
>
> He stinks. Drives people away.
>
> PROOF
>
> I don't stink.

4 -- Push in on Proof.

> PROOF
>
> I can control my pheremones to either drive people away or relax them.
>
> PROOF (cont'd)
>
> Like right now, I'm creating my own little umbrella around us.

5 -- Same.

> PROOF
>
> People aren't looking at us because they sense that there's something here they should avoid.
>
> PROOF (cont'd)
>
> Humans really aren't that different from other animals.

PROOF (cont'd)
You're ruled by your instincts.

6 -- Pull out a bit.
ELVIS
What do you mean you can relax people?
WAYNE
When you first met him in your mother's house...
WAYNE (cont'd)
Did you freak out?

Page 18 --
1 -- Pull way back and get some Seattle background in here. Maybe we're behind them, watching the three guys walk down the street.
ELVIS
Well, I pulled my gun on him right away.
PROOF
But then you calmed down, didn't you?

2 -- Proof is smiling at him.
PROOF
Don't worry about it.
PROOF (cont'd)
It's not mind control.
PROOF (cont'd)
More like aromatherapy.

3 -- Proof's holding open the door of a clothier's. It should look similar to the last place. Wayne's saluting him as they walk past.
PROOF
Here we are.

4 -- A small thin man with a goatee approaches with his arms open. Let's call him Jacques. If there's room, throw in a couple of assistants behind him. They can be folding clothes, measuring bolts of cloth or cutting cloth from the bolts, hanging things up, whatever.
JACQUES
Monsieur Prufrock!
PROOF
Hello, Jacques.
JACQUES (cont'd)
So good to see you again.

5 -- Wayne's leaning in to whisper at Elvis.
WAYNE
He's not really French.
WAYNE (cont'd)
His name's Jack, but Proof humors him.

6 -- Big panel. Pull back and there are racks and racks of suits and cubbies filled with slacks, jackets on mannequins and hats on wig blocks. It should look sort of overwhelming for someone like Elvis.

          JACQUES
Today my store is closed to all but you gentlemen.

Page 19 --
1 -- Elvis is leaning in to talk to Wayne.
          ELVIS
So Proof's making this guy smell something nice?
          WAYNE
No, Proof's been around long enough that there are people who know him and accept him.
          WAYNE (cont'd)
Jack here's one of those people.

2 -- Proof's talking to the little tailor.
          PROOF
Jacques, we just had my friend Elvis fitted for his first bespoke suit.
          JACQUES
How marvelous!

3 -- Same.
          PROOF
And now we're looking for something he can wear this weekend.
          JACQUES
What would be the gentleman's preference?
          PROOF (cont'd)
I think his current wardrobe probably runs toward sweatpants and flipflops.

4 -- Jacques looks confused.
          JACQUES
I do not know of these things.
          PROOF
Of course not.
          PROOF (cont'd)
Think of Elvis as a blank slate.

5 -- Jacques has turned around and is talking to his assistants, his arms thrown up in the air dramatically. If you left these two helpers out of the previous panels, he's summoning them from the back room.
          JACQUES
Pierre, Gaston! We are dining in today!
          JACQUES (cont'd)
Our work is cut out for us!

Pages 20-21 --
These two pages are a double-page spread of the guys trying on clothes. I imagine this thing would be divided in half horizontally, so you've got two tiers of panels that run across both pages. I don't think we should probably ride the gutter because I'm thinking

ahead about the trade and I always worry about these things lining up properly, but it's ultimately your call and if you wanna chance it... So, I'm thinking 12 panels total. Let me know if you have a better idea. I don't think that they necessarily have to have panel borders. In fact, it might be nice to have these things floating in one big space and over-lap them a bit. Let's talk about this on the phone and hash out some ideas. Anyway, pull outfits from the *Gentleman's Guide* and let's see Elvis trying on all sorts of different things, posing in each outfit for the other guys to see, so we'll have a panel or two of reaction shots. In one or two of these, Jacques is standing behind Elvis as Elvis poses. He's looking on, proud and excited as Elvis models his creations. And let's see a panel of Proof trying on a hat and one of Wayne standing there, looking bored as all hell, not trying on anything.

Page 22 --

1 -- The guys are leaving the shop. Elvis and Wayne are both carrying several huge bags. Elvis is wearing new tan corduroy slacks, brown shoes, a black shirt and a pea-colored overcoat that extends to his knees. The outfit second from the right on the cover of the *Gentleman's Guide*. Adam, remind me I'm gonna have to send you a copy of this book, so you can see what I'm talking about. There's still a slight drizzle and Proof's opening his umbrella.

> WAYNE
> Real men don't need umbrellas.
> PROOF
> Of course we do.
> PROOF (cont'd)
> Anyway, 1 don't like being wet.

2 -- Tight on Elvis.

> ELVIS
> Actually, I'm not too sure real men do anything we did today.

3 -- Wayne's laughing. Proof looks stern as he delivers a lecture. They're walking by now and Proof may not actually be looking at Elvis.

> WAYNE
> Hahahah!
> PROOF
> A man's appearance is the first and most lasting impression he makes.
> PROOF (cont'd)
> You can control that impression if you educate yourself.

4 -- Tight on Elvis.

> ELVIS
> Just seems a little gay to me.

5 -- Proof and Wayne are quiet, just looking at Elvis. They've stopped walking.

6 -- Pull back and get Elvis in here.

> ELVIS
> Oh man, I didn't mean...
> ELVIS (cont'd)
> I mean are you?

7 -- Small panel, tight on Wayne.
              WAYNE
       Nope. Proof's not gay.
              WAYNE (cont'd)
       I am, though.

Page 23 --
1 -- Elvis is talking to Wayne as they walk again. Proof's up ahead, out of earshot.
              ELVIS
       Well then why's this stuff so important to him?
              WAYNE
       You think if Proof ever finds his people he's still gonna be able to relate to 'em?

2 -- Tight on Wayne.
              WAYNE
       He's not really a cryptid anymore. Not an animal.
              WAYNE (cont'd)
       But he's not a person either.

3 -- Get Elvis in here too.
              ELVIS
       So this is all--
              WAYNE
       He really does care about his appearance.
              WAYNE (cont'd)
       He was raised in a time when all this stuff about clothes and grooming still
       mattered.

4 -- Same. They're still walking.
              WAYNE
       But if there are other sasquatches out there somewhere...
              WAYNE (cont'd)
       Well, I don't think they're gonna know what to make of our friend.

5 -- Same.
              WAYNE
       In a way, the guy who taught him all this stuff about how to dress...
              WAYNE (cont'd)
       That guy sorta ruined Proof's chances of ever being happy.

6 -- Same.
              ELVIS
       Who *did* teach him all this?
              WAYNE
       The third president of the United States...
              WAYNE (cont'd)
       Thomas Jefferson.

7 -- Small inset panel, colored in sepia tones, of a young Proof standing with (and slightly in front of) Thomas Jefferson. Jefferson has a hand on Proof's shoulder. Proof's

dressed in short pants and a buttoned blazer, imitating in miniature Jefferson's style of dress. (I'll send you reference.)

8 -- Back to the three guys walking down the street, but we're behind them and Proof's waving from up ahead to the other guys to catch up to him.
                    ELVIS
          Oh. Wow.
                    PROOF
          Come on, you guys. Let's get home before the sky opens up.

Page 24 --
1 -- Establishing shot of a farmhouse. We're hinting at the "Thunderbirds" story here, so the landscape is similar to what you've already drawn for the next issue.
                    CAPTION
          Illinois

2 -- We're inside a boy's bedroom. This is the little blond boy you drew for the first few pages of "Thunderbirds Are Go!" He's in bed, a blanket tucked around him. A window should be in the panel. The boy's mother, who should resemble your harpies, is sitting on the edge of the bed, stroking the boy's hair. Her name's Crystal. The boy's sleeping, sweaty and ill.
                    CRYSTAL
          You ain't gonna get any better, are you?

3 -- Push in on them.
                    CRYSTAL
          You been such a good boy since your daddy gone away.
                    CRYSTAL (cont'd)
          Such a big help to me.

4 -- Crystal stands and moves to the window.
                    CRYSTAL
          But I'm ready to let go of you now.
                    CRYSTAL (cont'd)
          It ain't right for me to keep you from taking your rightful place with our heavenly father.

5 -- She's opening the window. It should be one of those that swing open on hinges at both sides, so it makes a nice wide hole for something to come through. We're outside looking in at her and she's shouting.
                    CRYSTAL
          You hear me, Lord?
                    CRYSTAL (cont'd)
          You send them angels to take my boy home now.

6 -- Push in and she looks rapturous, her eyes half-closed. The tips and edges of wings are visible now, framing the panel as something big and feathery approaches the window. Don't show too much. We know these are Thunderbirds, but to the reader it should like angels are arriving.

CRYSTAL
You send us your heavenly host.
CAPTION
To be continued...

I eliminated the last page of art (indicated in the script here) from this collection. Because it led directly into the next story arc, it seemed more appropriate to include it in the next book, rather than this one.
-ALEX

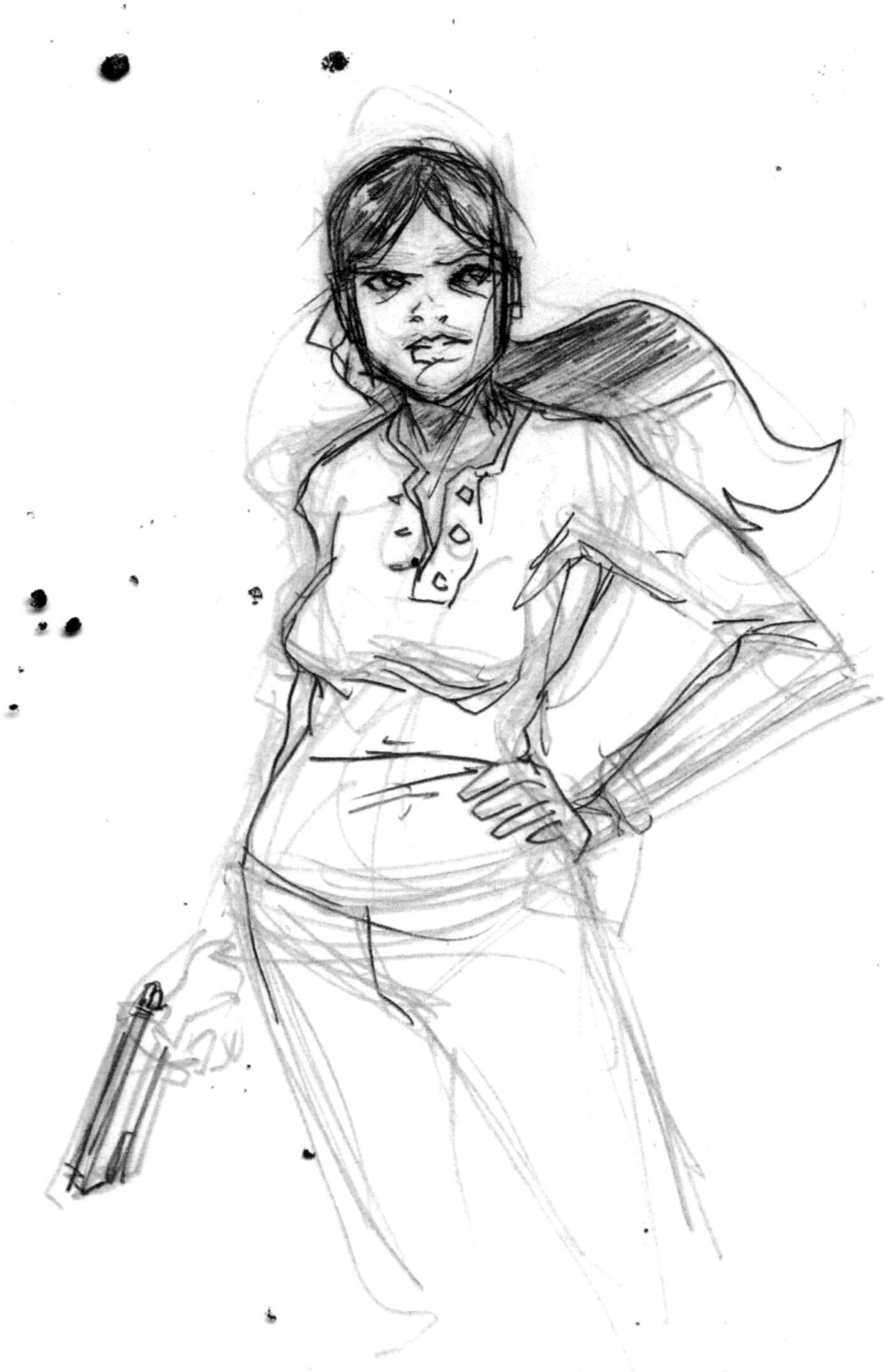

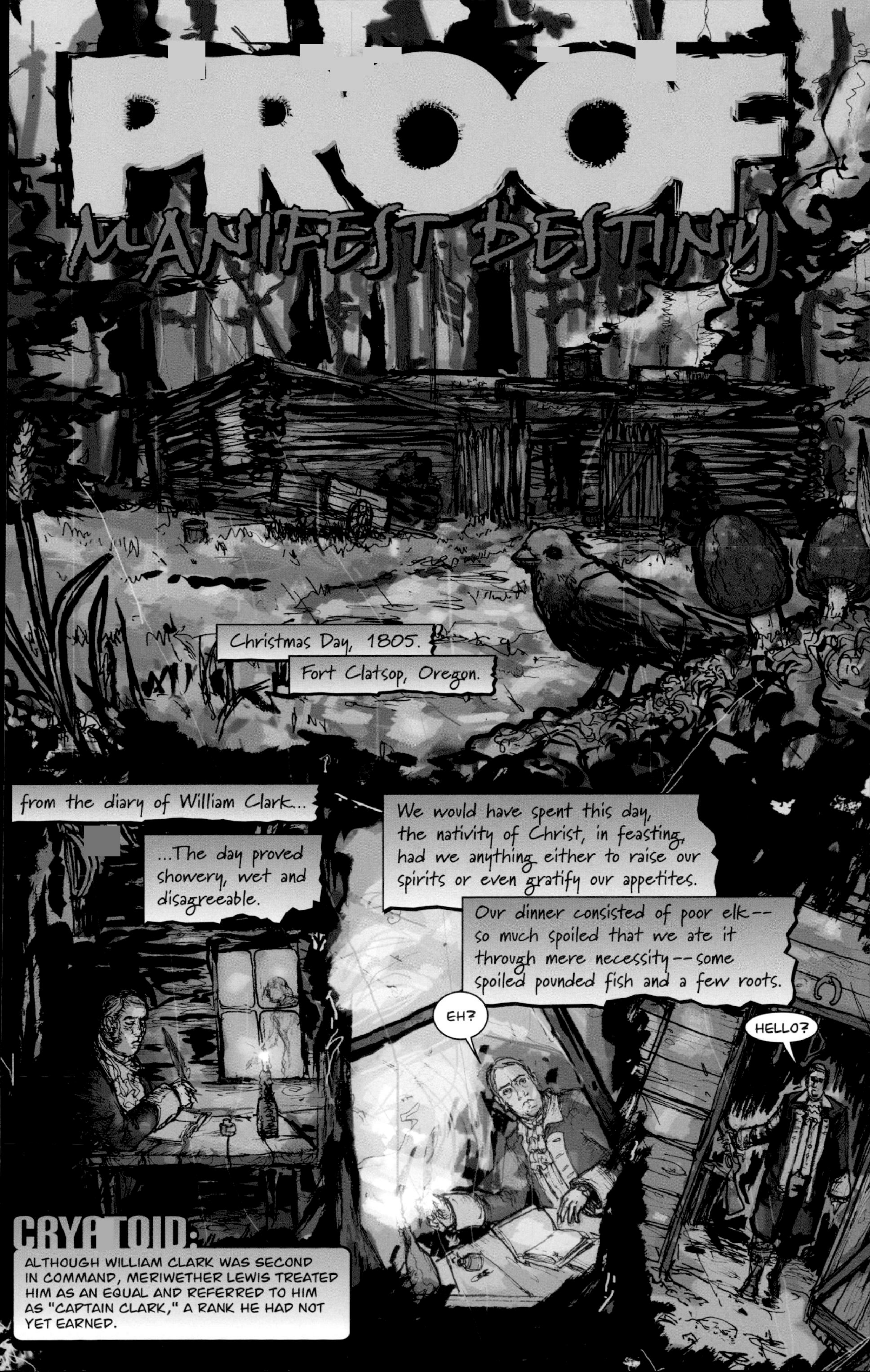
PROOF
MANIFEST DESTINY
Christmas Day, 1805.
Fort Clatsop, Oregon.
from the diary of William Clark...
...The day proved showery, wet and disagreeable.
We would have spent this day, the nativity of Christ, in feasting, had we anything either to raise our spirits or even gratify our appetites.
Our dinner consisted of poor elk -- so much spoiled that we ate it through mere necessity -- some spoiled pounded fish and a few roots.
EH?
HELLO?
CRYA TOID:
ALTHOUGH WILLIAM CLARK WAS SECOND IN COMMAND, MERIWETHER LEWIS TREATED HIM AS AN EQUAL AND REFERRED TO HIM AS "CAPTAIN CLARK," A RANK HE HAD NOT YET EARNED.

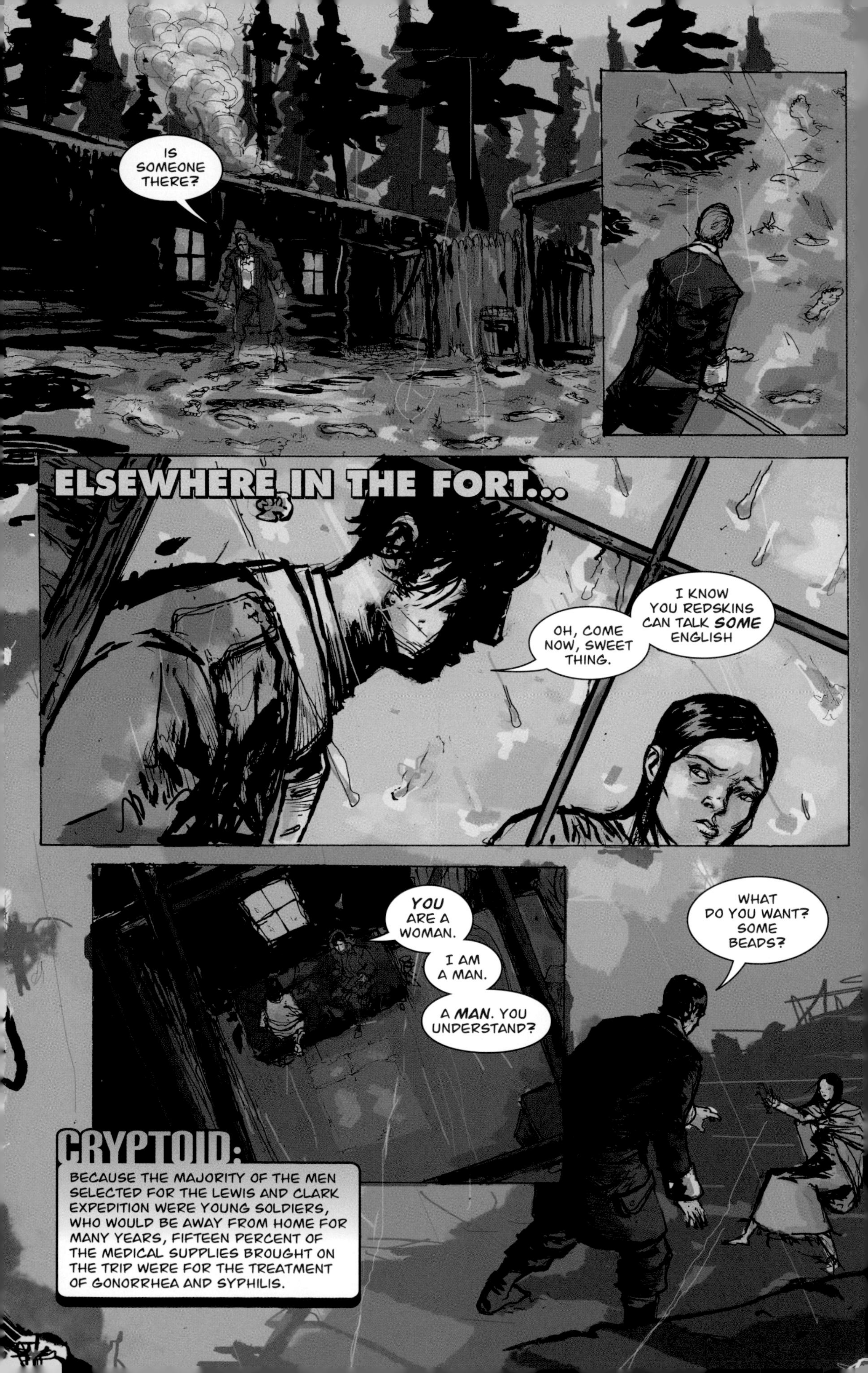
IS SOMEONE THERE?
ELSEWHERE IN THE FORT...
OH, COME NOW, SWEET THING.
I KNOW YOU REDSKINS CAN TALK SOME ENGLISH
WHAT DO YOU WANT? SOME BEADS?
YOU ARE A WOMAN.
I AM A MAN.
A MAN. YOU UNDERSTAND?
CRYPTOID:
BECAUSE THE MAJORITY OF THE MEN SELECTED FOR THE LEWIS AND CLARK EXPEDITION WERE YOUNG SOLDIERS, WHO WOULD BE AWAY FROM HOME FOR MANY YEARS, FIFTEEN PERCENT OF THE MEDICAL SUPPLIES BROUGHT ON THE TRIP WERE FOR THE TREATMENT OF GONORRHEA AND SYPHILIS.

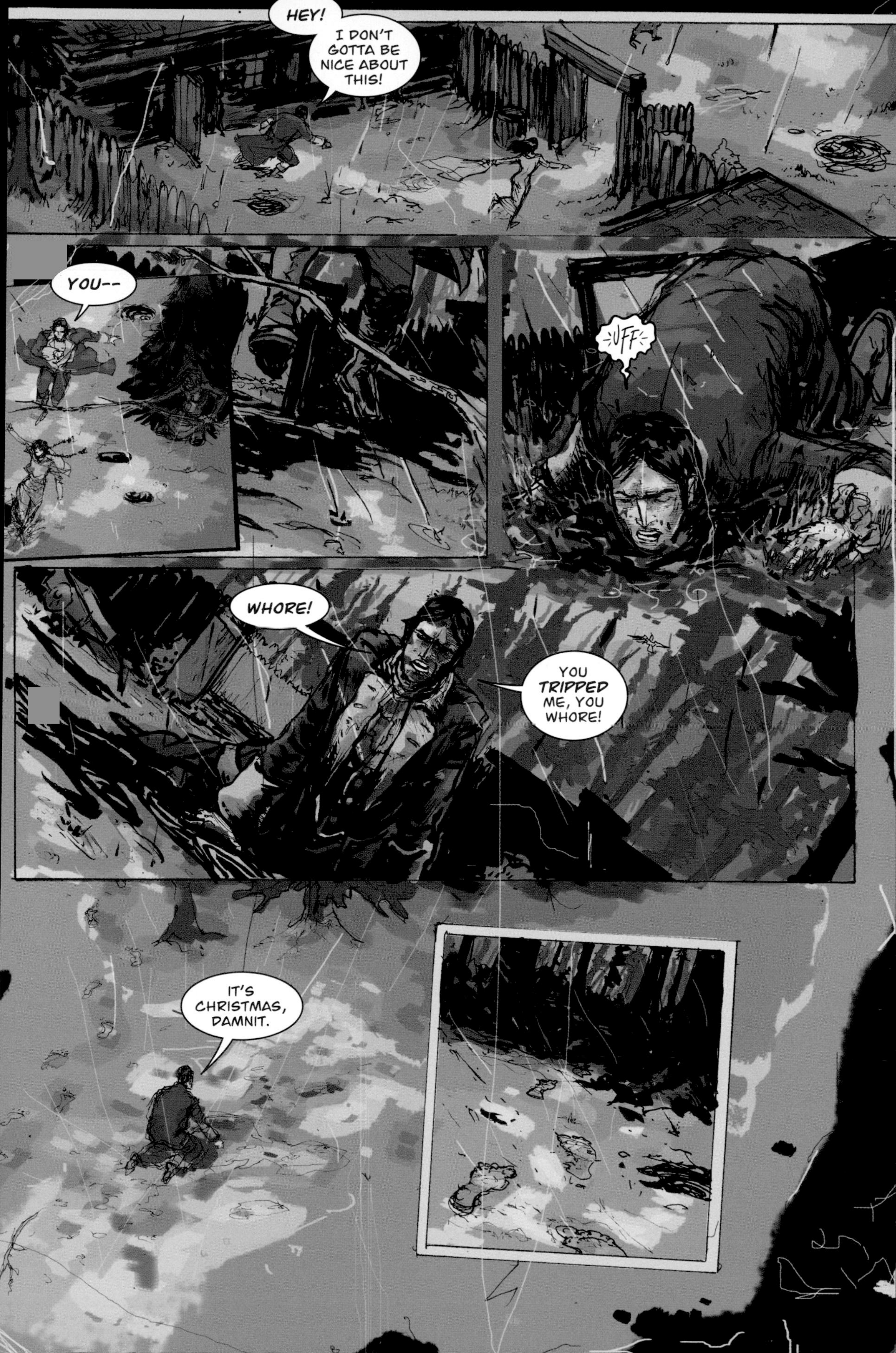
HEY!
I DON'T GOTTA BE NICE ABOUT THIS!
YOU--
UFF
WHORE!
YOU TRIPPED ME, YOU WHORE!
IT'S CHRISTMAS, DAMNIT.

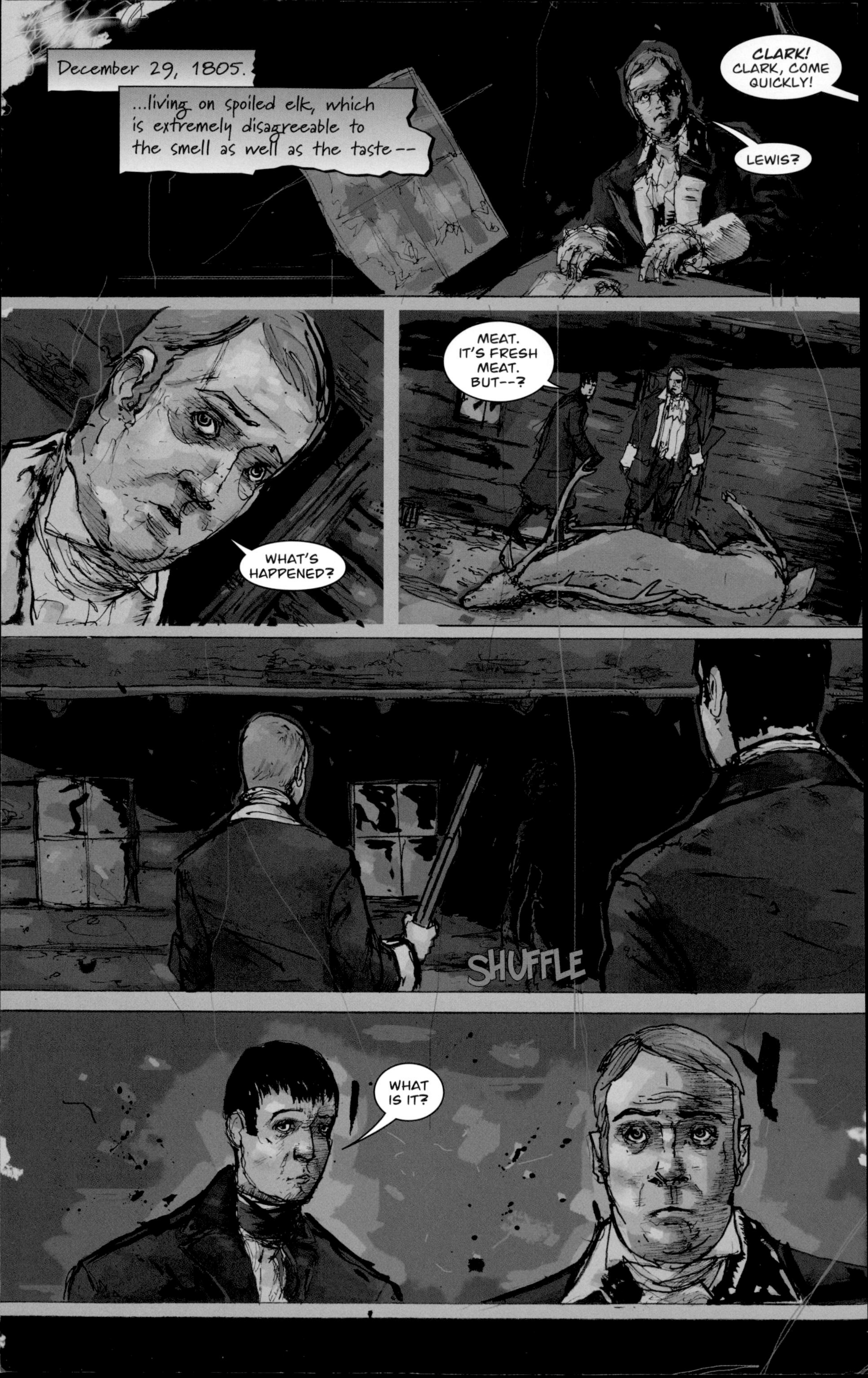
December 29, 1805.
...living on spoiled elk, which is extremely disagreeable to the smell as well as the taste--
CLARK! CLARK, COME QUICKLY!
LEWIS?
WHAT'S HAPPENED?
MEAT. IT'S FRESH MEAT. BUT--?
SHUFFLE
WHAT IS IT?

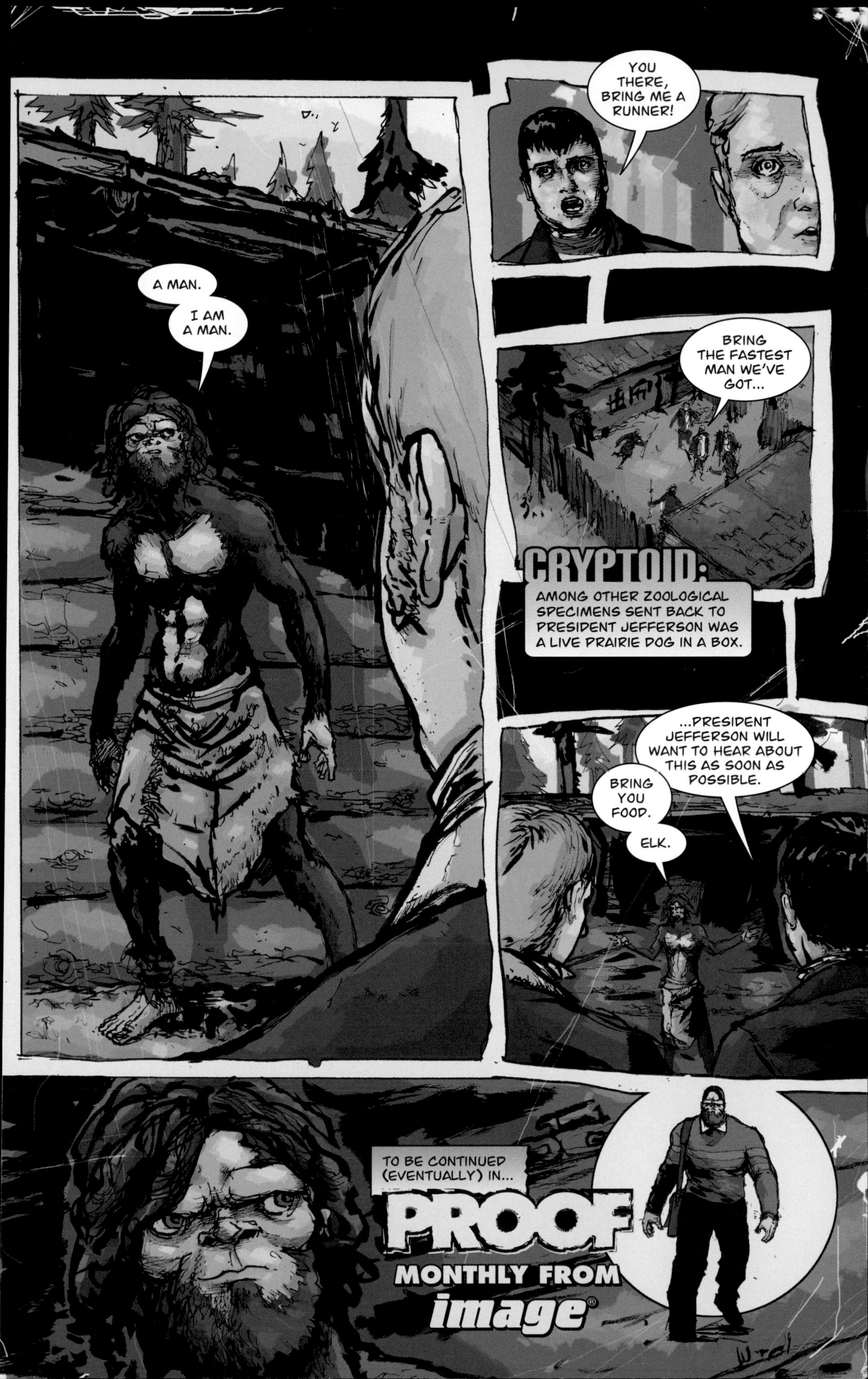
A MAN.
I AM A MAN.
YOU THERE, BRING ME A RUNNER!
BRING THE FASTEST MAN WE'VE GOT...
CRYPTOID:
AMONG OTHER ZOOLOGICAL SPECIMENS SENT BACK TO PRESIDENT JEFFERSON WAS A LIVE PRAIRIE DOG IN A BOX.
...PRESIDENT JEFFERSON WILL WANT TO HEAR ABOUT THIS AS SOON AS POSSIBLE.
BRING YOU FOOD.
ELK.
TO BE CONTINUED (EVENTUALLY) IN...
PROOF
MONTHLY FROM
image®